Understanding
Terror
Networks

UNDERSTANDING TERROR NETWORKS

Marc Sageman

PENN

UNIVERSITY OF PENNSYLVANIA PRESS

PHILADELPHIA

Copyright © 2004 University of Pennsylvania Press

All rights reserved

Printed in the United States of America on acid-free paper

10 9 8 7 6 5 4 3 2 1

Published by

University of Pennsylvania Press

Philadelphia, Pennsylvania 19104-4011

LIBRARY OF CONGRESS CATALOGING-IN-PUBLICATION DATA

Sageman, Marc

Understanding Terror Networks / Marc Sageman.

p. cm.

Includes bibliographical references and index.

ISBN 0-8122-3808-7 (cloth : alk. paper)

1. Terrorists–Social networks. 2. Terrorism. 3. Jihad. I. Title.

HV6431.S23 2004

303.6′25–dc22

2003070524

Contents

Preface

A NEW TYPE of terrorism threatens the world, driven by networks of fanatics determined to inflict maximum civilian and economic damages on distant targets in pursuit of their extremist goals. Armed with modern technology, they are capable of devastating destruction worldwide. They target the West, but their operations mercilessly slaughter thousands of people of all races and religions. Only a thorough understanding of these new terror networks and their social movement will enable the world to mount an effective defense.

As a step toward that understanding, this book combines fact with theory to go beyond the headlines and journalistic accounts and stimulate a more sophisticated discourse on the subject. Based on the biographies of 172 terrorists gathered from open sources, it examines this social movement, which I call the global Salafi jihad. It excavates the ideological roots of the movement and traces its evolution throughout the world. The data, broken down in terms of social, personal, and situational variables, challenge the conventional explanations of terrorism. They suggest instead that this form of terrorism is an emergent quality of the social networks formed by alienated young men who become transformed into fanatics yearning for martyrdom and eager to kill. The shape and dynamics of these networks affects their survivability, flexibility, and success.

I bring an unusual combination of experience and skills to bring to the study of terrorism. As a Foreign Service officer, I worked with Islamic fundamentalists on a daily basis during the Afghan-Soviet war, from 1986 to 1989. These interactions gave me some insight into the mujahedin's beliefs and practices. I also developed an appreciation of them as human beings, which ran counter to media portrayals of them in the aftermath of September 11, 2001. I was intrigued and decided to look into this phenomenon.

After leaving the Foreign Service in 1991, I returned to medicine and completed a residency in psychiatry. I am now in private practice and keep up with the literature of this rapidly changing field. Many of the old psychodynamic theories have been largely discredited in the modern field of psychiatry owing to lack of effectiveness or any empirical backing. Yet they still have an echo in the field of terrorism, where most of the "psychological" commentators provide psychodynamic accounts. I am a strong supporter of the new movement in medicine to base its practice on empirical science, which has started to eliminate some of the harmful practices stemming from age-old but misguided traditions. Empiricism should also inform the social science of terrorism. My subspecialty is forensic psychiatry. I have extensive experience interviewing, analyzing, and writing and testifying about murderers. I have learned that many of our popular concepts about them are mistaken. But nothing in my experience with solitary murderers, even mass murderers, helps me understand the collective murder-suicides of September 11, 2001. Their motivations and desire for martyrdom cannot be extrapolated from what is known about common criminals.

During my medical training I also acquired a doctorate in political sociology. I studied large-scale common good organizations such as political parties, unions, professional associations, and terrorist organizations. This helps me focus on larger social patterns even in my psychiatric practice, where I try to combine the statistical and analytical tools of social science with individual case study. Advances in social network analysis provided valuable insight into some of the surprising aspects of this global terrorist network.

In addition, extensive scholarship in the social psychology of genocide perpetrators over the past four decades has shed some light on this phenomenon. For several years I have taught a seminar at the University of Pennsylvania on this topic, which has sensitized me to the contributions of psychology, sociology, and social psychology to explanations of collective violence. The first meeting of my seminar on "The Moral Psychology of Holocaust Perpetrators" was held on September 12, 2001. During the seminar, the analogy between the Nazis and global Salafi terrorists became increasingly obvious to my students and me. This book is a continuation of my research into the origins of collective violence.

* * *

The data in this study are strictly derived from public sources. Since I left the government, I have neither security clearance nor access to government confidential files. Much of terrorism research is done under the cloak of secrecy. Often that is for legitimate national security reasons. However, research that is conducted in secret and not subject to rigorous peer review may be flawed and reach conclusions that are deleterious in their practical implications. My past experience in the Foreign Service made me well aware that the quality of "intelligence" is variable and depends on good sources and analysis. The competition and collaboration that mark the scientific method are mostly absent in the government, leading officials to an unwarranted sense of confidence in their analyses. Seclusion of the intelligence-gathering process shelters it from criticism, which affects the validity and reliability of its conclusions (Taylor, 1991: 123).

This book is an attempt to stimulate new ideas and perspectives in the study of terrorism. It raises as many questions as it answers. It aims at theoretical insights and practical applications for global security. My hope is that it starts a fruitful conversation that will help both specialists and laypeople better understand.

*Understanding
Terror
Networks*

ONE

The Origins of the Jihad

T HE GLOBAL Salafi jihad is a worldwide religious revivalist movement with the goal of reestablishing past Muslim glory in a great Islamist state stretching from Morocco to the Philippines, eliminating present national boundaries. It preaches *salafiyyah* (from *salaf*, the Arabic word for "ancient one" and referring to the companions of the Prophet Mohammed), the restoration of authentic Islam, and advocates a strategy of violent jihad, resulting in an explosion of terror to wipe out what it regards as local political heresy. The global version of this movement advocates the defeat of the Western powers that prevent the establishment of a true Islamist state.

Al Qaeda is the vanguard of this movement, which includes many other terrorist groups that collaborate in their operations and share a large support base (see Burke, 2003). Salafi ideology determines its mission, sets its goals, and guides its tactics. What sets the global Salafi jihad apart from other terrorist campaigns is its violence against foreign non-Muslim governments and their populations in furtherance of Salafi objectives.

Defending Islam: Jihad

Like other great, long-established religions, Islam is full of contentious issues, especially about some of its core concepts, such as *jihad*, which translates roughly as "striving" but denotes any form of activity, either personal or communal, undertaken by Muslims in attempting to follow the path of God. No single doctrine is universally accepted.

In a world full of iniquities, the greater jihad is the individual nonviolent striving to live a good Muslim life, following God's will. It includes adhering to the five pillars of Islam: profession of faith (*shahada*); praying regularly; fasting during Ramadan; being charitable; and performing the *hajj*, the pilgrimage to Mecca. It requires lifelong discipline and constant vigilance.

The lesser jihad is the violent struggle for Islam. Traditional Islamic jurisprudence saw jihad as an obligation in a world divided into the land of Islam (*dar al-Islam*) and the land of conflict (*dar al-harb*). The Muslim community, the umma, was required to engage in a jihad to expand dar al-Islam throughout the world so that all humankind could benefit from living within a just political social order. One school of interpretation diluted this belligerence by introducing the notion of the land of treaty (*dar al-suhl*), which had concluded a truce with dar al-Islam and was not subject to jihad.

There was a further distinction between defensive and offensive jihad. When infidels invade dar al-Islam and threaten the existence of Islam and its practices there, a legal opinion, fatwa, can sanction a state of jihad against the infidels. This implies an individual obligation (*fard ayn*) for all Muslims to take part in this defensive jihad, either through direct fighting or through financial contributions, charity, or prayers. In contrast, an offensive jihad to attack the land of the infidels (*dar al-kufr*) to submit it to Sharia, the strict Quranic law, implies a collective obligation (*fard kifaya*), which can be and often is discharged by Muslim governments without personal participation of individual Muslims. When the Soviets invaded Afghanistan in December 1979, several Muslim religious leaders issued fatwas compelling Muslims to take up the jihad to repel the infidels. This defensive version of jihad for the protection of Islam was one that Sheikh Abdallah Azzam preached with great success during the Afghan war.

Azzam was one of the first Arabs to join the jihad against the Soviets. He met with the Afghan resistance leaders and urged them to unify against the enemy. But his main success was in promoting the cause of the jihad worldwide. His message was simple; he issued fatwas proclaiming the fight against the Soviet invaders a defensive jihad. There was no ambiguity. The Afghan jihad was a fard ayn, a personal obligation for each Muslim, and as such it overrode the need to get parental, religious, or spousal permission to join the jihad. Many young people answered his call and came to Peshawar in Pakistan to join the jihad. Throughout the conflict, he remained uncompromising in his message: "Jihad and the rifle alone: no negotiations, no conferences, no dialogues." To him, Afghanistan was the first step in a worldwide jihad to recapture Muslim lands lost to infidels, especially his native Palestine:

> *This duty shall not lapse with victory in Afghanistan, and the jihad will remain an individual obligation until all other lands which formerly were Muslim come back to us and Islam reigns within them once again. Before us lie Palestine, Bukhara, Lebanon, Chad, Eritrea, Somalia, the Philippines, Burma, South Yemen, Tashkent, Andalusia. . . . Our presence in Afghanistan today, which is the accomplishment of the imperative of jihad and our devotion to the struggle, does not mean that we have forgotten Palestine. Palestine is our beating heart, it comes even before Afghanistan in our minds, our hearts, our feelings and our faith.* (Quoted in Kepel, 2002: 147)

Azzam was careful to confine this jihad to reclaiming formerly Muslim land lost to non-Muslim governments. He never advocated the overthrow of regimes in Muslim countries. Indeed, he tried hard to unify the various warring Afghan factions against the Soviets and the Communist Afghan government. He preached in most Muslim countries but never advocated the overthrow of any of their secular governments on the grounds of apostasy. His biography shows that he rejected internecine Muslim fights, like the Black September 1970 revolt in Jordan. He considered Afghan President Najibullah to be a Communist and not a Muslim, and saw no problem in continuing the fight against his government after the Soviets withdrew. Azzam's advocacy of jihad was a traditional one, albeit an aggressive, one demanding the return of formerly Muslim lands.

Restoring Islamic Prominence

The history of Islam, like that of Christianity or Judaism, is full of revivalist movements, restoring energy and vitality to the faith. Islam views itself as the latest and perfect revelation of God's message; the Prophet has been dubbed the "Seal of all Revelation." Implicit in this message is the destiny of Muslims to lead humanity and spread God's message throughout the world. Yet after a few centuries of spectacular gains, Islam reached a plateau and entered a long period of political and cultural decline. The disparity between its self-appointed mission and reality generated waves of revivalist movements to check this decadence and restore its grandeur.

Various diagnoses of the causes of this decadence have elicited a range of responses. These include personal redemption, withdrawal (*hijra* in Arabic), imitation, accommodation, and confrontation. Imitation has been a popular strategy and includes adoption of secularism and Westernization to transform Muslim societies. Accommodation and assimilation are programs of reform which include a reinterpretation of Islam in light of modern conditions, allowing it to catch up to the West while preserving an Islamic core. More confrontational strategies include peaceful political activism and, finally, the use of violent tactics, jihad, in defense of Islam.

The Salafi strategy is based on the following diagnosis: Islam became decadent because it strayed from the righteous path. The strength of the original and righteous umma flowed from its faith and its practices, for they were pleasing to God. Recapturing the glory and grandeur of the Golden Age requires a return to the authentic faith and practices of the ancient ones, namely the Prophet Mohammed and his companions.

Traditionally, Islamic religious and legal interpretations are based on four prongs. The first is the authority of the Quran. The second is the words and deeds of the Prophet as recorded in stories (*hadith*) by people who knew him. The third is an extension of the first two, based on analogies, to arrive at some opinion to deal with situations not encountered in the Quran or the hadith. The last is a consensus of Islamic scholars on a particular issue. Salafists reject the last two Islamic traditions as innovations (*bidah*) that have been corrupted by non-Islamic influences and that dilute the word of God. To them, only the first two are authentic messages from God, and the only legitimate beliefs and practices are strictly derived from them. This return to genuine Islam would please God who would once again bestow strength, glory, and dignity upon the umma. They reject modern Muslim traditions and practices as deviations from the path of God that lead to decadence.

Dawa

The Salafi diagnosis and prescription can accommodate several strate-gies. A nonviolent personal form was Muhammad Ilyas's creation of Tab-lighi Jamaat (Society for the Propagation of Islam) in 1927 in India. Es-chewing politics, Ilyas advocated intensive religious discipline to bring back Muslims who had succumbed to the temptation of Hindu or West-ern culture. This discipline is based on strict and literal imitation of the life of the Prophet and his companions as the model of Islamic virtue. Through these everyday practices, all forms of impious thoughts and be-havior corrupting true Islamic life would fade away. This "born again" movement seeks to break the links between faithful Muslims and their corrupting environment and forge them into the authentic umma of strict submission to God. This strategy proved to be successful in a setting where Muslims were in a minority, as in India or where they were expatriates in a non-Muslim land. With the urbanization of the second half of the twen-tieth century, it also became popular where young Muslims moved from the countryside to cities, away from their traditional customs and into a more disorienting and secular lifestyle. In the late twentieth century, it became the most important form of Muslim revivalism worldwide, in Western Europe as well as in developing countries.

Like other Salafi movements, the Tablighi movement rejected tradi-tional worship of saints or tombs. It is not well known because its adher-ents intentionally maintain a low profile. It advocates individual respon-sibility in spreading Islam to the rest of society through one's personal proselytism to convert others. Ilyas urged his disciples to travel widely throughout the world and promote the *dawa* (call to Islam in Arabic). This calls for reaffiliating Muslims to "true" Islam or converting non-Mus-lims. They operate informally at the grassroots level, shying away from undue publicity and staying away from politics. They wander on foot in imitation of the Prophet from one small mosque to another, spending adequate time among the faithful and leaving a trail of reaffiliated or "born again" Muslims. Over three-quarters of a century, it has formed a dense network around the globe and has become the major force in twentieth-century Muslim revivalism. Its headquarters are located near Lahore, Pak-istan. It is a patient strategy aimed at the slow transformation of Muslim society into an authentic umma (Khosrokhavar, 1997: 47-116). In recent years, Tablighi networks have become vulnerable to exploitation by more militant Salafists, who reject the unifying and nonviolent Tablighi vision of Islam rooted in the Indian subcontinent. To jump ahead, many future al Qaeda recruits got visas to Pakistan on the pretext of plans to study at Tablighi schools there while in reality, they intended to go to Afghanistan for terrorism training (Kherchtou, 2001: 1109).

A second Salafi strategy is peaceful political activism to change society through state organs. Dramatic decline of the umma in comparison to Western societies in the nineteenth century and the first half of the twentieth inspired this strategy. France directly conquered Muslim lands in North Africa. Britain established imperial domination over South Asia and parts of the Middle East. Economic exploitation, social discrimination, and lack of industrial development characterized this era of European colonialism. When colonial powers blocked various political venues to redress these humiliating trends, Muslims turned to religion to regain dignity, pride, and power. Political activism grounded in religious principles is traditional in Islam, which does not recognize the Western separation of religion and politics so painfully negotiated in Europe as a result of its calamitous religious wars.

In the late nineteenth century, Jamal al-Din al-Afghani (d. 1896) was the voice of this political form of Muslim revivalism. Originally from Persia, he resided in Afghanistan, India, Egypt, Persia, Iraq, and the Ottoman Empire, often one step ahead of state arrest. In his travels, Afghani became disgusted at the willingness of Muslims to accept Western ideas and domination. He believed that religion was a political force and tried to inspire them to unite to restore Islamic grandeur. He rejected godless Western materialism but admired modern science and technology. He believed that the strength of Islam resided in the values and practices of the Prophet and his pious companions, purged of later aberrations. He argued that a combination of modern science and the values of the ancient pious ones (salaf) would restore the Golden Age of Islam. He urged a pan-Islamic movement of political solidarity against the West (Hodgson, 1974, 3: 307-310).

More consistent with Salafi revivalism was the creation of Salafi political parties. Hasan al-Banna (1906-1949) established the Muslim Brotherhood in 1928 in Egypt, and Mawlana abu al-Ala Mawdudi (1903-1979) founded the Jamaat-i Islami (Islamic Society) in 1941 in India. The two men held similar beliefs, namely the unity of Islam as an all-encompassing guide for the life of the believer and his or her community. Their diagnoses and prescriptions were Salafi. They advocated the creation of a true Muslim state through imposition of the Sharia, which they viewed not only as the strict Quranic law but also as the practices of the salaf. Science and technology could be harnessed in an Islamic context. This new Golden Age would require personal and communal jihad to change the practices of the believers and bring about political reforms, creating the social and political conditions for such all-encompassing practices. To carry out this program, each created his organization as a vanguard of the righteous community that would serve as the nucleus of true "born again" Muslims spreading authentic Islam to the broader society. Violent jihad against the infidel colonizers was permissible, and these parties allied themselves with nationalist Muslims trying to gain independence from the colonizers.

Mid-twentieth-century decolonization restored Muslims to power and ushered in the promise of a true Islamist state. On the Indian subcontinent, the creation of Pakistan was based on the notion that true Muslims cannot live under infidel domination. But the new Muslim leaders chose the imitation strategy. Their ideas of secularism, popular sovereignty, nationalism, women's rights, and constitutionalism came into direct conflict with the Salafists, who raised questions about their legitimacy as Muslim leaders. This opposition between Muslim leaders and political Salafists made for an explosive situation. The state responded with a seesaw strategy of accommodation and repression. This strategy of peaceful Salafi political reform survives to this day in Egypt, Morocco, and Pakistan, but has been suppressed in many other countries.

Salafi Jihad

Repression by modern Muslim states convinced some Salafists that dawa and political reforms were not viable strategies for the establishment of an Islamist state. But any violence against the state would spread *fitna* (temptation or trial) in the community. Fitna refers to the chaos or disunity of the two civil wars that tore the Muslim community apart within half a century of the Prophet's death, resulting in the Shia-Sunni split. The candidate eventually selected as caliph specifically appealed to unity. Those who followed him became Sunni and those who rejected him became Shia. Sunni traditions universally condemn fitna within the umma. Even a bad Sunni ruler was still better than fitna. How could good Muslims revolt against a bad Muslim leader without causing fitna?

The legitimization of such a revolt lies in Sayyid Qutb's (1906-1966) concept of *jahiliyya*, the state of barbarism and ignorance that prevailed in the Arabic Peninsula before Mohammed's revelations. Qutb, an Egyptian ideologist for the Muslim Brothers, was imprisoned because of his opposition to President Nasser's secular policies. His views grew more radical in prison. Although he was not the first one to use this concept, he was the first to draw its radical implications.

In the eighteenth century, Mohamed ibn Abd al-Wahhab (1703-1791), an Arabian Peninsula preacher, had rejected the depravity of the prevailing popular beliefs and practices of the tribes of the peninsula. He claimed they had reverted back to a state of jahiliyya. As idolaters, they deserved death for abandoning Islam. He preached an austere form of Islam based on a strict interpretation of the Quran, purifying Islam from later deviations. His central doctrine was *Tawhid* (the Unity of God in Arabic), condemning as idolatry all signs of possible intermediaries to God, such as saints or shrines. He forged an alliance with a local tribal chief, Mohamed ibn Saud, forming a revivalist political movement to purify Islam and fulfill its godly promise. The charge of jahiliyya was the justification for waging war on fellow Muslims. The Wahhabi-Saudi alliance conquered most of the peninsula by the end of the eighteenth century. To the horror of the umma, it destroyed all the sacred tombs, including the tomb of the Prophet, massacred the Muslims of the Holy Cities, and imposed its own standards on Muslim pilgrims. The Ottomans intervened and, using Western European military tactics, pushed it back to its ancestral homeland around Riyadh. The Wahhabi-Saudi alliance survived for more than two centuries. By 1925, it had reconquered most of the peninsula and founded the kingdom of Saudi Arabia.

Ibn Abd al-Wahhab had based many of his Quranic interpretations on the fatwas of Taqi al-Din Ahmad ibn Taymiyya (1263-1328), who had lived in one of the most disruptive periods of Muslim history—the conquest of Muslim lands by the Mongols who had previously converted to Islam. The question was put to ibn Taymiyya whether it was legitimate for Muslims to declare a jihad against other Muslims. He responded that, since the Mongols continued to follow the Yasa legal code of Genghis Khan instead of the Sharia, they were not real Muslims, but apostates who should be punished with death according to the Sharia. It was the right, indeed the duty, of Muslims to wage jihad against them. Although often at odds with the Mamluk rulers and earning short prison sentences as a result, ibn Taymiyya in his other writings never condoned revolting against them despite their alleged depraved practices (Sivan, 1985: 90-101).

Mawdudi had resurrected the concept of jahiliyya in his writings as an abstract term to describe the system of beliefs and ideas of the times in India. There was no hint that he intended it as a justification for violent revolt. Qutb took both ibn Taymiyya's duty to wage jihad against apostates and Mawdudi's concept of jahiliyya out of context and combined them in a novel way, extending ibn Abd al-Wahhab's ideas even further.

Sayyid Qutb's influence on the Salafi jihad in general was crucial. Afghan resistance leaders like Burhanuddin Rabbani, who translated his works into Dari, were his disciples. Some of the founders of al Qaeda—Ayman al-Zawahiri, Ali Amin Ali al-Rashidi, and Subhi Muhammad Abu Sittah— were Egyptian disciples who had sought refuge from political persecution in the Afghan jihad. Qutb's writings later filled the ideological vacuum created when the catastrophic 1967 Arab defeat discredited imitation and pan-Arabism as strategies for catching up to the West. Qutb's *Milestones*, published in 1964, is the manifesto of the Salafi jihad and its later global variant. Deeper analysis of his arguments is necessary to understand this violent ideology and its widespread appeal.

Qutb started by stating the Salafi creed. Mankind was on the brink of a precipice. It was devoid of vital values necessary for its healthy development and real progress. Western civilization could not provide this guidance, for it had no such values. Only Islam possessed them. Unfortunately, the umma—that group of people whose manners, ideas and concepts, rules and regulations, values, and criteria are all derived from Islamic sources—had been extinct for years because later deviations had corrupted the original teachings. It was necessary to restore the umma to its original form in order for Islam to play its decisive role. The goal was a spiritual and practical change from the world of jahiliyya. Both communism, which humiliated man, and capitalism, which exploited him, were rebellions against God's authority and denied the dignity God gave to man: "To attain the leadership of mankind, we must have something to offer besides material progress, and this other quality can only be a faith and a way of life which on the one hand conserves the benefits of modern science and technology, and on the other fulfills the basic human needs on the same level of excellence as technology has fulfilled them in the sphere of material comfort. And then this faith and way of life must take concrete form in a human society—in other words, in a Muslim society" (Qutb, n.d.: 10).

To revive Islam, a vanguard was necessary to recapture the message of God. True Islam had existed only during the generation of the Companions of the Prophet, who were inspired exclusively by the Quran and the hadith. Later innovations diluted this message. This resulted in *jahili* society, no longer worthy of any compromise. "Our aim is first to change ourselves so that we may later change society. Our foremost objective is to change the practices of this society" (21). This task demanded great sacrifices.

The fundamental question for this revived religion was the relationship between God and man. The doctrine of Tawhid, the Unity of God, enshrined in the first part of the Islamic creed, "there is no God but God," addresses this relationship. Sovereignty can be ascribed only to God and not to humans, be they rulers, priests, or rich men. The original Companions were pure and there was no need to enforce laws, "for now conscience was the law-enforcer, and the pleasure of God, the hope of Divine reward, and the fear of God's anger took the place of police and punishments"(30). Through Islam, they had attained perfection. "All this was possible because those who established this religion in the form of a state, a system of laws and regulations had first established it in their hearts and lives in the form of faith, character, worship and human relationships" (21).

This state of perfection pleased God.

When God tried them and they proved steadfast, relinquishing their own personal desires, and when God Most High knew that they were not waiting for any reward in this world, now were they desirous to see the victory of this message and the establishment of this Religion on earth by their hands, when their hearts became free of pride of lineage, of nationality, of country, of tribe, of household—in short, when God Most High saw them

to be morally pure—then He granted them the great trust, the conscious
assumption of being God's representative on earth. . . . He knew they
would not use it to benefit their own selves or their families or tribe or na-
tion, but would dedicate this authority purely to the service of God's reli-
gion and laws, as they knew that the true source of authority is God alone
and that they were only trustees. (31)

Islam was not just a theory but a way of life based on deep faith. It was
this spirit of complete submission to God that transformed men to form
the umma. The first task was to implant this faith in the hearts of men
and translate this belief into a living reality. By acknowledging only the
sovereignty of God and his Sharia in all spheres of life, the call to Islam
(dawa) freed men from servitude to other men so that they might devote
themselves to God and delivered them from the clutches of human lord-
ship and manmade laws, value systems, and traditions.

So far, this was a traditional Salafi argument. But Qutb departed from
his predecessors when he insisted on jihad to establish the true Muslim
state. The second part of the Muslim creed, bearing witness that "Mohammed is the Messenger of God," was the guide to the formation of the
true umma. The revival of Islam and its society is based on the model of
this original umma, which under the leadership of the Prophet strove to
bring people to God's sovereignty, authority, and laws:

It cannot come into existence simply as a creed in the hearts of individual
Muslims, however numerous they may be, unless they become an active,
harmonious and cooperative group, distinct by itself, whose different ele-
ments, like the limbs of a human body, work together for its formation, its
strengthening, its expansion, and for its defense against all those elements
which attack its system, working under a leadership which is independent
of the jahili *leadership, which organizes its various efforts into one harmo-*
nious purpose, and which prepares for the strengthening and widening of
their Islamic character and directs them to abolish the influences of their
opponent, the jahili *life.* (48)

To strive for the cause of God is "to abolish all injustice from the earth,
to bring people to the worship of God alone, and to bring them out of
servitude to others into the servants [*sic*] of the Lord" (56). This implied

11

the abolition of those oppressive political systems which prevented people from freely choosing Islam. Islam could not be imposed by force, but this did not mean that Muslims had to tolerate political and material powers that prevented people from accepting it. Islam freed man from servitude to other men, for sovereignty belonged to God alone, and Islam challenged all systems through which man had usurped this divine attribute.

Qutb maintained that dawa, or preaching, could not by itself achieve God's dominion on earth. "Those who have usurped the authority of God and are oppressing God's creatures are not going to give up their power merely through preaching" (58-59). Only a vanguard Muslim movement could remove the political, ideological, social, racial, and economic obstacles to dawa's dissemination. "This is the only way in which 'the religion' can be purified for God alone. The word 'religion' includes more than belief; 'religion' actually means a way of life, and in Islam this is based on belief" (61). Striving through use of the sword (*jihad bis sayf*) must clear the way for striving through preaching. Jihad in its narrow or defensive war sense distorted the universal nature of Islam, which was a movement to wipe out tyranny: "If we insist on calling Islamic *Jihad* a defensive movement, then we must change the meaning of the word 'defense' and mean by it the 'defense of man' against those elements which limit his freedom. These elements take the form of beliefs and concepts, as well as of political systems, based on economic, racial or class distinctions. When Islam came into existence, the world was full of such systems, and the present-day *Jahiliyya* also has various kinds of such systems" (62).

Islam's universal mission is eternal and ubiquitous, not dependent on specific causes or "external reasons" such as invasion and defensive wars. "It is in the very nature of Islam to take initiative for freeing the human beings throughout the earth from servitude to anyone other than God; and so it cannot be restricted within any geographical or racial limits, leaving all mankind on the whole earth in evil, in chaos and in servitude to lords other than God" (73).

The message of Islam is universal: "Islam is not a heritage of any particular race or country; this is God's religion and it is for the whole world. It has the right to destroy all obstacles in the form of institutions and traditions, which limit man's freedom of choice. It does not attack individuals nor does it force them to accept its beliefs; it attacks institutions and traditions to release human beings from their poisonous influences, which distort human nature and which curtail human freedom" (75).

For Sayyid Qutb, Islam is not merely a set of beliefs, like Western religions. It is a way of life ordained by God for all mankind. As jahili societies do not allow the conditions for the Islamic way of life, "it is the duty of Islam to annihilate all such systems, as they are obstacles in the way of universal freedom" (75). Jihad is simply a name for making this system of life dominant in the world and implies practical steps to organize a movement for bringing it about. "Thus, whenever an Islamic community exists which is a concrete example of the Divinely-ordained system of life, it has a God-given right to step forward and take control of the political authority so that it may establish the Divine system on earth, while it leaves the matter of belief to individual conscience" (76).

This struggle applied against any jahili society. "The *jahili* society is any society other than the Muslim society; and if we want a more specific definition, we may say that any society is a *jahili* society which does not dedicate itself to submission to God alone, in its beliefs and ideas, in its observances of worship, and in its legal regulations. According to this definition, all the societies existing in the world today are *jahili*" (80). It was clear that "all the existing so-called 'Muslim' societies are also *jahili* societies" because their way of life is not based on submission to God alone. "Although they believe in the Unity of God, still they have relegated the legislative attribute of God to others and submit to this authority, and from this authority they derive their systems, their traditions and customs, their laws, their values and standards, and almost every practice of life" (82). They have completely abandoned Islam in their way of life. Full acceptance of the second part of the Muslim creed, witnessing, "Mohammed is the Messenger of God," implies imitation of Mohammed's way of life and obedience to Sharia, God's law. Islamic society is not one in which people call themselves Muslims but in which Sharia has no status. Just as Islam is not confined to ideas alone but includes a whole way of life, so is Sharia not strictly limited to laws, but includes "principles of belief, principles of administration and justice, principles of morality and human relationships, and principles of knowledge" (107).

By declaring present Muslim societies jahiliyya, Sayyid Qutb provides the rationale for rejection of and violent revolt (*jihad bis sayf*) against nominally Muslim regimes, bypassing the issue of fitna. The righteous Muslims were not fighting other Muslims, but idolaters. Shortly after publication of *Milestones*, Nasser's government rearrested Qutb for sedition and he was executed on August 29, 1966. Qutb's martyrdom bestowed instant credibility upon his ideas.

His disciples then had to work out the practical strategic implications of his theoretical arguments. The traditionalists tried to reconcile his arguments with dawa, holding that preaching alone would lead the corrupt Muslim society back to true Islam. Hasan al-Hudaybi, the leader of the Muslim Brothers, summarized this opinion in the title of his book *Preachers, not Judges*. Militants accepted the argument that violent overthrow of the regime was the only solution. Salih Sirriya, the leader of a radical Muslim Brotherhood offshoot called the Islamic Liberation Party, condemned the political system for imposing this state of jahiliyya. He viewed the decaying society at large as the victim of unscrupulous godless leaders. A coup overthrowing this top leadership therefore would trigger a spontaneous popular uprising restoring the Islamist state. The attempted coup on April 18, 1974, at the Technical Military Academy in Cairo was quickly subdued. Sirriya was arrested and later executed.

A more influential interpretation of Qutb's ideas was that of Shukri Mustafa, who drew the implication of the doctrine of jahiliyya to its logical extreme. If Egyptian society was jahiliyya and rotten to the core, then it must be excommunicated (*takfir*, a lapsed Muslim, from the Arabic root *kufr* for impiety). He advocated following the strategy of the Prophet, who, when faced with the jahiliyya in Mecca, went in exile (*hijra*) to Medina in order to build a society of Muslims, gather strength, and return to Mecca in triumph. Imitating the Prophet, Mustafa created the Society of Muslims (Jamaat al-Muslimin), righteous communes withdrawn from the corrupt society. At first, he built his communes in caves in Upper Egypt (the press called the movement "People of the Cave") before establishing communal apartments in cities. He hoped that withdrawal and isolation would protect the community from the impious society and allow it to grow strong enough to eventually conquer Egypt and establish a true Islamist society. To belong to the sect, one had to abandon one's ties to society, including family, former friends, state employment, and what was considered useless education. Communal living in city apartments was also open to women, and Mustafa encouraged early marriage among his members. This contrasted with the rest of Egyptian society, where poverty postponed departure from the parental home and marriage. Many objections to the Society of Muslims came from parents whose daughters had disappeared to marry into the sect. Information about joining the sect was spread through siblings and friends, as Mustafa was prohibited from publishing his ideas. The sect sustained itself through agricultural labor, petty commerce, and remittances from members sent to work in oil-rich Persian Gulf states. After a government crackdown in 1977, this sect disappeared from Egypt. Its ideas survived among future global terrorists.

By far, the most influential disciple of Qutb was Muhammad Abd al-Salam Faraj (1954-1982), who was head of the Cairo branch of the Tanzim al-Jihad (Jihad Organization) that killed President Anwar al-Sadat. Faraj articulated his ideas in a pamphlet, *The Neglected Duty*. He quickly built on Qutb's argument:

> *The establishment of an Islamic State is an obligation for the Muslims, for something without which something which is obligatory cannot be carried out becomes (itself) obligatory. If, moreover, (such a) state cannot be established without war, then this war is an obligation as well.... The laws by which the Muslims are ruled today are the laws of Unbelief, they are actually codes of law that were made by infidels who then subjected the Muslims to these (codes).... After the disappearance of the Caliphate definitely in the year 1924, and (after) the removal of the laws of Islam in their entirety, and (after) their substitution by laws that were imposed by infidels, the situation (of the Muslims) became identical to the situation of the Mongols.* (Faraj, 1986: 165-167)

This analogy with the Mongols made the fatwas of ibn Taymiyya relevant to the present day. Faraj simply stated that the rulers of this age were in apostasy from Islam despite their profession of faith, and the Islamic punishment for apostasy was death (169). His pamphlet addressed the traditional objections to this argument. Faraj rejected out of hand the argument that benevolent societies might bring about the establishment of an Islamist state through their acts of devotion. Similarly, individual piety and education of Muslims abrogated the highest form of devotion, which is jihad (after the prescribed five pillars of Islam, of course). He liked Islamic political parties better than benevolent societies, "because a party at least talks about politics" (184). However, even this strategy failed for it collaborated with and thereby supported the "pagan" state.

Faraj rejected the strategy of using dawa to build a broad base that would bring about the foundation of an Islamist state. The wicked state's control of all means of mass communication prevented the true implementation of dawa. He repudiated the quest for knowledge without the use of violence as not addressing the needs of the community. Faraj also dismissed waiting for the liberation of former Muslim lands like "the liberation of Jerusalem" or defeat of imperialism before overthrowing one's government. Muslims must give priority to "radical definitive" solutions. "To fight an enemy who is near is more important than to fight an enemy who is far" (192). Fighting the "far enemy" would benefit the interests of local "Infidel Rule" and set back the Islamist cause through the shedding of Muslim blood. Fighting had to be only under the banner of Islam and under Islamist leadership:

> The basis of the existence of Imperialism in the Lands of Islam are (precisely) these rulers. To begin by putting an end to imperialism is not a laudatory and not a useful act. It is only a waste of time. We must concentrate on our own Islamic situation: we have to establish the Rule of God's Religion in our own country first, and to make the Word of God supreme. . . . There is no doubt that the first battlefield for jihad is the extermination of these infidel leaders and to replace them by a complete Islamic Order. From here we should start. (193)

Faraj noted that Islam had been spread by the sword, showing that jihad in Islam was not defensive. He quoted the Quranic "sword verses" to support his view: "When the sacred months have passed, slay the idolaters wherever you find them, and take them, and confine them, and lie in wait for them at every place of ambush" (Quran 9:5).

> With regard to the lands of Islam, the enemy lives right in the middle of them. The enemy even has got hold of the reins of power, for this enemy is

*(none other than) these rulers who have (illegally) seized the Leadership
of the Muslims. Therefore, waging* jihad *against them is an individual
duty. . . .*

Know that when jihad *is an individual duty, there is no (need) to ask
permission of (your) parents to leave to wage* jihad, *as the jurists have
said; it is thus similar to prayer and fasting.* (Faraj, 1986: 200)

Faraj also dismissed as a dangerous recent innovation the distinction
between the great jihad (against one's soul) and the small jihad (against
the enemy) because it reduced the value of fighting with the sword. Nor
was the absence of a caliph an excuse for postponing jihad. This made it
all the more urgent to organize jihad activities to return Islam to Muslim
nations. The price of neglecting jihad was the "lowness, humiliation, di-
vision and fragmentation in which the Muslims live today" (205).

The rest of Faraj's pamphlet is a discussion of military ethics and tactics, such as the legality of deceit, surprise attacks, and destruction of prop-
erty, and specifies that the killing of children, women, and innocent bystanders should be generally avoided.

Copies of the pamphlet were discovered in the houses of the perpetrators during the wave of arrests after the assassination of President Sadat.
It was clear that the pamphlet was a clandestine document for internal
and not public consumption. It was published only after the Egyptian
government directed Al-Azhar University scholars to refute its theses. The
debates around the accusation of jahiliyya and takfir go to the core of the
dispute between traditionalist and militant Salafists about the meaning
of jihad and the legitimacy of internal violent rebellion given the prohi-
bition against fitna. The militants, like Faraj, used selective quotes from
the Quran to support their positions. For instance, in his use of the "sword
verses," he quoted only the first part. The Quran continues, "but if they
repent and fulfill their devotional obligations and pay the *zakat* [tax for
alms] then let them go their way, for God is forgiving and kind" (Quran,
9:5). This last part undermines the militants' advocacy of indiscriminate
slaughter of Islam's enemies.

The Salafi jihad is thus a Muslim revivalist movement advocating the
violent overthrow of local Muslim government, the "near enemy," to establish an Islamist state.

Global Salafi Jihad

The Afghan war against the Soviet Union was a watershed in militant Muslim revivalist movements. Militants from all over the Muslim world finally met and interacted for lengthy periods of time. The common fight forged strong bonds among them. After the Soviets withdrew, the militants started to analyze their common problems with a more global perspective, transcending their countries of origin. Sheik Abdallah Azzam advocated a traditional jihad to roll back Christian encroachment on former Muslim lands. He rejected internal Muslim infighting as fitna. He supported conflicts in the Philippines, Palestine, and even Spain, but not in Muslim lands such as Egypt, Jordan, and Syria. The Egyptian Salafi mujahedin (from the Arabic root *jihad*, jihad fighters; the singular is *mujahed*), intoxicated with the ideas of Qutb and Faraj, sought help in overthrowing their government and wanted to use the Afghan jihad resources to that end. Osama bin Laden, Azzam's popular and fabulously wealthy deputy, gradually came to espouse their views. After Azzam's death in 1989, the organizations he had created survived, but lacked a common enemy to focus their energies. This changed with the appearance of U.S. troops in Saudi Arabia and later Somalia, both solid Muslim lands.

The Muslim militants' reaction to infidel troops on Muslim soil was originally a call to traditional jihad to throw the infidels out of Muslim lands. Under the now global gaze of the community of "Afghan Arabs" (also referred to as "Arab Afghans") however, a more global analysis of Islam's problems was gradually taking shape. Local *takfir* Muslim leaders were seen as pawns of a global power, which itself was now considered the main obstacle to establishing a transnational umma from Morocco to the Philippines. This in effect reversed Faraj's strategy and now the priority was jihad against the "far enemy" over the "near enemy." With the demise of the Soviet Union, the only such global power left was the United States. The discussions leading to this analysis took place during al Qaeda's Sudanese exile in the 1990s. Parallel discussions took place in New York, leading to the 1993 World Trade Center bombing, and in Algeria and France, prior to the wave of bombings there in 1995-96.

A step toward the global Salafi jihad was Osama bin Laden's August 8, 1996, declaration of "War Against the Americans Occupying the Land of the Two Holy Places (Expel the Infidels from the Arab Peninsula)." As the subtitle indicates, this fatwa kept Azzam's notion of defensive jihad to expel infidels from Muslim lands. The basis of the reversal of Faraj's strategy is captured in a metaphor: "The situation cannot be rectified (the shadow cannot be straightened when its source, the rod, is not straight either) unless the root of the problem is tackled. Hence it is essential to hit the main enemy who divided the *Ummah* into small and little countries and pushed it, for the last few decades, into a state of confusion."

Bin Laden went back to the Mongol analogy and ibn Taymiyya's fatwas in support of this strategy: "People of Islam should join forces and support each other to get rid of the main '*Kufr*' who is controlling the countries of the Islamic world, even to bear the lesser damage to get rid of the major one, that is the great *Kufr*." To bin Laden, there was no more important duty than pushing the American enemy out of the Holy Land. Again, citing ibn Taymiyya, "to fight in defense of religion and Belief is a collective duty; there is no other duty after Belief than fighting the enemy who is corrupting the life and the religion."

A year and a half later, on February 23, 1998, the fatwa of the World Islamic Front declaring "Jihad against Jews and Crusaders" became the manifesto of the full-fledged global Salafi jihad. In this document, bin Laden extended his previous concept of jihad from a defensive to an offensive one. The global Salafi jihad now carried the fight to the "far enemy" (the United States and the West in general) on its own territory or in third country territory. The justification for this new type of jihad was that U.S. "occupation" of Saudi Arabia, support for Israel, and the killing of Iraqi children was a "clear declaration of war on Allah, his Messenger, and Muslims":

The ruling to kill the Americans and their allies—civilians and military—is an individual duty for every Muslim who can do it in any country in which it is possible to do it. . . . We—with Allah's help—call on every Muslim who believes in Allah and wishes to be rewarded to comply with Allah's order to kill the Americans and plunder their money wherever and whenever they find it. We also call on Muslim ulema, leaders, youths, and soldiers to launch the raid on Satan's U.S. troops and the devil's supporters allying with them, and to displace those who are behind them so that they may learn a lesson. (bin Laden et al., 1998)

The clearest elaboration of this new global Salafi jihad is Ayman al-Za-wahiri's *Knights Under the Prophet's Banner* (al-Zawahiri, 2001: part 11). Here al-Zawahiri declared that the new jihad was a struggle between Islam and hostile global forces: the Western powers and Russia, using a "number of tools," including "(1) The United Nations. (2) The friendly rulers of the Muslim peoples. (3) The multinational corporations. (4) The international communications and data exchange systems. (5) The international news agencies and satellite media channels. (6) The international relief agencies, which are used as a cover for espionage, proselytizing, coup planning and the transfer of weapons." Opposed to this enemy was a new Islamist fundamentalist coalition, consisting of the jihad movements in the various lands of Islam. "It represents a growing power that is rallying under the banner of jihad for the sake of God and operating outside the scope of the new world order." Al-Zawahiri described this as a new phenomenon of young mujahedin, who had left "their families, country, wealth, studies, and jobs in search of jihad arenas for the sake of God." In his view, there was no solution without jihad. The betrayal of the peaceful Algerian fundamentalist movement demonstrated the futility of "all other methods that tried to evade assuming the burdens of jihad" (al-Zawahiri, 2001: part 11).

Loyalty to leadership was a duty that should not be allowed to deteriorate into a personality cult, for sovereignty belongs only to God. "The loyalty to the leadership and the acknowledgement of its precedence and merit represent a duty that must be emphasized and a value that must be consolidated. But if loyalty to the leadership reaches the point of declaring it holy and if the acknowledgement of its precedence and merit leads to infallibility, the movement will suffer from methodological blindness. Any leadership flaw could lead to a historic catastrophe, not only for the movement but also for the entire nation" (al-Zawahiri, 2001: part 11).

Mobilization of the Muslim masses was critical for the global Salafi jihad, which needed to get close to the masses, be in their midst or slightly ahead of them, and not isolated from them:

> The jihad movement must dedicate one of its wings to work with the
> masses, preach, provide services for the Muslim people, and share their
> concerns through all available avenues for charity and educational work.
> We must not leave a single area unoccupied. We must win the people's

confidence, respect and affection. The people will not love us unless they feel that we love them, care about them, and are ready to defend them. . . . We must not blame the nation for not responding or not living up to the task. Instead we must blame ourselves for failing to deliver the message, show compassion, and sacrifice. (al-Zawahiri, 2001: part 11)

This message had to be communicated in simple terms, so all could grasp its religious origins. This meant a strong dawa mission. The umma would not participate in the jihad unless it understood the slogans of the mujahedin.

The one slogan that has been well understood by the nation and to which it has been responding for the past 50 years is the call for the jihad against Israel. In addition to this slogan, the nation in this decade is geared against the U.S. presence. It has responded favorably to the call for the jihad against the Americans. A single look at the history of the Mujahedin in Afghanistan, Palestine, and Chechnya will show that the jihad movement has moved to the center of the leadership of the nation when it adopted the slogan of liberating the nation from its external enemies and when it portrayed it as a battle of Islam against infidelity and infidels. . . . The fact that must be acknowledged is that the issue of Palestine is the cause that has been firing up the feelings of the Muslim nation from Morocco to Indonesia for the past 50 years. In addition, it is a rallying point for all the Arabs, be they believers or non-believers, good or evil. (al-Zawahiri, 2001: part 11)

Al-Zawahiri declared that the jihad must expose the treason of the Muslim rulers and their apologists, which is based on their lack of faith and their support of the infidels against the Muslims. The movement must establish an Islarnist state in the Muslim heartland, from which to launch its battle to restore the Caliphate based on the traditions of the Prophet. "If the successful operations against Islam's enemies and the severe damage inflicted on them do not serve the ultimate goal of establishing the Muslim nation in the heart of the Islamic world," he argued, "they will be nothing more than disturbing acts, regardless of their magnitude, that could be absorbed and endured, even if after some time and with some losses" (al-Zawahiri, 2001: part 11).

This was not an easy goal that could be reached in the near future. Patience was needed for the jihad movement to build its structure until it was well established with enough resources and support to select the time and place to fight its battles. If local regimes uncover the movement's plans and arrest its members, withdrawal to the safety of a shelter should be sought "without hesitation, reluctance, or reliance on illusions." It was better to be on the move than spend time in the humiliation of captivity. Since the goal of the jihad is comprehensive change, the path is a long one, full of sacrifices. The movement must not despair of repeated setbacks and recurring calamities, and must never lay down its arms regardless of the casualties. If retreat is cut off and collapse is imminent, the mujahed should fight "so that nobody is captured or killed for nothing." But sometimes hostile circumstances dictated another strategy. If forced by local forces to fight under adverse circumstances, "we must respond in the arena that we choose; namely, to strike at the Americans and the Jews in our countries." This would accomplish three things. First, it would be a strike at the "great master" enemy hiding behind its local agents. Second, it would help win over the Muslim people by striking at "a target it favors, one that it sympathizes with those who hit it." Third, it would expose the regime before the Muslim people when it retaliates in defense of its "U.S. and Jewish masters, thus showing its ugly face, the face of the hired policeman who is faithfully serving the occupiers and the enemies of the Muslim nation" (al-Zawahiri, 2001: part 11).

Al-Zawahiri pressed his case to target the far enemy:

> *The masters in Washington and Tel Aviv are using the regimes to protect their interest and to fight the battle against the Muslims on their behalf. If the shrapnel from the battle reach their homes and their bodies, they will trade accusations with their agents about who is responsible for this. In that case, they will face one of two bitter choices: Either personally wage the battle against the Muslims, which means that the battle will turn into clear-cut jihad against infidels, or they reconsider their plans after acknowledging the failure of the brute and violent confrontation against Muslims. Therefore, we must move the battle to the enemy's grounds to burn the hands of those who ignite fire in our countries.* (al-Zawahiri, 2001: part 11)

Thus, al-Zawahiri argues, the struggle for the establishment of a Muslim state cannot be confined to a regional struggle and cannot be postponed:

> It is clear from the above that the Jewish-Crusade alliance, led by the
> United States, will not allow any Muslim force to reach power in any of
> the Islamic countries. It will mobilize all its power to hit it and remove it
> from power. Toward that end, it will open a battlefront against it that includes the entire world. It will impose sanctions on whoever helps it, if it
> does not declare war against them altogether. Therefore, to adjust to this
> new reality we must prepare ourselves for a battle that is not confined to a
> single region, one that includes the apostate domestic enemy and the Jewish-Crusade external enemy. . . . The mujahid Islamic movement must escalate its methods of strikes and tools of resisting the enemies to keep up
> with the tremendous increase in the number of its enemies, the quality of
> their weapons, their destructive powers, their disregard for all taboos, and
> disrespect for the customs of wars and conflicts. In this regard, we concentrate on the following:
>
> 1. The need to inflict the maximum casualties against the opponent, for
>   this is the language understood by the west, no matter how much
>   time and effort such operations take.
> 2. The need to concentrate on the method of martyrdom operations as
>   the most successful way of inflicting damage against the opponent
>   and the least costly to the Mujahedin in terms of casualties.
> 3. The targets as well as the type and method of weapons used must be
>   chosen to have an impact on the structure of the enemy and deter it
>   enough to stop its brutality, arrogance, and disregard for all taboos
>   and customs. It must restore the struggle to its real size.
> 4. To reemphasize what we have already explained, we reiterate that
>   focusing on the domestic enemy alone will not be feasible at this
>   stage. (al-Zawahiri, 2001: part 11)

This was a battle that every Muslim must face to defend his creed, society, values, honor, dignity, wealth, and power. To mobilize, the masses needed a leadership that they could trust, understand and follow; a clear enemy to strike at; and removal of the shackles of fear and weakness in their souls. The jihad movement must get its message across to the masses by breaking the media siege imposed on it. Al-Zawahiri described the basic objective of the Islamic jihad movement, regardless of the sacrifices and the time involved, as follows: "Liberating the Muslim nation, confronting the enemies of Islam, and launching jihad against them require a Muslim authority, established on a Muslim land, that raises the banner of jihad and rallies the Muslims around it. Without achieving this goal our actions will mean nothing more than mere and repeated disturbances that will not lead to the aspired goal, which is the restoration of the Caliphate and the dismissal of the invaders from the land of Islam" (al-Zawahiri, 2001: part 11).

The foregoing makes it clear that the present wave of terrorism directed at the far enemy is an intentional strategy of a Muslim revivalist social movement. Its ideology comes from Egypt, as its major contributors were Qutb, Mustafa, Faraj, and al-Zawahiri. It focuses on internal Islamic factors rather than non-Islamic characteristics. Unlike its portrayal in the West, it is not based on hatred of the West. It certainly preaches a message of hate for Western values, and the mention of Israel is a rallying point for the masses. But this hatred is derived from a particular Islamic version of love for God and true Muslims in general. Its appeal lies in its apparent simplicity and elegance that resonate with concerned Muslims not well schooled in traditional Muslim teaching, which it rejects. The next three chapters address how this movement evolved, who participates in it, and how they joined.

TWO

The Evolution of the Jihad

HE GLOBAL Salafi jihad is popularly conceived as a "blowback" (the alleged CIA neologism referring to unintended consequence of covert operations) of the U.S. government training and support of "Afghan Arabs" during the Afghan-Soviet war. This view appears again and again in the media and in books written by journalists. "The CIA had funded and trained the Afghan Arabs during the war, and now their former 'assets' appeared to be turning on their old ally" (Reeve, 1999: 55; see also Harding, 2000: 24; and many others). There is a tragic irony to the blowback thesis, from the hubris of 1980s U.S. policy for Afghanistan to the jihadi nemesis of September 11, 2001. Other commentators take the opposite tack, however, and accuse the CIA of doing too little and blame it for failure to prevent Pakistani support and training of militants, who later exported jihad and terrorism around the world (Bergen, 2001: 67). Only a close look at the historical evolution of the global Salafi jihad will resolve this dispute.

Egyptian Origins

Many of the founders of the global Salafi jihad came to Afghanistan in the 1980s from different countries and without prior connection to each other. This was not true of the Egyptians, who had known each other from their antigovernment activities in Egypt before seeking refuge in Afghanistan. This network of Egyptians went on to constitute the leadership of the global jihad.

The history of the Egyptian Salafi jihad is confusing, not least because the same names are recycled to label different groups, leading the inattentive reader to assume an erroneous genealogy. Only by putting labels aside and strictly following the actual network of the relationships involved can we start to see the origins of these movements and how the structure of these networks influenced doctrinal disputes, and later alliances, that eventually gave rise to global organizations such as al Qaeda or the Egyptian Islamic Jihad (EIJ).

The key person in this analysis is Ayman al-Zawahiri, the leader of the EIJ, and the deputy of al Qaeda. Ayman al-Zawahiri was born on June 19, 1951, and came from one of the most prestigious Egyptian families in Cairo. His father was a professor of pharmacology, his maternal grandfather held prestigious ambassadorial posts and academic positions, and an uncle had been the founding secretary general of the Arab League. Although educated in a secular school, al-Zawahiri was devout and regularly went to the mosque with his younger brother Mohammed. At an early age he was strongly influenced by the writings of Sayyid Qutb, and in 1966, he, his brother, and three high school friends made a secret pact to oppose the Nasser regime along the lines advocated by Qutb. The formation of such clandestine groups among high school friends, searching for a cause to give meaning to their young lives, is a common phenomenon. Usually, these groups are unconnected to a larger movement and fade over time, as people grow up and get on with their lives. In this case, circumstances and al-Zawahiri's obstinate perseverance sustained the group. The friends met at each other's homes and at the mosque. They wanted to be revolutionaries but did not know how to proceed. Many such groups formed all over Egypt, made up mainly of restless and alienated students. They were small, disorganized and largely unaware of each other because the repressive political climate of Egypt prevented them from advertising their existence and reaching out to each other.

The humiliating defeat by Israel in 1967 completely discredited the Nasserite government and its secular socialist policies. It fueled the alternative view, that "Islam is the solution." In his memoirs, al-Zawahiri (2001) described how he and his friends participated in the ensuing demonstrations protesting the catastrophe. They had decided to stage a demonstration at a mosque where they heard a young deputy prosecutor, Yahya Hashim, loudly challenge the government after services. Later, al-Zawahiri met and befriended him. Al-Zawahiri went on to medical school, where he slowly continued to expand his clandestine group, stressing secrecy and security. After Nasser's death, Anwar al-Sadat's government courted Islamic movements to help confront remnants of Nasser's leftist policies. He released imprisoned Muslim Brothers and sponsored Islamic associations or groups (Jamaat Islamiyya, usually referred to in the plural) at universities to challenge their leftist peers, who had control of university social associations.

This new freedom inaugurated a period of extensive experimentation among Islamist groups, each deriving its own strategy to achieve the Islamic state. The traditional Muslim Brothers preached dawa in an effort to peacefully transform civil society into a mass movement that would successfully demand and implement an Islamist state. Hasan al-Hudaybi, the Supreme Guide of the Muslim Brothers, championed this long-term strategy from below. He repudiated Qutb's call for violence in a book aptly titled *Preachers, not Judges*. The voice for this group was the monthly magazine *Al-Dawa*, which demanded the immediate application of Sharia by the state. Its analysis was that the main obstacle to the Islamist state was the Jews. The magazine opposed peace overtures with Israel, crusaders and their colonial variants, communists and their socialist variants, and finally secularists, like Mustafa Kemal Ataturk and his secular project in Turkey.

Impatient younger militants were not satisfied with this long-term strategy and demanded a more rapid creation of the Islamist state from above, through the activities of a vanguard of Muslims as advocated by Qutb, who had become a legend after his martyrdom. With the relaxation of repression after Nasser's death, small groups of Islamist militants spontaneously surfaced in university towns throughout Egypt. Each pursued its own strategy without bothering to coordinate or even gather support from other Jamaat Islamiyya.

Some were convinced that an Islamic society would form spontaneously if the iniquitous ruler were removed. This was the message of Salih Sirriya, a Palestinian who had come to Egypt from Jordan in 1971, after the failure of the Black September coup there in 1970. His eloquence and persuasiveness in religious and political affairs attracted students from Cairo and Alexandria. He organized them into a group called the Islamic Liberation Organization (ILO). His only message was that the violent overthrow of the godless Egyptian government would lead to the establishment of a righteous Muslim society. On April 18, 1974, about one hundred ILO members stormed the armory at the Technical Military Academy and seized weapons and vehicles to go to the nearby Arab Socialist Building, where Sadat and other top officials were attending an official event. The intent was to kill them all, capture the nearby radio and television buildings, and announce the birth of the Islamic Republic of Egypt. Security forces intercepted the conspirators before they were able to leave the school. The ensuing firefight killed eleven and wounded twenty-seven people. Ninety-five ILO members were arrested and tried; thirty-two were convicted. Sirriya and one of his lieutenants were executed on November 9, 1976.

The ILO failure did not discredit the idea of a coup d'état from above. Hashim advocated such a strategy and urged those close to him to wage a guerrilla war. Al-Zawahiri tried to dissuade his friend from pursuing this strategy, which required places of sanctuary from the government. Egypt was basically a narrow river valley sandwiched between two deserts without any good places to hide. Hashim persevered and tried to recruit the imprisoned ILO conspirators for his campaign. Using his position as deputy prosecutor, he planned their escape during a transfer between prisons. When the plan was discovered, Hashim and a few companions fled to a mountainous region in Upper Egypt. Police forces easily discovered them, and Hashim was killed in the ensuing firefight.

Another strategy was the creation of pure Islamic commmunities living outside the impure society, as advocated by Shukri Mustafa. His Society of Muslims ran afoul of the law in November 1976, after a few members left to form their own independent group. Declaring them apostate, a crime punishable by death, Mustafa led a group of disciples in a raid to kill them, probably to discourage future dissent. The police intervened, arrested a few members, and detained them without charging them. Mustafa demanded their release, but the government ignored him. His group earned the ridicule of the press, which portrayed them as a bunch of fanatics or criminals and latched onto the twin concepts of excommunication and exile (al-Takfir wa'l Hijra). The label stuck and this is how the Society is remembered. Mustafa protested the caricature in press releases which were never printed.

Out of frustration, Mustafa kidnapped a former minister, Muhammad al-Dhahabi, on July 3, 1977, and demanded the release of his followers, public apologies from the press, the publication of his book explaining his philosophy, the printing of the Society's communiqués and a modest amount of money. The government ignored the demands and Mustafa killed his hostage to maintain credibility. After the corpse was found, the police cracked down on the Society and several people on both sides were killed in the confrontations. The government arrested and tried hundreds of members, but convicted only a few. Mustafa and four others were sentenced to death and executed on March 19, 1978 (Ibrahim, 1980 and 1982; Kepel, 1993). The press coverage portrayed Mustafa as a fanatic criminal who sought to overthrow the regime and who had duped young innocent people under the cloak of religion. In Salafi circles, he became a cause célèbre, and his ideas later became influential among segments of the global Salafi jihad.

The main movement for the establishment of an Islamist state was the Jamaat Islamiyya at prominent universities in Cairo, Alexandria, and the provincial capitals of Asyut, Minya, Sohag, Qena, and Fayyum in Upper Egypt. These Islamic student associations organized services such as transportation for students, cheap copies of course notes, and even summer camps. By 1977, the Islamists completely dominated political and social life in the universities. They controlled student newspapers and printed Islamist literature, including Qutb's *Milestones*, which introduced Salafi ideas to the student body. Their alliance with Sadat's government dissolved because of their opposition to the peace process with Israel. The conclusion of the 1979 Camp David Accords added to their progressive disillusionment with the government's continuing secular policies and inspired the proliferation of clandestine Islamist cells preaching deeds over words.

Al-Zawahiri's group was probably typical of this gradual radicalization. Perhaps inspired by Hashim, it focused on jihad and the necessity of a coup rather than the slow process of a mass movement establishing an Islamist state. This strategy needed absolute secrecy and security to escape government notice. But it also required military skills and access to weapons, and hence a way to infiltrate the military. The vigilance of Egyptian counterintelligence services made this strategy especially perilous. Al-Zawahiri's group proceeded with great caution, using friendship or kinship ties to protect against potential denunciations. The recruitment of Issam al-Qamari illustrates this play of friendship and kinship bonds. A member of the group was Ulwi Mustafa Ulaywah. His brother Muhammad Mustafa Ulaywah had gone to the military college, where he befriended al-Qamari. Al-Qamari wanted to play a role in the overthrow of the Egyptian regime and had passed up opportunities to go to more prestigious schools and study for a more lucrative occupation in order to attend the military college and join the army. With increased intimacy and trust, Muhammad Ulaywah and al-Qamari discussed their religious and political views. Through the Ulaywah brothers, al-Qamari joined the group and became very close to al-Zawahiri. Al-Qamari rose quickly in the ranks of the Armed Corps. For his clandestine group, he drew up the major foci of security and military presence in the capital upholding the regime and analyzed the most vulnerable points. At the same time, his greater access to the military allowed him to divert some weapons from his base and store them in al-Zawahiri's clinic. Other members of al-Zawahiri's group included his brother Mohammed al-Zawahiri and Sayyid Imam al-Sharif, another surgeon, who later became known as Dr. al-Fadl.

Four to six such clandestine groups coalesced in Cairo under the overall leadership of Mohammed Abd al-Salam Faraj. His book about the neglected duty of jihad provided their common strategy and the label later applied to them by the authorities, the Tanzim al-Jihad (jihad organization). It is not clear how these clandestine groups found each other, but it appeared that Kamal Habib played a role. Faraj's group included some military members, such as Lieutenant Colonel Abud al-Zumur, an intelligence officer who led the military wing of the group. Rather than concentrate on the universities, Faraj focused on relatively deprived urban groups. He preached in a private mosque built for him by his in-laws and stressed the necessity of armed jihad to establish the Islamist state. His disciples in turn brought in their friends and families, expanding the group. Each Cairo group was autonomous, but their leaders met regularly to work out a general strategy. Although Faraj, like al-Zawahiri, favored recruitment of military officers, al-Zumur discouraged any special efforts in that direction for fear of exposure since he knew that internal security within the military was very vigilant. Some officers did join, but they had to be carefully vetted through friends or family. Al-Zumur's strategy was a popular uprising and revolution, based on the Iranian model of 1979.

The militant groups of Upper Egypt (Said) were of different composition and had different aims. Students constituted a majority (64 percent) in the Saidi groups, as opposed to a minority (43 percent) in the Cairo counterparts. Karam Zuhdi in Minya was the overall leader of the Upper Egypt groups. Najih Ibrahim Abdallah Sayyid was the leader in Asyut; Mohammad al-Islambuli, the leader in the business faculty at Asyut University; and Hamdi Abdel Rahman, the leader in Sohag. The Saidi groups remained embedded in their society, an important distinction which will be examined in Chapter 5. Upper Egypt had traditionally resisted central government control and maintained order according to a code of honor, blood feuds, and vendettas. Social groups fleeing from central control had historically found refuge there. For instance, the Copts, members of a Christian sect, were able to survive for centuries and constituted about 20 percent of the population there in contrast to 6 percent nationwide. Islamists in Upper Egypt resented this group, whom they believed to be overrepresented in provincial business and political institutions. This conflict between Islamists and Copts degenerated into open violence. For Zuhdi and his colleagues, the priority was to wage jihad first against the Copts for they considered Christian proselytism the major obstacle to the propagation of Islam. In their view, the regime was under the influence of this Christian cabal.

People who had connections to both the Cairo and Saidi groups engineered a first meeting between them around March 1980. Faraj tried to convince Zuhdi of the imperative of jihad against the regime and unveiled Zumur's plan to attack vital government installations and homes of public officials in Cairo. Zuhdi advocated instead the purging of Christian influence from Egyptian society. Despite this disagreement, they decided to continue to meet regularly, alternating their sites between Cairo and Upper Egypt. In June 1980, they decided to coordinate their activities, each faction retaining freedom of action within its own region. They established a twelve member shura (council). Their ideology required the sanction of a mufti, certifying that their operations conformed to the precepts of the Quran. Zuhdi proposed the blind Sheikh Omar Abdel Rahman, who had just returned to Fayyum from Saudi Arabia and whom he knew from his student days in 1974 when he had invited the sheikh to preach in Minya and Asyut. Sheikh Omar agreed to become the mufti of the shura in the spring of 1981 and promptly sanctioned robbery and killing of Copts in furtherance of the jihad.

The origin of Tanzim al-Jihad was therefore based on the loose associations of local groups from Cairo and Upper Egypt. This explains the surprising total absence of Alexandrian militants in its midst, despite the fact that Alexandria had been a hotbed of Islamist activities and had been prominent in the 1974 ILO uprising. Sirriya, the ILO leader, had taught in Alexandria and had been able to attract militants locally.

Meanwhile, al-Zawahiri had come into contact with Afghan resistance fighters when he accepted an invitation from the Red Crescent Society to care for Afghan refugees in Peshawar during the summer of 1980. He had been preoccupied with the problem of finding a secure base from which to launch the Egyptian jihad and hoped to find it in Peshawar. During his short stay there, he was converted to the jihad against the Soviet invaders and even crossed into Afghanistan to witness some of the fighting. He returned to Cairo that fall, full of stories about the "miracles" taking place in Afghanistan. In February 1981, his clandestine group suffered a security breach. The police had intercepted and arrested a courier carrying weapons from al-Qamari along with his plans identifying military targets in Cairo. Al-Qamari went underground, and al-Zawahiri returned to Peshawar for a two-month tour of duty with the Red Crescent Society.

The assassination of President Sadat was the result of the sudden appearance of an irresistible target of opportunity rather than a carefully planned operation. On September 3, 1981, Sadat had cracked down on Islamists, who had previously escalated both their fighting against the Copts and their opposition to his government's international and domestic policies. Among the 1,536 arrested was Mohammed al-Islambuli, the Asyut leader. His brother, Khaled, whose own activism was an attempt to emulate his brother, was distressed by the news of Mohammed's arrest and alleged torture and swore to avenge him. Khaled was a lieutenant in the military and, in the spring of 1981, had been posted to Cairo, where Faraj had invited him to join his group. Three weeks after the arrests, Khaled was selected to command an armored transport vehicle in the upcoming October 6 victory parade commemorating the 1973 crossing of the Suez Canal. Khaled immediately contacted Faraj and suggested that he could try to kill the president. On the evening of September 26, Faraj held a meeting with some of the leaders, including Zuhdi and al-Zumur, to discuss this possibility. There was a strong difference of opinions. Al-Zumur believed that the assassination was premature, for it could not be followed by a popular uprising. He doubted the ability of his group to take over the security nerve centers in the capital. Zuhdi in contrast promised that he could take control of Asyut in the aftermath. The conspirators decided to go ahead with al-Islambuli's plan despite al-Zumur's objections. The four members of the action commando unit met for the first time shortly before the operation.

The other Tanzim al-Jihad leaders were informed of the plot shortly before its implementation. Al-Zawahiri learned about it a few hours before it took place. The successful assassination of Sadat took these leaders by surprise. Reacting to the situation, al-Qamari and al-Zawahiri contacted al-Zumur to try to coordinate the aftermath. The three of them finally met for the first time the evening after the assassination. They planned to follow up with another attempt during Sadat's funeral to finish off the political leadership, but were caught in the wave of arrests before they could carry out their plans. The Asyut branch launched its insurrection on the morning of October 8, a holiday during which only a skeleton crew protected security headquarters and armories. They controlled the city for a few days before paratroopers flown in from Cairo crushed the rebellion. Two trials took place in the aftermath of Sadat's assassination. The first was held in camera and consisted of the twenty-four suspects directly involved in the assassination. Khaled al-Islambuli, his three accomplices, and Faraj were sentenced to death and were executed on April 15, 1982. The second trial consisted of 302 defendants charged with conspiracy and being members of the illegal Tanzim al-Jihad and lasted almost three years.

In prison, cleavages developed among the defendants. On the one hand, the Cairo branch under the leadership of al-Zumur maintained that the correct strategy for establishing an Islamist state would be a violent coup carried out by a small, dedicated vanguard of Islamist mujahedin to the grateful acclamation of the nation. This was an Islamist version of the putsch scenario advocated by Leninists and successfully executed by nationalist army officers throughout the Arab world in the preceding decades. On the other hand, the Saidi group advocated a more traditional armed resistance scenario focusing on mobilization of the population to overthrow the government. This involved a combination of dawa and violence, which would be used to provoke ever more repressive governmental measures against the population, alienating and mobilizing it against the regime until a popular uprising would topple it. Sheikh Omar Abdel Rahman sided with his colleagues from Upper Egypt.

The factions broke along the lines of previously established networks. The Cairenes, who included al-Zumur, al-Qamari, and al-Zawahiri, tried to discredit the Saidis by arguing that a blind person (referring to Sheikh Omar) could not lead a group of the faithful. The Saidis, who included Zuhdi, Talat Fuad Qasim, Mohammed al-Islambuli, Osama Rushdi, Hamdi Abdel Rahman, and Rifai Taha, replied that a prisoner, referring to al-Zumur, could not lead such a group. These rival networks never reconciled in the course of the next two decades. Indeed, the rivalry resulted in two distinct surviving groups: the Islamic Jihad (*al-jihad islamiyya*, referred to as the Egyptian Islamic Jihad, EIJ) under al-Zawahiri; and the Islamic Group (*jamaa islamiyya*, in singular, referred to as the Egyptian Islamic Group, EIG) ruled by a shura. During the trial, al-Zawahiri became a spokesman for the defendants because of his eloquence and his knowledge of foreign languages. This pushed him into the limelight. The state showed itself lenient at the second trial. Despite the prosecution demand of 299 death sentences, the judges gave out none. Only fifty-eight prison sentences were given, despite the fact that the Asyut revolt resulted in the death of sixty-eight policemen and soldiers. Except for the senior leaders in the shura and actual perpetrators, most of the defendants were released after three years in prison. Many left Egypt and went to Afghanistan to join the jihad against the Soviets.

The Afghan Jihad Period and the Creation of al Qaeda

In 1985, al-Zawahiri left for Jeddah, where his brother Mohammed had fled, and then went on to Peshawar in 1986. Sayyid Imam al-Sharif (a.k.a. Dr. al-Fadl) from his Cairo group joined him there. In 1987 they established the EIJ and published a monthly magazine, called *The Conquest* (*al-Fath*) under the leadership of al-Sharif. They expanded and included Ali Amin Ali al-Rashidi (a.k.a abu Ubaydah al-Banshiri), a former policeman who was the brother-in-law of Abdel Hamid Abdel Salam, one of Sadat's assassins. Al-Rashidi had been arrested but was released quickly. He went to Afghanistan in late 1983 and fought alongside Ahmad Shah Massoud in the Panjshir Valley (hence his Arabic nom de guerre). Other new members included Subhi Mohammed abu Sittah (a.k.a, abu Hafs al-Masri or Mohammed Atef), whose past is mysterious, and Ali Abdel Suud Mohammed Mustafa (a.k.a. Ali Mohammed), a former military officer from Alexandria who went on to enlist in the U.S. Army.

While the senior leadership of the Tanzim al-Jihad remained in prison, several of the mid-level leaders of the Saidis were released and went to Saudi Arabia, on the way to Peshawar and Afghanistan. Among the most prominent were Mohammed al-Islambuli, Rifai Taha, Osama Rushdi, Mustafa Hamza, and Talat Fuad Qasim. Although the leadership remained in the hands of the imprisoned shura, the spiritual leader was still Sheikh Omar, and Qasim assumed the position of deputy leader. They reconstituted their organization as the EIG and published a newsletter, *Al Murabitun*. The disputes that had arisen in prison resurfaced in Peshawar along the lines of their social bonds. The Saidis became the EIG, while the Cairenes and Alexandrians became the EIJ. Both met the rest of the Arab expatriate community while fighting the Afghan jihad.

By the time the Egyptians arrived in Peshawar, Sheikh Abdallah Azzam, with the help of Osama bin Laden, had organized the Afghan jihad for foreign Muslim volunteers. They had created the Mekhtab al-Khidemat (Service Bureau) to facilitate administrative problems for the volunteers and the Bait al-Ansar (House of Supporters) to house them. At first, they assigned all the volunteer expatriate mujahedin to the four fundamentalist Afghan resistance parties. The common Soviet enemy had united the various mujahedin factions; eventually, its withdrawal exposed their differences. Both Egyptian groups viewed Afghanistan as temporary and dreamed about fomenting an Islamist jihad back in Egypt. It appears in retrospect that al-Zawahiri's strategy was to get close to bin Laden, the fundraiser for the Afghan jihad, in order to gain his exclusive support for the EIJ. Al-Zawahiri had an opportunity to care for bin Laden medically, and through this rapport, gradually suggested trusted members of the EIJ for key positions in bin Laden's growing organization. Beginning in 1987, Azzam and bin Laden created a training camp for the foreign mujahedin near Khowst, at Ali Kheyl in Jaji, and named it Masada (the lion's den). When Soviet forces attacked Masada in the spring 1987 offensive because it was sitting on the mujahedin supply lines, bin Laden and his small group held their ground and repulsed several waves of assaults by Soviet Spetznaz special forces. After the Soviets withdrew with heavy losses, bin Laden's reputation spread over the Muslim world and especially his native Saudi Arabia.

The announcement of the Soviet withdrawal from Afghanistan in early 1988 was a turning point for the expatriate mujahedin community. In response to Azzam's fatwa and recruitment efforts, they had come from all over: core Arab countries, such as Saudi Arabia and Egypt; Maghreb Arab countries such as Algeria and Morocco; Southeast Asian countries such as the Philippines and Indonesia; and the Muslim immigrant community of the United States and Europe. The end of the Soviet presence in Afghanistan eliminated the legitimacy of the jihad in the traditional sense and started a debate about what to do next. The consensus among the hardcore leaders of the expatriate mujahedin was to establish a base (*al-qaeda*), or a social movement, to carry out a worldwide jihad. They disagreed about the essence of this jihad, however. On the more traditional side were Azzam and most of the expatriate mujahedin he had recruited through the Mekhtab al-Khidemat. Although most did return home after the fulfillment of their individual duties, some stayed on. Azzam suggested that they turn their attention to other areas where infidels had conquered or threatened former Muslim lands, like the Philippines, Kashmir, the central Soviet republics, Bosnia, and Somalia. He proposed that the role of this social movement, *al-qaeda*, should be to establish a Muslim state in infidel lands. Azzam's dream of liberating former Muslim lands would shift the jihad to the periphery of the Muslim world, such as the Philippines, central Asia, Kashmir, and, of course, Palestine (al-Fadl, 2001; Kherchtou, 2001). Those who stayed to fight further became disillusioned with the Afghans' degeneration into infighting among rival factions. Many, including Osama bin Laden, reluctantly returned home (al-Banyan, 2001). Others, particularly the Egyptians whose goal was the overthrow of the Egyptian government along the lines advocated by Faraj, could not return home because of fears of political persecution. By a process of elimination, therefore, the most radical elements remained in Afghanistan or Peshawar. They felt that the traditional jihad advocated by Azzam, however, would not advance their goal of overthrowing the Egyptian government. Azzam's rejection of Faraj's arguments and refusal to sanction the overthrow of a Muslim government conflicted with their strategy.

Azzam and two of his sons were murdered in Peshawar on November 24, 1989, by a remote controlled car bomb. His murder is still unsolved. In the hagiographies later disseminated on Islamist Internet sites and in the public declarations of the leaders of the global Salafi jihad, it is difficult to re-create the context of his death. I suspect it has much relevance to the creation of the global Salafi jihad and its present vanguard, al Qaeda. Azzam advocated unity within the Muslim community and disliked the notion of takfir, which spread fitna within this community. Osama bin Laden originally pursued this strategy of tolerance among Muslims. He expelled from Camp Masada an Egyptian follower of Shukri Mustafa who had branded as takfir other trainees at the camp. Yet the notion of takfir is central to the argument that nonpious Muslim leaders should be overthrown, as the Egyptians advocated. This doctrinal dispute between Azzam and the Egyptians led by al-Zawahiri is well documented (al-Zawahiri, 2001; Rushdi, 2001; al-Shafii, 2001; al-Banyan, 2001). There may also have been disputes over the use of the Mekhtab al-Khidemat funds and the Masada camp. The EIJ, sensitive to news of Egyptian crackdowns on Islamist movements, wanted to use both for a terrorist campaign back home. Azzam was opposed to this program of terrorism against Muslim governments and issued a fatwa stating that using jihad funds to train terrorists would violate Islamic law (Gunaratna, 2002: 21-24). Azzam's son-in-law, Abdallah Anas, accused the EIJ of killing his father-in-law on the grounds that it "considered Sheikh Abdullah Azzam to be a rogue who had strayed from the right path of the faith. . . . Sheikh Abdullah Azzam was murdered because he had issued a *fatwa* in which he stated that once the Russians were ejected from Afghanistan, it would not be permissible for us to take sides" (al-Shafii, 2001). The death of Azzam deprived the newborn al-qaeda social movement of its strongest advocate for a traditionalist jihad. The remaining leaders of this vanguard were now all Salafi mujahedin. Even Azzam's protégé, Osama bin Laden, was progressively being won over by the EIJ arguments. At the time of his mentor's murder, however, he was back in Saudi Arabia.

Saddam Hussein's invasion of Kuwait in August 1990 was a turning point for the jihad. It further divided the Muslim camp, which was caught between two unsavory choices. Salafi mujahedin hated Hussein, the epitome of a secularist ruler who rejected Islam. Salafists everywhere at first condemned the invasion. Shortly after the invasion, Osama bin Laden offered to bring over his faithful mujahedin to fight off the apostate Hussein. However, the Saudi royal family chose to call on the United States and other non-Muslim forces to defend the kingdom, and the presence of infidels on Arabian sacred soil was too much for Salafists and Osama bin Laden to bear. They roundly condemned this presence, and many who had originally condemned Hussein now rallied to his cause as the lesser of two evils.

Meanwhile, the fighting in Afghanistan continued. Contrary to Islamist complaints, U.S. and Saudi support continued until the fall of Kabul in 1992, as part of the U.S. and Soviet governments' positive symmetry of supporting their respective sides. More Muslim expatriates flocked to Afghanistan to receive military training. The expatriates now had at least four camps where they learned their skills. They were allied with three of the four Afghan fundamentalist factions, headed by Gulbuddin Hikmatyar, Yunis Khalis, and Abdal Rabb Rasul Sayyaf. Because the traditionalist mujahedin had retired, the Salafists now dominated this group. They fought in Afghanistan against the communist forces and spread the jihad back in their homelands. They joined their Afghan brothers in attacking Afghan government strongholds, such as Jalalabad, Khowst, and Kabul. Janjalani returned to the Philippines, where he founded the Abu Sayyaf Group against the Christian central government. Osama bin Laden seems to have been involved in fomenting a jihad in South Yemen. Kashmir became a favorite target of some Pakistani mujahedin. The Indonesians secretly formed the Jemaah Islamiyah to establish a Muslim state in Southeast Asia stretching from the Philippines to Indonesia. Both the EIJ and EIG started campaigns of terrorism against Egyptian officials; the EIG also targeted the Copts. At this point, the militant Islamist movement was not a coordinated global jihad but a collection of local jihads, receiving training and financial and logistic support from the vanguard of the movement, al Qaeda. Al Qaeda now became a formal organization consisting of a cluster of terrorists, the central staff supporting the global Salafi jihad, the religious social movement (see also Burke, 2003). There were very few full-time paid staff members of al Qaeda. Instead, the jihad fellow travelers were given training and seed money to go and carry out their own jihad. They then had to raise their own money or receive support from Muslim charity organizations.

After the Soviet withdrawal, Peshawar lost its appeal as the central site for the Salafi jihad. The central staff was restless about having little to do locally now that Soviets had left. There was grumbling about the distance to the Arab world, where the Salafi jihad was to take place (al-Fadl, 2001: 216). Meanwhile, the EIG was still carrying out operations in Egypt. In October 1990, it tried to assassinate Interior Minister Abdel-Halim Moussa but killed Parliamentary Speaker Rifaat el-Mahgoub by mistake. To get closer to the areas of struggle, al Qaeda leaders explored the option of moving to the Sudan, where an Islamic government under General Omar Hassan al-Bashir, in alliance with Hassan al-Turabi's National Islamic Front, had taken power in June 1989. After a visit with al-Turabi, they resolved to move their headquarters to Khartoum in late 1990. Some infrastructure was left in Afghanistan in the areas controlled by friendly local Afghan warlords and in Peshawar outside direct federal Pakistani control. Some training sites were moved to remote areas of Yemen. Osama bin Laden, who had been under house surveillance after his criticism of the Saudi's reliance on U.S. troops, was sent to Kabul in March 1992 to help stop the internecine fighting among Afghan resistance factions. Instead of returning to Jeddah, he flew to Khartoum, completing the transfer of the movement leadership to the Sudanese capital.

At this point, there is no evidence that al Qaeda, the base of this religious movement, was targeting the "far enemy," the United States. It concentrated on providing training and logistics and financial support for jihad à la Azzam at the periphery of the Muslim world and jihad à la Faraj against the "near enemy" in Egypt and Yemen. There is no doubt that among al Qaeda members there was a strong streak of anti-Western and specifically anti-American sentiment, which stems from Salafi attitudes. Qutb was strongly anti-American as a result of his two years' experience in the United States, but he saved his venom for the Egyptian regime. Faraj was also anti-American, but he nevertheless advocated the priority of jihad against the "near enemy" over that against the "far enemy." During the Afghan war, future global Salafi jihad leaders were also hostile to the United States, but tolerated its help in the jihad against the Soviets. Only after the Sudanese exile did the virulent brand of anti-Americanism arise in the organization, culminating in the 1996 declaration of war.

The Sudanese Exile

The 1990-1991 Gulf War brought U.S. troops to the Arabian Peninsula. The movement that became the global Salafi jihad might have faded but for the continued presence of these troops. The Salafi mujahedin interpreted this presence as an infidel invasion of the Land of the Two Holy Places. It became the focus of Salafi resentment against the West and breathed new life into the movement. The appearance of U.S. troops in Somalia (as part of a United Nations peace mission to equitably provide food to the starving population) further fueled the fears of al Qaeda's leaders, now in nearby Sudan, that this constituted a U.S.-led secret grand strategy to conquer Muslim lands. They reacted by sending trainers to Somalia to teach techniques acquired in the Afghan-Soviet war to forces that were hostile to the American presence. They also explored the possibility of carrying out bombings of Western targets in Kenya. Their objective at the time was to attack Western targets in the Middle East or East Africa to force Western forces to withdraw from Muslim lands. Their model was the 1983 Beirut bombings against U.S. and French military personnel that brought about their withdrawal from Lebanon (Mohamed, 2000: 27-30). In October 1993, the shooting down of a U.S. helicopter in Mogadishu, using techniques from the Afghan war, and the consequent and unexpected U.S. withdrawal from Somalia put these plans on hold.

The skirmishes against the U.S. were still a minor aspect of the jihad during the Sudanese exile. Most of the effort was directed at liberating former Muslim lands (Kashmir and the Philippine island of Mindanao), resisting aggression against Muslim lands (Bosnia and Chechnya), and fighting secular Muslim government repression in Egypt and Algeria. These efforts seem to have been more reactive than offensive, and al Qaeda's role was to support and coordinate local movements that started spontaneously. These local movements included graduates of the Afghan jihad who had both military skills and connections with their former expatriate mujahedin. The Algerian Groupe Islamique Armé (GIA, Armed Islamic Group) received a boost when, in January 1992, the government cancelled the second round of elections, which would have brought an Islamist party to power. This played into the hands of the Salafi jihad position that trying to gain power through legal means was useless because the apostate government would never voluntarily relinquish power. The

Egyptians in al Qaeda (and probably bin Laden) paid close attention to developments in Algeria and supported the nascent GIA. Many of the original leaders of this organization—Qari Said, Tayyeb al-Afghani and Djafar al-Afghani—were Afghan Arabs. Al Qaeda also supported the propaganda branch of the organization with the publication of *Al Ansar* in London and contemplated direct operational support for GIA, as some of its staff members in Nairobi were tasked to case potential French targets locally, in Djibouti and in Senegal (Kherchtou, 2001: 1220). There is evidence that funding for the wave of bombings in France in the summer of 1995 came from al Qaeda as well (Macintyre and Tendler, 1996).

Al Qaeda encouraged these terror networks that arose spontaneously and locally with funding, training, and sometimes weaponry. Some members of these networks, especially the Egyptians, had dual membership in their own organizations and al Qaeda. Despite bin Laden's urging them to do so, they did not coordinate their operations. They continued to squabble publicly even though bin Laden became exasperated with them, and sometimes cut off their financial support.

There was much fighting within the ranks of the two groups as well, especially the EIJ, which was more removed from a strong popular base of support. In the early 1990s, al-Zawahiri won an internal power struggle within the EIJ and sidelined the previous leaders. His old companion Sayyid Imam al-Sharif (a.k.a. al-Fadl) stayed in Yemen and went into voluntary isolation. The imprisoned al-Zumur, now rejected by his own group, was invited to join the shura of the rival EIG in prison. This is the only instance I ever discovered of someone from one network jumping to another. In 1992, an EIJ leader was captured with a computer containing information on all the members in Egypt. More than eight hundred members were arrested and tried in the "Vanguards of Conquest" case. This devastating setback further split the EIJ. Al-Zawahiri stayed in charge of the remnants of the organization. Ahmad Ujaysah and Osama Ayyub, who had belonged to the same terrorist cell in Bani Suwayf, Egypt, stayed in Yemen and formed an EIJ splinter group. Mohammed Makkawi supported them but decided to devote all his energy to al Qaeda. The EIJ became increasingly invested in al Qaeda, with most of its highest-ranking officers also doubling as al Qaeda's top management.

The EIG was more of a mass movement, socially embedded in the Said and better able to conduct operations in country, especially against the

41

Copts. It also targeted government officials, tourists, and secular writers like Faraj Foda and even Naguib Mahfouz. This did not prevent it from conducting operations outside of Egypt, like Mustafa Hamza's attempt on President Hosni Mubarak's life in Addis Ababa on June 26, 1995. Because of the involvement of the Sudanese government in this operation, the United Nations condemned it and imposed economic sanctions against it.

Another influential network of terror, connected to both al Qaeda and the EIG, was that headed by Khalid Sheikh Mohammed. This network is difficult to classify for it spans several countries. Mohammed and his nephew Abdul Basit Karim were Baluchi, born and raised in Kuwait, and they studied abroad, in the United States and Britain, respectively. They were religious but not rigidly so, and willing to taste the sins of the West. They came to Peshawar, where Mohammed's brother was the head of one of the main Muslim relief organizations. Their friendliness was contagious. Karim became friends with Janjalani and spent some time in the Philippines training the latter's recruits. Karim also recruited his childhood friends into the jihad, whose targets were not limited to Western interests, but included Prime Minister Benazir Bhutto and Iranian Shii as well. In 1992, the followers of Sheikh Omar, the mufti of the EIG, invited Karim to join them in New York to strike a blow against the United States. The result was the first bombing of the World Trade Center on February 23, 1993. The extent of al Qaeda's involvement in this plot is unclear. The two leaders of this network traveled in the same circles and stayed at the guesthouses funded by al Qaeda. Mohammed provided the funding (perhaps from al Qaeda), and Karim planned and executed out the operations. But they both seemed too unpredictable at the time to have been part of a larger, more rigid organization. Indeed, Karim's premature attempt to recruit Ishtiaque Parker, a stranger, backfired and resulted in his arrest.

The full-time staff at the al Qaeda organization constituted a different network. In the early days, they appeared to do multiple tasks: raising money through bin Laden's enterprises in the Sudan, setting up logistic support cells in Nairobi for potential operations in East Africa, and casing potential targets. High-ranking members of al Qaeda, such as Ali Amin al-Rashidi (Abu Ubaydah al-Banshiri, the chair of al Qaeda's military committee), Ali Abdel Suud Mohammed Mustafa (the trainer of bin

Laden's personal bodyguards) and Wadih el-Hage (bin Laden's personal secretary) were personally involved in this operation and lived in Nairobi at various times. This Central Staff cluster was involved in hands-on operations at the time, which indicates that the organization was very fluid, without rigid organizational roles. As al Qaeda grew in importance, the Central Staff cluster would never again be involved in the day-to-day operations in the field.

The Sudanese exile was marked by financial concerns. Since the fall of Kabul, support for the Afghan jihad had faded. To keep one thousand staff members of al Qaeda and to house and feed their families would cost the organization $6 million each year, leaving no money for operations. Osama bin Laden invested heavily in Sudanese industry and required his staff members to work in his companies in order to raise money. When operations were planned elsewhere, al Qaeda members were again required to raise the money needed locally. New operations and new groups were given seed money but then left to further fund their operations on their own. Senior al Qaeda members went on fund-raising tours, including those of al-Zawahiri in California in the spring of 1993 and Ahmed Said Khadr in Toronto in 1994 and 1996. At a 1995 general meeting of EIJ in Yemen, al-Zawahiri announced that there was no money left for their organization. He urged his subordinates to become financially self-sufficient. Many started to work for Islamic relief organizations and used their salaries to fund the jihad. A large contingent gathered in Tirana, Albania, where they worked for an Islamic nongovernmental organization.

Meanwhile, the war in Bosnia attracted many Muslim volunteers against Serb aggression. Azzam.com advertised the ones who came from Saudi Arabia. But many came from Maghreb countries and France. People who wanted to continue the jihad worldwide could meet and organize in the Balkans. The most significant terrorist network to come out of this war was the one around Fateh Kamel from Montreal, who had connections to both the Montreal Maghreb network and the Roubaix gang. This would become the kernel of what I call the Maghreb Arab cluster. Its main logistic support base was in Milan under Sheikh Anwar Shaban, who had been sending young people to train in Afghanistan before the eruption of the war next door. Milan was to remain the main logistic support cell in Europe for a decade, facilitating the travel to Afghanistan and supporting operations in Germany, France, and Italy.

In Southeast Asia, the Abu Sayyaf Group fell from favor with bin Laden when it degenerated into a criminal group interested primarily in kidnap for ransom. Instead, the Moro Islamic Liberation Front became the favorite Filipino group with al Qaeda and its ally in Southeast Asia, the Jemaah Islamiyah. It provided training camps for Southeast Asian recruits. The Indonesian network was tightly organized around Pesentren Luqmanul Hakiem, an Islamist boarding school in Malaysia, under Abu Bakar Baasyir and Abdullah Sungkar. Most of the future leaders of the Jemaah Islamiyah were faculty members—Riduan Isamuddin (a.k.a. Hambali) and Ali Ghufron (a.k.a. Mukhlas, whose three brothers were also involved in the 2002 Bali bombing)—or students there—Abdul Aziz (a.k.a. Imam Samudra), Amrozi bin Nurhasym, and Ali Imron (two brothers of Ali Ghufron).

Al Qaeda was headquartered in the Sudan, with training camps in Afghanistan (the more advanced ones), Bosnia, Yemen, the Philippines, and the Sudan. During the exile in the Sudan, its leaders held intense discussions about the jihad. Globalists like Mamdouh Mahmud Salim argued that the main obstacle to the establishment of a Muslim state and the main danger for the worldwide Islamist movement was the United States, which was seen as moving in on Muslim lands such as the Arabian Peninsula and East Africa. It was the "head of the snake" that had to be killed. He argued that the priority had to be switched from the "near enemy" to the "far enemy." This included the United States and France, which was viewed as standing behind the Algerian power elite. The GIA had already come to this conclusion and started operations against France in late 1994. Osama bin Laden and Ayman al-Zawahiri came to adopt this new strategy. Members debated these issues. The EIG as a group rejected this focus on the "far enemy," repeating Faraj's argument that the priority was the "near enemy." Some members of the EIJ were also reluctant to tackle the United States because its greater power might defeat the movement.

In the mid-1990s, two significant bombings took place in Saudi Arabia. On November 13, 1995, the National Guard training center in Riyadh was bombed. Four suspects confessed to having been inspired by Osama bin Laden and receiving training in Afghanistan or Bosnia. Saudi authorities executed the four before they could be interrogated by U.S. agencies. The Khobar Towers explosion in Dhahran, which killed nineteen

U.S. personnel on June 25, 1996, was carried out by Shiite Saudis. Not much is known about the networks behind these two attacks. However, these explosions coincided with the change of target from the "near enemy" of the Salafi jihad to the "far enemy" of the global Salafi jihad.

The Sudan location's proximity to Egypt helped the two Egyptian organizations but, in the end, hindered further al Qaeda operations because of international pressure on the Sudan. Egypt protested to Sudanese authorities about all the operations conducted from its southern neighbor. The 1995 Addis Ababa attempt on President Mubarak's life was the last straw. It earned the Sudan international condemnation at the United Nations and economic sanctions. At the same time relations between the Sudanese intelligence service and the EIJ soured quickly when the Sudanese handed over to the EIJ for interrogation the son of an EIJ leader, who had been collaborating with the Egyptian intelligence services. Al-Zawahiri ordered the boy's execution shortly after his confession. When the Sudanese found out about the execution in its territory, al-Zawahiri was ordered to leave the Sudan within a few days. Trying to rehabilitate itself in the international community, the Sudanese government put pressure on bin Laden to leave the country. In May 1996, Osama bin Laden with about 150 followers and their families returned to Afghanistan. Many people stayed behind and left the jihad, which they believed was taking an uncomfortable turn. The return to Afghanistan was the occasion for another large purging of al Qaeda of its less militant elements, who hesitated to take on the United States, with whom they had no quarrel and no legitimate fatwa. The two large movements out of and into Afghanistan in 1991 and 1996, respectively, radicalized the organization through a self-selecting mechanism of keeping the most militant members.

Bin Laden quickly established a close relationship with Afghanistan's new ruler, Mullah Mohammed Omar, whom he publicly acknowledged as the Amir ul-Momineen (Commander of the Faithful). In response, the Taliban government allowed bin Laden a freedom to move about and conduct operations inside Afghanistan that he had never had in the Sudan. In the safety of his new refuge, bin Laden issued a long fatwa on August 23, 1996, declaring war against the "Americans Occupying the Land of the Two Holy Places (Expel the Infidels from the Arab Peninsula)." This final step marked the emergence of the true global Salafi jihad.

The Global Salafi Jihad from the Afghan Refuge

The return to Afghanistan allowed bin Laden to consolidate his grip on jihad activities worldwide. Organizationally, bin Laden incorporated many of the independent Muslim terrorist organizations under his umbrella Salafi movement. He helped funnel new potential members through Zain al-Abidin Mohammed Hussein (a.k.a. abu Zubaydah) in Peshawar, who established contact with militant Muslims of Maghreb Arab origin in Europe, first through Mustafa Kamel and later through Amar Makhlulif. This group constitutes the Maghreb Arab cluster of the global jihad. Bin Laden invited Khalid Sheikh Mohammed to join the military committee under Subhi Mohammed abu Sittah (a.k.a. Mohammed Atef or abu Hafs al-Masri). The nature of bin Laden's network in Saudi Arabia is still unknown. The group of terrorists joining the global jihad from Saudi Arabia, Yemen, and other oriental Arab countries in the 1990s constitute the Core Arab cluster of the jihad. Bin Laden also increased cooperation with the Southeast Asian Salafi militants through Omar al-Faruq, Mohammed, and Isamuddin. The Southeast Asian mujahedin, mostly from Indonesia, Malaysia, and the Philippines, make up the Southeast Asian cluster of the jihad. The global jihad propaganda arm was up and running in London with the quartet of Yasir Tawfiq al-Sirri, Khalid al-Fawwaz, Omar Mahmoud Othman (abu Qatada), and Mustafa Kamel (abu Hamza al-Masri).

Bin Laden also established greater control over the EIJ. After leaving the Sudan, al-Zawahiri went clandestinely to visit former Soviet Caucasian republics. A Russian patrol arrested him in Dagestan in December 1996. He stuck to his cover story and was released in May 1997 without ever being identified by the Russians. His followers chastised him for his carelessness, and bin Laden expressed his disapproval by reducing the subsidy for the EIJ to $5,000 for the six months he was absent (Wright, 2002: 81). This left al-Zawahiri no choice but to move closer to bin Laden in order to put EIJ members on al Qaeda's payroll.

Meanwhile, the EIG chose the opposite path. The arrest of their mufti, Sheikh Omar, in New York in the summer 1993 and al Qaeda's inability to do anything to get him out of jail had alienated many EIG dual members, who left al Qaeda as a result. The decision to change the priority from Egypt to the United States antagonized others. The leadership shura in prison announced a unilateral ceasefire in Egypt in July 1997. They reasoned that the terrorist campaign in Egypt had been a failure, for it had turned the population against them. Their strategy of mobilizing the population to overthrow the government had backfired. The outside leadership of al-Islambuli and Taha rejected this new initiative, but Sheikh Omar supported it from his U.S. prison cell. To force the hand of the imprisoned leaders, Taha directed the Luxor massacre, which killed more than sixty people on November 11, 1997. The leadership condemned him and insisted on the ceasefire initiative. This was the last EIG terrorist activity.

Osama bin Laden's consolidation of the global Salafi jihad was proclaimed, on February 23, 1998, in the formation of the World Islamic Front declaring a jihad against Jews and crusaders, signed by himself, al-Zawahiri, and Taha on behalf of the EIJ and EIG, respectively. In this fatwa, he sanctioned the ruling "to kill the Americans and their allies—civilians and military—is an individual duty for every Muslim who can do it in any country in which it is possible to do it." The rank and file of both Egyptian organizations rebelled against their leaders. Taha published a retraction within a week of his signature. The shura replaced him as chair with Mustafa Hamza, who supported the ceasefire initiative. Al-Zawahiri also faced a rebellion of EIJ members for signing onto bin Laden's fatwa, sanctioning this change of priority from the "near" to the "far" enemy. At a general meeting in Qandahar, most criticized him for signing the fatwa without consulting them. He threatened to resign but eventually stayed on as their leader. Many members left the organization, including his loyal brother Mohammed, who wanted to maintain the priority against Egypt rather than the United States. Shortly thereafter, in early summer 1998, the EIJ suffered another setback with the arrest in Albania and extradition to Egypt of many EIJ members. They had been under surveillance, and with the Kosovo crisis heating up, Washington had asked Albanian authorities to arrest them before the deployment of a large contingent of U.S. troops. They were tried the next year in the "Returnees from Albania" trial, resulting in several death sentences, including one in absentia for al-Zawahiri.

The August 7, 1998, twin bombings of the U.S. embassies in Nairobi and Dar es Salaam marked a new milestone in al Qaeda operations. Previously, it had targeted enemies on Muslim soil to force their withdrawal, as in Saudi Arabia or even Somalia. Here, the targets were in Kenya and Tanzania, not Muslim lands, and the victims were mostly civilians, as threatened in the fatwa. These attacks marked a shift from defensive operations on Muslim soil to offensive operations on enemy soil. In retrospect, the next step was clearly to take the fight onto U.S. ground. The ineffectual U.S. response to the attack only increased the popularity of bin Laden in the Muslim world and encouraged al Qaeda to carry out more daring operations. Bin Laden gained fame as the man who dared take on the only remaining superpower. With the abandonment of Egypt as a target and the decrease in intensity of the Algerian civil war, the global Salafi jihad concentrated on the Western targets, specifically the United States.

The East Africa operations, which inaugurated a worldwide wave of bombings and plots against Western targets, involved a great deal of central planning by the full-time al Qaeda staff. This would be unique in the organization's operations. Over the next two years, operations were more decentralized, and planned with a great deal of local autonomy. Instead of direct participation, al Qaeda's involvement consisted of training potential terrorists for their tasks in Afghanistan, giving them seed money to get the ball rolling, and providing some logistic support. The exact targets and details of the operations were left to local initiative. For three years after the East Africa operations, a wave of terrorist activities spanned the globe, until U.S. forces eliminated Afghanistan as a safe heaven for al Qaeda. Chronologically, the major plots were the millennial plots in Amman and the Los Angeles airport in December 1999; the two attacks against U.S. naval ships in Aden (USS *The Sullivans* and USS *Cole*) in January and October 2000; the Christmas Eve 2000 bombings against churches throughout Indonesia; the bombings in Manila in December 2000; the Strasbourg Christmas market plot in December 2000; the September 11, 2001, airplane attacks in the United States; the U.S. embassy plot in Paris in the fall of 2001; the shoe bombing attempt in December 2001; and the Singapore bombing plots in December 2001. I have included the last two because they were planned before al Qaeda lost its sanctuary in Afghanistan. The plots involved all three clusters of mujahedin: the Maghreb Arabs based in the Western world were involved in the Amman and Los Angeles millennial plots, the Strasbourg Christmas market plot, the Paris U.S. embassy plot, and in the shoe bomber plot; the Core Arabs based in the

Middle East and Germany were involved in the two naval vessel plots in Aden and in the September 11, 2001, events; and the Southeast Asians were involved in the two December 2000 bombings in Indonesia and Manila as well as the Singapore December 2001 plot.

The same major characters were involved within each cluster. Zain al-Abidin Hussein (abu Zubaydah) was involved in all five Maghreb Arab plots as the central coordinator for al Qaeda. Fateh Kamel was his link for the two millennial plots. Amar Makhlulif gradually took over his role as field coordinator for operations around 1999 and was involved in the Los Angeles, Strasbourg, Paris, and shoe bombing plots. Many of the terrorists involved in the Strasbourg, Paris, and shoe bombing plots knew each other from London, after the center of global Salafi jihad operations in the West shifted from Montreal to London. The Core Arab operations also involved the same set of characters under Khalid Sheikh Mohammed's leadership. His lieutenants met in Kuala Lumpur to put the finishing touches to their operations. They included Ramzi bin al-Shibh, Abd al-Rahim al-Nashiri, Waleed Tawfiq bin Attash, Khalid al-Midhar, and Nawaf al-Hazmi. Al-Nashiri and bin Attash were primarily involved against the naval targets, while the other three were involved in the September 11 plot. The Southeast Asians started their operations after their return from their Malaysian exile following the fall of the Suharto regime. The operations involved Isamuddin as the overall field commander, Omar al-Faruq, Fathur Rahman al-Ghozi, and Faiz bin abu Bakar Bafana. The major leaders were generally informed of the broad outlines of the plots but were not involved in the day-to-day operations, which their field lieutenants executed. Within each cluster, the arrest of one person might have led to others, who were plotting new operations. However, there were no links between clusters with two known exceptions. The Maghreb and Core Arab clusters intersected through their common Syrian members, who knew each other from past decades: Imad Eddin Barakat Yarkas (a.k.a. abu Dahdah) in Madrid and Mamoun Darkazanli and Mohammed Heidar Zammar in Germany. The Core Arab cluster also intersected with the Southeast Asian cluster through the personal bonds between Khalid Sheikh Mohammed and Riduan Isamuddin. The latter hosted the January 2000 summit of the Core Arab principals in Kuala Lumpur at Yazid Sufaat's condominium. Mohammed also sent Mohammed Mansur Jabarah to help the Jemaah Islamiyah coordinate the Singapore bombing plot. Otherwise, each cluster was completely independent of the others and penetration of one would not have revealed operations by another.

The evolution of the three main clusters followed a pattern of growth through friendship, kinship, worship, and discipleship. In Chapter 4, I outline the evolution of the Montreal and Hamburg networks. A similar pattern holds for the rest of the Maghreb Arab cluster as well. Djamel Beghal, the field commander for the Paris plot, met Kamel Daoudi, later his deputy, at a mosque in a suburb of Paris. They both drifted to London's Maghreb community around the Salafi preachers Othman and Kamel. There they met Habib Zacarias Moussaoui, Nizar Trabelsi, the brothers David and Jérome Courtailler, and Richard Reid. The two trained in Afghanistan around the same time, where they met Yacine Akhnouche. The Southeast Asian cluster continued to be connected to Abu Bakar Baasyir's two boarding schools in Malaysia and Indonesia. This connection may be unique to Southeast Asia, where extraordinarily strong teacher-student bonds, not seen elsewhere in the world, are forged.

The Core Arabs from Saudi Arabia are more difficult to trace because of the general lack of information from the kingdom. Yet, even the "muscle" involved in the September 11, 2001, operation can be linked through friendship and kinship. Salim al-Hazmi followed in the footsteps of his older brother Nawaf. Likewise, Wail and Waleed al-Shehri were brothers. The al-Shehri brothers and their two friends, Ahmed al-Nami and Saeed al-Ghamdi, swore an oath to commit themselves to jihad in the spring of 2000 at the al-Shehri family mosque (Seqely Mosque in Khamis Mushayt). They then went on to Afghanistan for training. Ahmed al-Haznawi al-Ghamdi was a cousin of two other hijackers, Ahmed al-Ghamdi and Hamza al-Ghamdi. Majed al-Harbi and Satam al-Suqami were roommates at King Saud University in Riyadh. Fayez Ahmed al-Shehri (a.k.a. Fayez Rashid Ahmed Hassan al-Qadi Banihammad) studied at King Khaled University in Abha, in Asir Province, along with Muhammad al-Shahri and Ahmed al-Nami (the friend of the al-Shehri brothers). They all went to train at al-Faruq camp in Afghanistan. The imam of the camp was Abdul Aziz al-Omari, who became the last of the hijackers (Senott, 2002a and 2002b; Khashoggi, 2001a and 2001b; Murphy and Ottaway, 2001; Lamb, 2002; "Hijackers were from Wealthy Saudi Families," 2001; "The Highway of Death," 2002). The 9/11 operation was also unique in that it was totally funded by al Qaeda, freeing the operators from having to raise money themselves through petty crime and allowing them to keep a low profile.

This period constitutes the apogee of the global Salafi jihad. Osama bin Laden was finally able to consolidate his hold on the global jihad by incorporating the EIJ into a new entity called al-Qaeda al-Jihad in June 2001. Al-Zawahiri had weathered the internal turmoil of the EIJ. He had resigned as emir of this organization in the summer of 1999, when EIJ members kept up their criticism of his leadership in the face of continued operational disasters. Some advocated the peaceful initiative of the EIG. After a few months, his ineffective successor relinquished his post and al-Zawahiri resumed his leadership, now more firmly in control. With little opposition from his subordinates, he engineered the merger with al Qaeda to resolve the financial problems of the EIJ. Meanwhile, the EIG completely disappeared from the jihad, and the imprisoned traditional leaders started preaching a more peaceful message and apologized for past violence. The exiled al-Islambuli publicly rejected this new initiative and defended the actions of his brother in killing Sadat. Sheikh Omar may also have believed that the traditional shura was going too far and withdrew his support for their initiative during the summer of 2000.

This phase of the global Salafi jihad includes its most ambitious operations, most of which failed. Two operations brought on massive carnage (the bombings of U.S. embassies in Nairobi and Dar es Salaam and the 9/11 operations) and two were of questionable success (the December 2000 Indonesia and Manila bombings) because of the low number of deaths despite the ambitious multiple bombings. The USS *Cole* operation succeeded in disabling the ship and killing dozens of sailors but did not sink the ship, which was later restored. The other seven operations, discovered before any damage was done, were outright failures.

The Decentralized Global Salafi Jihad

The success of the 9/11 operation backfired on al Qaeda. There is some evidence that al Qaeda leadership anticipated a limited U.S. response to the operation, on the order of the Clinton administration's response to the East Africa embassy bombings and its lack of response to the USS *Cole* bombing. This turned out to be a serious miscalculation; the Bush administration decided to freeze al Qaeda funds and invade Afghanistan to change its regime and deny al Qaeda any refuge. U.S. forces, however, did not succeed in eliminating the leadership of al Qaeda, which escaped through allied Afghan lines during Operation Anaconda. The capture of al Qaeda documents and videotapes in safe houses provided a better understanding of the structure and dynamics of the organization and helped foil at least the Singapore plot in December 2001. U.S. forces dispersed the leadership, eliminated the training camps, and greatly reduced the means of communication among members, their leaders, and the central office, which handled logistical support for local operations.

The absence of a sanctuary to train new recruits prevents the dissemination of terrorist skills and tactics for the global jihad. The freezing or confiscation of financial assets deprives the jihad of needed resources. Mujahedin are being aggressively pursued and prosecuted worldwide. The only operation against an official Western target, the plot to strike at U.S. or British naval vessels in the Straits of Gibraltar in the summer of 2002, was discovered before it got off the ground and seems to have been unraveling on its own because of communication difficulties between the field commander and more central control. All the other major operations with great damage potential in this phase of the jihad were against soft targets: tourist destinations in the developing world (Djerba Synagogue, Bali nightclubs, Mombasa hotels, foreign housing in Riyadh, and Jewish and tourist sites in Casablanca and Istanbul); and commercial shipping (SS *Lemburg*). Most of these seem to have been initiated locally.

Some governments, including those of Indonesia, Saudi Arabia, and Morocco, were initially hesitant to aggressively prosecute the war on terror. They denied that they had native-bred terrorism on their soil. This created local pockets of safety for terrorism. After suffering from spectacular bombing operations, however, they finally joined the war with enthusiasm and have further denied refuge and resources to the global Salafi mujahedin.

After the elimination of al Qaeda headquarters in Afghanistan, the Indonesian Jemaah Islamiyah was not significantly disrupted because the Indonesian government hesitated to pursue a potentially unpopular policy. Indonesia is the world's largest Muslim country, and its population is suspicious of government claims, after decades of Suharto's regime. As a result, the global Salafi jihad was still able to offer training camps in Suluku province, Indonesia, as well as on the Island of Mindanao, in the Philippines run by the Moro Islamic Liberation Front. The usually authoritative International Crisis Group issued a comprehensive briefing on terrorism in Indonesia on August 8, 2002, concluding: "Indonesia is not a terrorist hotbed. Proponents of radical Islam remain a small minority, and most of those are devout practitioners who would never dream of using violence" (International Crisis Group, 2002a). The situation changed drastically after the carnage of the Bali bombings in October 2002. The Indonesian government aggressively pursued the perpetrators and even arrested, tried, and convicted the popular Abu Bakar Baasyir. In December 2002, the International Crisis Group completely reversed itself and issued a comprehensive briefing, "How the Jemaah Islamiyah Terrorist Network Operates" (International Crisis Group, 2002b).

Likewise, despite the fact that fifteen of nineteen perpetrators of the 9/11 operation were Saudi nationals, Saudi Arabia refused to acknowledge its citizens' involvement in the global Salafi jihad. The Saudis believed they were safe from terrorism on their own soil. They provided refuge for fleeing mujahedin, allowed business contributions to the jihad, and tolerated violent sermons from Salafi preachers in support of the jihad and condemning the West. These conditions helped maintain a reservoir of potential future mujahedin. The May 12, 2003, Riyadh bombing shattered this complacency, and the kingdom started to crack down on locally bred terrorism and began an internal discussion about the contribution of its culture and finances to terrorism.

Moroccan authorities, at the forefront of the fight against terror, had detected and prevented the Gibraltar plot. But they believed that terrorism was just a foreign import, confined to the three Saudis convicted of the plot. The May 16, 2003, multiple bombings in Casablanca dispelled this belief and prompted the government to crack down on its locally bred Salafi jihad organizations, which had perpetrated the bombings. The Moroccan pattern was different from that of other global Salafi jihad operations. Elsewhere, the terrorists had been trained in Afghanistan before the camps were eliminated. In Casablanca, the bombers received only hasty local training over weekends in nearby caves. As a result they had difficulty manufacturing their bombs, which were too heavy and unreliable. The leader had to postpone the operations. Finally, after finding a lighter and more reliable formula on the Internet, they quickly built the bombs the day before the operation. They tried to carry out a sophisticated plan of five simultaneous bombings, but four of them more or less failed, resulting in the deaths of the bombers. Only one bombing resulted in mass casualties.

The Casablanca bombing may be a preview of operations to come during this phase of the jihad. Some of the leaders are well trained to conduct sophisticated operations, but are on their own to train their foot soldiers. These may be enthusiastic but lack skills and knowledge of how to carry out operations, resulting in a serious degradation of the jihad's lethal capability. Difficulties with communication and a lack of support for training and logistics will further diminish their ability to carry out sophisticated operations on the order of September 11, 2001. The heightened vigilance of most governments eliminates mujahedin mobility, especially travel to Western nations from countries where they can maintain a refuge. Monitoring of communications by the West has already resulted in the arrest of multiple leaders who used cell phones to communicate with subordinates. The full-time pursuit of safety by the leadership prevents them from coordinating sophisticated large-scale operations with local cells around the world. Small-scale operations may never be eliminated because singletons with little training can execute them. Although such attacks may be lethal, they will not result in mass carnage, which requires coordination, skills, and resources. The lack of training facilities will diminish the level of skill of the post-Afghanistan cohort of mujahedin. The crackdown by Western and now Saudi banking authorities and Arab states on private financial contributions to the jihad will further diminish its available resources. Heightened vigilance at border entry points and monitoring of communications worldwide diminish the ability to effectively coordinate operations from a central point. Without any more spectacular successes, the appeal of the jihad will fade with time.

Conclusion

The global Salafi jihad evolved through a process of radicalization consisting of gradual self-selection, manipulation of resources from above, and recognition of the single common target of the jihad. At the end of the Afghan-Soviet war in 1989, the traditional mujahedin, who could go back, returned home. Those who remained in Afghanistan joined by default. The second milestone was the move to the Sudan in 1991 when the most militant actively pledged their commitment to the global jihad. During the Sudanese exile, there was intense discussion leading to a gradual shifting of target from the near to the far enemy. Witnesses at the East African embassy bombings trial and the "Returnees from Albania" trial mentioned that there was then a target common to all the disparate groups. The move back to Afghanistan in 1996 was the third milestone. Only about 150 made the journey back. Many left the organization through disillusionment or rejection of the new mission against the United States. When the global jihad was formally announced in February 1998, the EIG quickly rejected it and the EIJ split over it. All through this evolution the most militant component, as represented by Osama bin Laden, controlled the resources (Saudi wealth) and was able to guide the direction of the jihad.

The evolution of the global jihad was also characterized by a succession of sites, which attracted multiple militant networks of diverse perspectives. These small networks interacted with each other in intense debates and generated excitement and a sense of purpose. These sites were "where the action was." Progressive ideological extremism and a heightened sense of commitment emerged from these intense interactions (see Collins, 1998, for a similar argument about the importance of "scenes" in intellectual creativity). Egyptian prisons and university campuses in the 1970s were the places where the concept of the Salafi jihad was developed. In Peshawar in the late 1980s, militant Muslims from all over the world debated the future of a worldwide jihad. They continued this dialogue in Khartoum in the 1990s and finalized the ideology of the global Salafi jihad.

There were also the usual internal disputes. In 1991, al-Zawahiri took over the EIJ, setting Abud al-Zumur aside. He also renewed the EIJ-EIG rivalry despite the efforts of some EIG members to forge a common bond between these organizations. He seems to have been the most contentious of the lot. In 1993, there were more internal divisions within the EIJ because of the large-scale "Vanguards of Conquest" disaster. In 1997, there was an EIG split over the nonviolent initiative, with the prisoners in favor and the outsiders opposing it. In 2001, the EIJ merged with al Qaeda. This type of radicalization is similar to that of other terrorist organizations such as the Algerian Armée Islamique du Salut, Groupe Islamique Armé, and Groupe Salafiste pour la Prédication et le Combat. Despite their internal problems, they still managed to conduct successful operations.

The loss of the Afghan sanctuary degraded the operational capability of the global Salafi jihad. Its inability to strike official targets in the West forced it to shift to operations on "soft targets" in their own sanctuaries (Indonesia, Saudi Arabia, and Morocco). These bombings prompted the thus far reluctant governments to crack down on the jihad, eliminate some of its last areas of refuge, and discourage private solicitation of support for the jihad. In the summer of 2003 came early indications that the Iranians might join the war on terror through house arrest of al Qaeda leaders in Iran. These developments will further decentralize the jihad and degrade its operational capabilities.

Blowback?

To return to the blowback thesis, the above account shows that the global Salafi jihad emerged through a process of evolution. This implies that the traditional Afghan Arabs of 1988 were not the same people or had a different mentality from the global Salafi mujahedin of 1998. This undermines the blowback thesis.

The global Salafi jihad is without doubt an indirect consequence of U.S. involvement in that Afghan-Soviet war. Without the U.S. support for that jihad, the Soviets would probably not have withdrawn from Afghanistan. U.S. covert action supported a *traditional* jihad, which included foreign Muslim volunteers. Toward the end of the war, the Egyptian Salafists subverted the Mekhtab al-Khidemat, the organization supporting the participation of the traditional foreign mujahedin, and possibly killed Azzam, its leader, who stood in the way of their mission. They created their own organizations, for which they recruited a minority of the foreign volunteers and none of the Afghan mujahedin, who had been the real recipients of U.S. support. Only after their return from the Sudanese exile, many years after the end of U.S. support for the Afghan jihad, did the essence of the global Salafi jihad emerge.

At no point during the Afghan war or since was there direct U.S. support for the foreign mujahedin. The U.S. government, through the Central Intelligence Agency, funneled all its aid through the Pakistani Inter-Services Intelligence Directorate (ISID). The U.S. government trained the

Pakistanis, who trained the mujahedin. The Pakistanis insisted that the weapons and money go through them, and rightly so, as they did not want to have potentially unsavory characters trained by a foreign government running wild in their territory. The notion that U.S. personnel trained future al Qaeda terrorists is sheer fantasy. The authority on this topic is Brigadier Mohammad Yousaf, who ran the ISID Afghan Bureau from 1983 and 1987 and was no friend of the United States. He was categorical about the fact that everything went through ISID hands (Yousaf and Adkin, 2001). The foreign Muslim volunteers received support from the Afghan mujahedin, not from ISID, further removing them from any direct U.S. support. Bin Laden and al-Zawahiri (2001: part 2) denied receiving any U.S. aid, support, or training.

Peter Bergen, bin Laden's biographer, is correct to point out that the Pakistanis favored the fundamentalist mujahedin, but there is no evidence that they later exported jihad and terrorism around the world. These *Afghan* mujahedin were quite different from the foreign volunteers. I am not aware of any major Afghan participant in the global Salafi jihad except for Wali Khan Amin Shah, a personal friend of Osama bin Laden. Al Qaeda, EIJ, and their allies in the global Salafi jihad recruited exclusively from the foreign volunteers: with the exception of Shah, no Afghan, no matter how fundamentalist, who was trained and supported by the ISID later joined al Qaeda. Indeed, Afghans are conspicuous by their absence from the global Salafi jihad, all the more surprising since al Qaeda kept training camps in Afghanistan for more than a decade. By the end of the Soviet-Afghan war, a great deal of mutual antagonism existed between the Afghan mujahedin and the expatriates, whom the Afghans called *Ikhwanis* (Arabic for "brothers," as in the Muslim Brothers organization) or Wahhabis (a pejorative term from their perspective). The Afghans resented the foreigners, who were telling them that they were not good Muslims. Jumping a decade ahead, this hostility played an important role in the quick U.S. victory in 2001 when Afghans turned against these foreigners.

No U.S. official ever came in contact with the foreign volunteers. They simply traveled in different circles and never crossed U.S. radar screens. They had their own sources of money and their own contacts with the Pakistanis, official Saudis, and other Muslim supporters, and they made their own deals with the various Afghan resistance leaders. Their presence in Afghanistan was very small and they did not participate in any significant fighting (al-Shafii, 2001; Bearden, 2001; Bearden and Risen, 2003: 243). Contemporaneous accounts of the war do not even mention them. Many were not serious about the war. Some Saudi tourists came to earn their jihad credentials. Their tour was organized so that they could step inside Afghanistan, get photographed discharging a gun, and promptly return home as a hero of Afghanistan. The major contribution of the more serious volunteers was humanitarian aid, setting up hospitals around Peshawar and Quetta and providing funds for supply caravans to travel to the interior of the country.

Very few were involved in actual fighting. For most of the war, they were scattered among the Afghan groups associated with the four Afghan fundamentalist parties. Examples of these fighters were Essam al-Ridi, al-Rashidi, and Abdallah Anas. For the most part, Afghans welcomed them. But with time, more sectarian volunteers (Salafi and Wahhabi) came. They stayed aloof from the Afghans and criticized their hosts for not being good Muslims. Afghans traditionally practiced a Sufi Islam, which is thought to be an abomination by Wahhabis and Salafists alike. Afghans used the derogatory term "Wahhabi" to refer to these newcomers and began to avoid them. Their only significant fighting as a group in the war was in the fighting around Masada in the spring of 1987, when Osama bin Laden distinguished himself.

After the Soviet withdrawal from Afghanistan, the foreigners might have inadvertently prolonged the Afghan civil war and postponed for three years the fall of Kabul. When the Soviets withdrew, the traditional mujahedin were on their way back home and the Salafists had stayed on. Two of their camps were in the vicinity of Jalalabad, and they became involved in the battle for the city that took place in March 1989. The campaign started well for the mujahedin, who captured several strategic points. The Communist government forces were in the process of negotiating their surrender and guarantee of safety in the usual Afghan tradition. Anticipating the usual resolution of these issues, several governmental troops had surrendered to the mujahedin after a token resistance. These prisoners were divided among the various fighting groups. About sixty of them went to a contingent of foreigners, who promptly executed them, cut them into small pieces, and sent the remains back to the besieged city in a truck with the message that this would be the fate awaiting the infidels (Akram,

1996: 272-277). This put an end to the negotiations of surrender, despite apologies and assurances of safety from Afghan resistance leaders. It rejuvenated the fighting spirit of the besieged and resulted in the first major government victory. This success reversed the government's demoralization from the withdrawal of Soviet forces, renewed its determination to fight on, and allowed it to survive three more years.

The departure of the Soviet infidels invalidated the fatwas for the traditional jihad (al-Banyan, 2001). The new crops of volunteers responded to Salafi urgings. At that early stage of the Salafi jihad, the training consisted of regular guerrilla tactics—the use of assault rifles, land mines, and antiaircraft weapons (see al-Fadl, 2001; Kherchtou, 2001)—useful for fighting a war of insurgency. Terror tactics useful for the Salafi jihad—explosives, casing a target, and analysis of its vulnerability—were introduced much later, around 1992 (Mohamed, 2000; Kherchtou, 2001). By this time, new al Qaeda members were quite different from the early volunteers, who had come to fight in the traditional jihad.

In summary, the United States indirectly supported the Afghan mujahedin, who did all the fighting, paid dearly for it, and deserved the full credit for their victory over the Soviets. The expatriate contribution to this victory was minimal at best, for they spread dissension among Muslim resistance ranks. Usually, the victors write the history. For the Soviet Afghan war, there is no Afghan account, perhaps due to the high illiteracy rate or the later developments in Afghanistan. Instead, the foreign bystanders got to write the history. These foreigners expropriated the native Afghan victory over the Soviet Union, created the myth that they had destroyed a superpower by faith alone, and argued that the same fate would lie ahead for the only remaining superpower (al-Zawahiri, 2001: part 2). Thus the global Salafi jihad was able to hijack the Afghan mujahedin victory for its own ends.

THREE

The Mujahedin

Defining the Terrorists and Their Organizations

THE GLOBAL Salafi jihad is a new development in the annals of terrorism. It combines fanaticism, in its original sense of "excessive enthusiasm in religious belief" (Taylor, 1991), with terrorism against a "far enemy," a global target to bring about a utopia. This fanaticism embraces an eagerness to die and kill for the cause. This glorification of the notion of *shahada* (literally the testimony of faith, but now also meaning martyrdom) is an inherent aspect of this new form of global terrorism, and can be understood only in its religious context. I submit that the new global Salafi mujahedin are sufficiently distinct from other terrorists that an in-depth study of their specific characteristics, patterns of joining the jihad, and behavior is needed. So far, the statements about them are based on anecdotal evidence or speculations derived from popular prejudice and conventional wisdom about evil people in general and terrorists in particular. My aim is to provide a general empirical study of these individuals to add to what is known and to correct some widely disseminated misconceptions.

The discussion here includes only those Muslim terrorists who target foreign governments and their populations, the "far enemy," in pursuit of Salafi objectives, namely the establishment of an Islamist state. Drawing these boundaries removes many terrorists from consideration, but my concern is that an overly inclusive sample may obscure important factors that might help us to understand this phenomenon.

Specifically, I eliminate all non-Muslim terrorists, as well as Muslim terrorists involved in domestic insurgency and in urban warfare against their own governments. I do not include Muslims fighting for the "liberation" of Kashmir or Chechnya, for these seem to be straightforward jihads, like the former Afghan or Bosnian jihads as defined by Azzam. Likewise, many Muslims fighting in Central Asia seem to be fighting an internal insurgency, a simple domestic Salafi jihad rather than a global one. Algerian terrorists who confine their activities to Algeria are likewise involved in a domestic Salafi jihad, which resembles an insurgency against their government based on a mixture of domestic grievances and religious fanaticism. I do include, however, those Algerians who committed terrorist attacks against French targets, as in the waves of terrorism in France in 1995 and 1996. They clearly did so not to change the French government but to fight the "far enemy" that prevented the establishment of an Islamist state in their own country.

The empirical world is rarely as tidy as we want it to be. It does not easily fit into our analytical categories and requires us to make difficult decisions in the selection of our data. Palestine is one such difficult choice. Azzam defined the struggle for the liberation of Palestine as a straightforward jihad rather than as an effort to establish a Salafi Islamist state. Indeed, many Palestinian terrorists have traditionally been secular rather than religious, although religious fanaticism seems to be ascendant. Furthermore, the Palestinian struggle involves complex social, economic, and political grievances as well as the goal of "liberation" of a former Muslim land. To include the Palestinians, therefore, would muddy the more purely ideological waters of the global Salafi jihad. I suspect that Palestinian terrorism is significantly different from the global Salafi jihad in terms of the people it attracts and their behavior. The global Salafi mujahedin in my sample have a very different profile from that of the extensive sample of Palestinian suicide terrorists described by Ariel Merari (1990).

Perhaps the most controversial decision I made was to exclude from this analysis the imprisoned leadership of the Egyptian Islamic Group (EIG). The EIG has been blamed for many terrorist acts in Egypt and abroad against Egyptian targets. The imprisoned leadership approved of these operations. But it was quite clear that they were part of a simple Salafi jihad. The terrorizing of tourists in Egypt in the 1990s was not an end in itself but an attempt to discredit the state. By demonstrating to the

world the government's inability to protect tourists, the terrorists succeeded in undermining the economy by disrupting the major national
industry. The leadership believed that this campaign would increase the
hardship of the masses, who would blame the government and mobilize
to overthrow it. When this strategy backfired and turned the population
against the EIG, the imprisoned EIG leadership recognized their error
and completely reversed tactics in 1997, initiating a nonviolent strategy,
which is still holding up. In the process, the EIG leadership has even abandoned its jihad and has become closer to the dawa strategy.

Despite the exclusion of the imprisoned EIG leadership, I have included the expatriate EIG leadership, for it played an important role in the
ideological development of the Muslim revivalist movement from a simple jihad in Afghanistan to a Salafi jihad to the global Salafi jihad. Throughout the past decade the exiled EIG leaders have flirted with the global
Salafi jihad at many points. They have supported its operations, met and
plotted with their global colleagues, and in turn received support from
the global Salafi jihad in terms of funds and logistics for their in-country
operations. They had dual membership in al Qaeda and the EIG. The targeting of tourists started to become an end in itself, because of both their
corrupting effect on society and their financial support for the Egyptian
government. When the EIG leadership imprisoned in Egypt issued its
nonviolent initiative, the expatriate leaders rejected it. There is evidence
that the Luxor massacres that took place after this initiative were an attempt by the exiled leadership to undermine it and force the continuation of the strategy of violence. Eventually, they resigned from the ruling
council of the EIG to make room for leaders supporting the new strategy. They earned a place in my sample, alongside their rivals from the
Egyptian Islamic Jihad (EIJ), who had made the transition from a Salafi
jihad to a global Salafi jihad. The EIJ has been a significant part of the
global Salafi jihad. Its leader al-Zawahiri is the jihad's main ideologist,
and its leadership comprises the majority of al Qaeda's ruling council
(shura). Indeed, in June 2001, the EIJ and al Qaeda merged to form al-
Qaeda al-Jihad.

The global Salafi jihad is an Islamic revivalist social movement. It consists of people and organizations in various degrees of formalization who
share the same ideology and mission. Al Qaeda and EIJ are well-defined
organizations whose leadership supports terrorist operations. So are the

Jemaah Islamiyah in Indonesia and Malaysia, the Moro Islamic Liberation Front in the Philippines, and the Groupe Salafiste pour la Prédication et le Combat (GSPC) in Algeria. Other groups such as the Abu Sayyaf
Group in the Philippines and the Groupe Islamique Armé (GIA) in Algeria have lapsed into pure criminality and lost the support of al Qaeda,
the vanguard of this movement. Less well defined are the small illegal Moroccan clusters around charismatic preachers, which have various names
but are grouped under the amorphous social movement called the Salafia
Jihadia. The global Salafi jihad also includes apparently unaffiliated individuals who pursued the goals of the jihad, such as Abdul Basit Karim
(Ramzi Yousef), who received support from the jihad for his operations.
His role in the 1993 World Trade Center bombing and the 1995 Bojinka
plot to blow up airplanes over the Pacific leaves no doubt that he was a
part of this global movement without being a formal member of any of
its organizations.

With the above considerations in mind, I kept the sample focused exclusively on the global Salafi jihad in order to reveal some specific patterns that might have been obscured by a more inclusive selection (see
Pape, 2003).

Problems in Gathering Information

Collecting data on global Salafi mujahedin presents a series of challenges,
mostly resulting from a general lack of information. I included only those
mujahedin on whom enough background information was available to
include them in empirical generalizations as to age, origin, religious commitment, and education. Although several hundred mujahedin have been
arrested in the past several years, there is not enough information to include most of them in this study. There is evidence that those on whom
enough information exists are not a representative sample of the rest. This
inevitably slants this study in specific directions, which I will shortly discuss, and affects the validity of some of my conclusions.

My sources of information were all in the public domain. I did not have
direct access to the mujahedin or to any government's secret reports. Global Salafi jihad organizations like al Qaeda are clandestine organizations,
very secretive about their members and operations. Often, they deny or
obfuscate their very existence and do not take official credit for success-

ful operations. They do not grant access to their members, and their leaders' few interviews are well-orchestrated propaganda exercises with poor documentary value. There are no available official documents on their members and organizations, making it difficult to gather representative information. Even captured mujahedin have been reluctant to speak freely with academics or journalists for fear of betraying their cause, putting themselves at risk of retaliation from former comrades or undermining their criminal defense or post-trial appeals. They reject any social science project that would diminish the validity of their mission—jihad in the path of God.

But even assuming no intent to deceive, the rare prison interviews must be viewed with skepticism. Acceptance of responsibility does not protect from a tendency to distort the past to make it consistent with one's present self-concept; "confessions" may not accurately reflect historical events or states of mind. Nevertheless, when transcripts of such interviews exist, they cannot be ignored because of their potential to shed light on clandestine events and on states of mind. Governments have also been reluctant to grant access to those they have captured. Their priorities are to protect information that might be vital to their fight against terror, including the extent of their knowledge about terrorist organizations and operations, and to prevent communication between the prisoners and their former comrades.

My sources included the documents and transcripts of legal proceedings involving global Salafi mujahedin and their organizations, government documents, press and scholarly articles, and Internet articles. The information was often inconsistent. I considered the source of the information in assessing facts. In decreasing degrees of reliability, I favored transcripts of court proceedings subject to cross-examination, followed by reports of court proceedings, then corroborated information from people with direct access to the information provided, uncorroborated statements from people with that access, and finally statements from people who had heard the information secondhand. "Experts" fall into the last category for their reliability as sources of information depends on their diligence as historians.

The collected information suffers from several limitations. First, the mujahedin selected are hardly representative of the global Salafi jihad as a whole. Although the judicial system might prosecute all involved, journalists and scholars tend to focus on leaders, people they can investigate, and unusual cases. Leaders set the tone and direction for these groups, but usually are not representative of the overall membership. Lack of investigative opportunity also slants a sample because of the neglect of significant portions of a group. Little is known about the perpetrators of the November 13, 1995, bombings of the Saudi National Guard training center in Riyadh, the June 25, 1996, bombing of the Khobar Towers in Dhahran, and the Saudis involved in the September 11, 2001, atrocities because the Saudi government has not allowed independent investigation on its soil. Finally, by definition, unusual cases are not representative. For instance, the presence of members of the elite and Western converts to Islam in jihad organizations arouses interest by challenging the conventional wisdom. Their inclusion in this sample detracts from the more mundane militants. Since much of my data comes from journalists, the result is somewhat biased toward leaders and unusual cases, and tends to ignore those who cannot be investigated and downplay the rank and file.

Second, reliance on journalistic accounts is fraught with danger. There is much misinformation in the press. Information about clandestine groups is truly difficult to acquire. Many journalists do not seem to distinguish explicitly between sources who had access to the information and those who did not. For instance, many have accused the U.S. government of directly funding or even training the original global Salafi mujahedin in Afghanistan. This is based on a complete misunderstanding of the U.S. role during the war. As noted in the previous chapter, the only two people who had real access to this type of information and went public are Brigadier Yousaf, head of the Pakistani ISID Afghan Bureau, and Milton Bearden, the CIA chief of station in Islamabad at the time. They both categorically deny any direct link between the U.S. government and the early mujahedin. Indeed, al-Zawahiri's book denies it as well. Yet this has not stopped many journalists, who should know better, from continuing to make this claim.

Lack of direct access to information feeds the wildest rumors. During the Soviet-Afghan war, many journalists in Peshawar retired to the USAID guesthouse, which was the only bar in town. Between drinks, they exchanged outlandish stories, some of which found their way into print later on. When challenged on publication of a story without additional confirmation, one of them told me, "The story is too good to check." The practice of interviewing other journalists or scholars with a similar lack of access for confirmation is no more valid. This second "source," more likely than not, has heard the same information from the same original source, leading to a false sense of confirmation and a rehash of the rumor mill.

Furthermore, journalists are born storytellers. Unfortunately, information is typically received in fragments. There is a strong tendency to fill in the gaps between facts in order to construct a better narrative, a practice that leads to many inaccuracies when the fillers assume lives of their own in later accounts. This uncomfortably disjointed nature of an evolving story may also lead to speculations, which later turn out to be erroneous. It is important to follow the developments of a story to correct original inaccuracies. For instance, Ahmed Ressam, the Millennial Bomber (more on whom in Chapter 4), had made up a story of militancy and imprisonment by Algerian authorities to support his application for political asylum when he first came to Canada to avoid deportation back to Algeria. Laidi (2002: 231-232) and Gunaratna (2002: 110), in their otherwise excellent accounts of the global jihad in Europe and around the world, uncritically repeated this tale and added various details. At his trial, Ressam admitted that he made up this story (Ressam, 2001: 537), and Bernton and colleagues (2002) convincingly refuted the political discrimination story in a comprehensive investigation of Ressam's life prior to his leaving Algeria.

Likewise, in the post-9/11 hysteria, many people were arrested and suspected of terrorism merely because of often unwitting association with known terrorists. Many Muslims share Salafi beliefs but stop far short of violence. Often journalists and law enforcement officers do not distinguish between Tablighis, peacefully preaching dawa, and mujahedin conducting violent operations. Although arrests are front-page news, there is rarely any fanfare about exoneration. More sinister was the use of this hysteria to settle personal accounts. Abderrezak Besseghir, a baggage handler at the Paris Charles de Gaulle airport, was set up as a terrorist by his in-laws as retaliation for his presumed involvement in his wife's death. False accusations of terrorism have also been used in custody disputes; in such a dispute disguised as a terror case, Hany Kiareldeen was incarcerated in New Jersey for nineteen months. No evidence of wrongdoing was ever presented, ostensibly for reasons of "national security" (Purdy, 2003). These cases underline the importance of following the developments of a story.

67

Third, a more pervasive problem I encountered is reliance on retrospective accounts from principals and witnesses, which are subject to the biases of self-report and flawed memory. Even when there is an attempt to provide information as factually as possible, accuracy is limited because of the reconstructive nature of human memory (Schacter, 1995, 1996, 2001). People reconstruct their experience as narratives consistent with their present beliefs, which may be at variance with the actual past. This is usually done inadvertently, due to the natural distortions of memory. Less innocent are the intentional distortions in self-presentation. Even the most racist person does not portray himself as a bigot. In gathering the data, I have not encountered any admission of pure prejudice against the West, Jews, or the United States. Mujahedin and their sympathizers' attitudes toward this trio are usually couched in terms of an unavoidable defense forced upon them by the violent exploitation of or discrimination against Muslims. These self-serving retrospective accounts contrast sharply with the transcripts of terrorists' conversations recorded secretly by the police in Milan, Hamburg, and Montreal, in which the violence of the words and the prejudices of the speakers are disturbing. These elements do not surface in retrospective accounts.

Perhaps the greatest limitation on this inquiry is the lack of a relevant control group, specifically Muslims with similar background and activities who did not participate in the jihad despite having had an opportunity to do so. Finding such a group would be extremely difficult in our present culture. Most governments have taken a punitive strategy toward people who toyed with the idea of joining the jihad. Like the Lackawanna Six, a group of Yemeni-American men suspected of belonging to an al Qaeda terror cell in western New York who were sentenced to a decade in prison, they have been prosecuted for simply undergoing training in al Qaeda camps despite the fact that they eventually decided to walk away from the jihad. In this punitive environment, it is not surprising that few people come forward and tell about their past association with the jihad. A focus on this group, however, and an understanding of how its members are systematically different from those who joined the jihad would be very relevant for countering the jihad. Although the absence of a control group means that any findings and interpretations based on the data are necessarily suggestive hypotheses, there is still a great deal to be learned from an empirical examination of the global Salafi jihad.

Profiles of the Mujahedin

What sets global Salafi mujahedin apart? On the surface, they are all Muslims who accept the Salafi interpretation of Islam. The temptation is therefore strong to blame Islam, or its Salafi variant, for this type of terrorism. But this common feature is based on the definition guiding my selection and its explanatory value is therefore tautological.

The search for common features explaining why individuals become involved in global terrorism may be divided into three general approaches. The first is that the terrorists share a common social background. The second is that terrorists share a common psychological make-up. The third is that some people became terrorists because of their particular situation at the time of recruitment. The rest of this chapter will be an empirical analysis of each of these sets of variables as a potential explanation for why people join a movement of global terrorism.

The unavoidable problem in the common features approach to the study of terrorism is what might be called the fundamental issue of specificity. Although numerous people share many of the postulated individual features or are exposed to the same social factors, very few go on to carry out terrorist acts. The inability of specific factors, singly or in combination, to distinguish future mujahedin from nonmujahedin limits our ability to make statements that are specific to terrorists. Identification of variables specific to the creation, maintenance, and demise of terrorists requires comparison with a relevant control group of nonterrorists.

Social Background

The focus on the background of the mujahedin gives us the opportunity to empirically test the popular social explanations of global terrorism. The common stereotype is that terrorism is a product of poor, desperate, naïve, single young men from third world countries, vulnerable to brainwashing and recruitment into terror. Unpacking this formula, the geographical origins of the mujahedin should be not only the third world, but some of the poorest countries of the third world. It also implies that they come from the lowest socioeconomic strata. Their naïve vulnerable dimension implies that they either are brainwashed early into hatred of the West or are relatively uneducated and susceptible to such brainwashing as young adults. In this sense, they are relatively unsophisticated and local in their outlook. A broad experience of the world might be protective against the alleged brainwashing that presumably led to their conversion to terrorism. The desperation implies that either they have no occupational opportunities or these are extremely limited. They are single, for any strong family responsibility might prevent their total dedication to a cause that demands their ultimate sacrifice.

Geographical Origins

Where are the mujahedin from? Looking at the sample as a whole, about two-thirds of the 172 mujahedin in the sample come from Saudi Arabia (31), Egypt (24), France (18), Algeria (15), Morocco (14), and Indonesia (12). Parsed this way, we would be hard pressed to find a common pattern among them. Analyzing the various linkages among the terrorists, four large clusters emerged in the previous chapter on the evolution of the jihad. The first consists of the Central Staff of al Qaeda and of the global Salafi jihad movement in general. The terrorists in this cluster form the leadership of the movement. Most of them were involved in the Afghan-Soviet war and were the founding members of al Qaeda. They are not usually directly involved in operations, but inspire and approve them from afar. They provide training, some financing, and sometimes logistical support for the global Salafi jihad in general. They are also responsible for propaganda in support of the jihad. The second large cluster includes terrorists coming from Core Arab states (Saudi Arabia, Egypt, Yemen, Kuwait). The third cluster represents jihad members coming from North Africa, also known as the Maghreb (Morocco, Algeria, Tunisia) but also people whose families were from the Maghreb but who were born and grew up in France. The fourth cluster is Southeast Asian and consists of the members belonging to the Jemaah Islamiyah centered in Indonesia and Malaysia.

Although I define these clusters geographically, assignment to a cluster is not based solely on geographical origin. It is based on the pattern of interaction among the terrorists. For instance, four members of the Hamburg clique that was responsible for the 9/11 operation were Moroccans (Mounir al-Motassadeq, Abdelghani Mzoudi, Said Bahaji, and Zakarya Essabar). Because they interacted with other members of the Core Arab cluster and were supported by the Central Staff responsible for this cluster, I classified them with the Core Arabs, despite the fact that three of them were born in the Maghreb. There was a lot of interaction among members of the same cluster, but almost none between them and members of different clusters. I will return to the emergence and structure of these clusters in Chapters 4 and 5.

Reorganizing the data according to the pattern of interactions, the Central Staff cluster contains 32 members; the Southeast Asian cluster, 21; the Maghreb cluster, 53; and the Core Arab cluster, 66. Each cluster has its distinctive profile, which I will develop in this chapter.

Almost two-thirds of the terrorists forming the Central Staff come from Egypt (20, or 63 percent). The rest come from Saudi Arabia (3), Kuwait (3), Jordan (2), Iraq, the Sudan, Libya, and Lebanon (1 each). The Egyptian representation at the leadership level is notable because Egyptians constitute only 14 percent of the overall sample. The Egyptians at the leadership level joined al Qaeda during its formation in the late 1980s and early 1990s. They were mostly Islamist militants, imprisoned after the assassination of President Sadat (see Chapter 2). When they were released from prison, they went to Afghanistan because of continued government persecution. They were already dedicated terrorists before coming to Afghanistan as illustrated by their imprisonment for political reasons. Of the first cluster, 15 of 26 (58 percent) on whom I have data had been imprisoned prior to joining the jihad. This contrasts sharply with the other

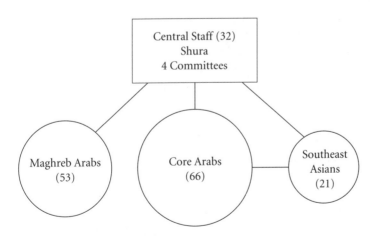

Figure 1. The Global Salafi Jihad

three clusters (only 9 of 118, or 8 percent). The Egyptian militants brought their Qutbian ideology with them and expanded it into the global Salafi jihad. They also constitute the backbone of the leadership of the global jihad, dominating in numbers and ideas the rest of the cadres of this movement, who come almost exclusively from the Core Arab world. Contrary to popular belief, the roots of the global Salafi jihad are therefore not Saudi or Afghan, but Egyptian.

Indonesians (12 of 21) dominate the Southeast Asian cluster, which also includes Muslims from neighboring states: Malaysia (3), Singapore (2), and the Philippines (2). Most of the members of the Jemaah Islamiyah were connected to two Islamic boarding schools in Indonesia and Malaysia, founded by the group's leaders.

The largest clusters are from the two Arab regions. The Core Arab cluster is dominated by a large Saudi contingent (28, or 42 percent) with smaller contributions from Egypt (4), Yemen (4), Kuwait(4), Morocco (4), England (3), Pakistan (2), Syria (2), the United States (2), Canada (2), and the United Arab Emirates (2). The Maghreb Arab cluster comes from France (18), Algeria (15), Morocco (10), and Tunisia (5). Most of the French contingent consists of second-generation Frenchmen of Maghreb origin, although there are a few French converts to Islam in this group.

The global Salafi jihad has evolved over time. It originated in Egyptian Muslim militancy. The Indonesian contingent is probably the second oldest and developed during its exile in Malaysia in the 1990s. It conducted no significant terrorist operations until its return to Indonesia in 1999 after the overthrow of the Suharto regime. The two Arab clusters came later to the jihad. The Maghreb Arab cluster joined when its peaceful political aspirations were thwarted in Algeria. After an Islamist victory in the first-round legislative election in December 1991, the second round was cancelled in January 1992 to prevent an Islamist takeover of the legislative body. The Bosnian war in the early 1990s became another rallying point for joining the jihad. This war also inspired the Core Arab cluster, although that group seems to have responded more to the direct appeal of Osama bin Laden in the late 1990s.

Before leaving this topic, let us look at the countries not represented. Perhaps the biggest surprise is the lack of representation from Afghanistan, with the exception of Wali Khan Amin Shah, who was a personal friend of bin Laden and Abdul Basit Karim. Afghanistan was the site where the jihad started and the place of training and refuge for the jihad for more than a decade. Somehow, the global mujahedin did not mix with the Afghans. This underscores the fact that the global Salafi jihad is not an Afghan phenomenon. Other countries not represented in the global jihad despite their large Muslim populations include India, Bangladesh, Turkey, and Palestine (not counting the Palestinians from the diaspora). Pakistan, the country of so many madrassas (Islamic schools), is also greatly underrepresented, with the exception of its Baluchi minority, who are generally hostile to the Punjabi majority, and expatriate Pakistanis who grew up in Britain.

Not surprising is the fact that Iranians and Shia Muslims in general are not represented at all in the global Salafi jihad. This jihad is strictly a Sunni affair run by people who consider the Shia to be heretics. This did not prevent the government of Iran from collaborating with the global jihad now and then, but their clashing ideologies prevented any formal or sustained partnership from forming.

Socioeconomic Status

The conventional wisdom is that terrorism is fueled by poverty in an asymmetrical power situation. Terrorism is the weapon of choice of the dispossessed and powerless against an all-powerful state. Although this argument arose in national liberation struggles, it has been too easily generalized in discussions of global terrorism.

I have divided my sample into upper, middle, and lower class, according to the socioeconomic status of the terrorists' families of origin. Even taking into consideration all the information available, this required sometimes crude judgments on my part.

Of the 102 people on whom I was able to gather data, 18 were upper class, 56 were middle class, and 28 were lower class (Table 1). This overall pattern hides significant differences among the various clusters. The Central Staff and Core Arab clusters are similar and skewed toward overrepresentation of the upper and middle classes. The leadership and the largest cluster of the jihad therefore come principally from the upper and middle classes. The Southeast Asian cluster is solidly middle class whereas the Maghreb Arab cluster is evenly divided between the middle and lower classes. Most of the people who came from the lower classes were

Table 1. Socioeconomic Status of Family of Origin

	Upper Class	Middle Class	Lower Class	Total
Central Staff	5	7	2	14
Southeast Asian	–	10	2	12
Maghreb Arab	–	16	15	31
Core Arab	13	23	9	45
Total	**18**	**56**	**28**	**102**

from the "excluded" second generation from the Maghreb or had emi-
grated from the Maghreb. The converts to Islam also came from the lower classes. But overall, about three-fourths of global Salafi mujahedin were
solidly upper or middle class, refuting the argument that terrorism aris-
es from poverty. The exception was the "excluded" Maghreb Arabs in
France and half of the Western Catholic converts to Islam.

Education

A common complaint in the West, directed especially at Pakistan and Saudi Arabia, is that both countries encourage a system of education that
preaches hatred of the West, and makes young people susceptible to the
Salafi message of global jihad against the West. In our sample of 137 terrorists, only 23 (17 percent) had an Islamic religious primary and sec-
ondary education (Table 2). The rest went to secular schools. These schools
in a country such as Saudi Arabia include a heavy dose of Islamic preaching. In most other countries, however, they are indeed secular. Half (11)
of those who had an Islamic religious education were Indonesians who
went to private Islamic boarding schools, specifically the two schools connected with Abu Bakar Baasyir and Abdullah Sungkar, the Pondok Ngruki in Indonesia and the Pesentren Luqmanul Hakiem in Malaysia. Half of
the rest went to madrassas, because they seemed to be the only available
school for poor people in their area of the world (sub-Saharan Africa and
the Philippines). Again, the data refute the notion that global Salafi terrorism comes from madrassa brainwashing, with the exception of the Indonesian network. Even if we add to this subsample all the Saudis, who
receive a large dose of religious teaching in their education, the total (56
or 41 percent) still does not reach a majority of the sample.

Table 2. Type of Education

	Secular	Religious	Total
Central Staff	24	3	27
Southeast Asian	8	11	19
Maghreb Arab	49	–	49
Core Arab	33	9	42
Total	**114**	**23**	**137**

Another argument linking education and future terrorism is that the potential terrorists were relatively ignorant and therefore susceptible to later brainwashing by a terrorist organization (Table 3). In our sample, there is information on the level of education of 132 terrorists: 22 (17 percent) did not graduate from high school; 16 (12 percent) graduated from high school only; 38 (29 percent) had some type of college education; 44 (33 percent) graduated from college; 7 (5 percent) had the equivalent of a master's degree; and 5 (4 percent) had the equivalent of a doctoral degree. Over 60 percent have had at least some college education, which makes them, as a group, more educated than the average person worldwide, and especially more educated than the vast majority of people in the third world.

From a cluster perspective, the Central Staff of the global Salafi jihad was fairly well educated—88 percent had finished college and 20 percent had doctorate degrees. The Southeast Asian cluster featured mostly people who had gone to Islamic boarding schools, namely the two schools run by Baasyir and Sungkar. Many went on to teach and preach. In the Core Arab cluster, the Saudis were the least educated. Those who went to Europe to pursue advanced studies were, of course, better educated than

Table 3. Educational Level Achieved

	Less Than High School	High School	College	B.A/B.S.	M.A.	Doctorate	Total
Central Staff	1	1	1	16	1	5	25
Southeast Asian	–	2	3	8	4	–	17
Maghreb Arab	13	8	9	6	1	–	37
Core Arab	8	5	25	14	1	–	53
Total	**22**	**16**	**38**	**44**	**7**	**5**	**132**

those who stayed home. The Maghreb Arabs were the least educated and most likely to have dropped out of school prematurely.

It appears that the global Salafi mujahedin were much better educated as a group than their parents. As such, they aspired to rise above their original socioeconomic background; the majority had gone to college. This refutes the image of this group as a relatively ignorant, naïve group, unsophisticated in the ways of the world. On the contrary, the data better support the opposite argument that this group is composed of truly global citizens, familiar with many countries—the West as well as the Middle East—and able to speak several languages with equal facility. This refutes the hypothesis that ethnocentrism produces terrorism. It does not mean that the global mujahedin were equally at home in the West and in their original countries, as we shall see later on. But their cosmopolitan outlook undermines the argument that ignorance of and lack of contact with the West was a precondition for terrorism. On the contrary, their world experience contrasts sharply with that of most Western students, who are not familiar at all with the Middle East and could be more aptly charged with ethnocentrism.

It might be assumed that the terrorists were drawn mostly from faculties of religious studies. This is true for the Southeast Asian cluster, as most of its members were closely tied to one of two Islamic boarding schools. But most of the other terrorists came from technical faculties such as science, engineering, or computer science, with little representation from the humanities or social sciences. Even their ideologues were not trained clerics. Qutb was a journalist, Faraj an engineer, al-Zawahiri a physician, and Mustafa Kamel (a.k.a. abu Hamza al-Masri) a civil engineer. This Muslim revivalist social movement relied on direct interpretation of the Quran and hadith, unmediated by any traditional Islamic interpretative school. This autodidact attitude toward the scriptures is encouraged by Salafi ideology, which rejects centuries of Islamic thought. The greater religiousness in technical/scientific disciplines is consistent with surveys of faith among faculty in the West (Stark and Finke, 2000).

The data on the socioeconomic and educational background of the mujahedin in this sample empirically refute the widespread notion that terrorism is a result of poverty and lack of education. On the contrary, the global Salafi mujahedin came from relatively well-to-do families and were much better educated than the average population, both in their home countries and in the West. This middle-class, relatively well-educated back-ground of the terrorists is consistent with studies of many other forms of terrorism, and contrary to popular conceptions. Merari's sample of PLO terrorists captured during the 1982 Lebanon War, however, came from poor refugee camps and were relatively uneducated (Merari, 1990 and 1991). This difference between the global Salafi mujahedin and Palestin-ian terrorists challenges the assumption that terrorists are fundamental-ly similar and can be lumped together for analysis (see Pape, 2003).

Faith as Youth

Contrary to the notion that the mujahedin had been brainwashed into extremist religious beliefs from childhood (the "green-diaper" baby the-ory), there might have been a shift in devotion to Islam from childhood to early adulthood among the individuals in the sample (Table 4). There was information on childhood faith of 117 people; of those 9 were Chris-tians, who must be removed from the sample. Of the rest, 53 (49 percent) were described as religious children. Breaking down this sample accord-ing to clusters, as expected in terms of consistency with their early reli-gious life, 13 of 16 global Salafi jihad Central Staff were considered reli-gious as children. This pattern is identical to that of the Southeast Asian cluster, linked together by their attendance at two Islamic boarding schools. The Core Arab cluster showed religious devotion early, as 24 of 39 (62 percent) were described as religious. The overwhelming exception to this was of course the Maghreb Arab cluster. France is a strongly secular coun-try, objecting even to the wearing of veils in school. Likewise, the three Maghreb Arab countries of Algeria, Tunisia, and Morocco have stressed secularism over Islam. It is no wonder then that only 3 of 37 (8 percent)

Table 4. Devotion As Youth

	Religious	Secular	Christian	Total
Central Staff	13	3	1	17
Southeast Asian	13	3	1	17
Maghreb Arab	3	34	6	43
Core Arab	24	15	1	40
Total	**53**	**55**	**9**	**117**

showed any Islamic religious devotion as youths. This strong secularism coupled with the size of this cluster skews the overall sample to reject the green-diaper baby theory. The other three clusters robustly support this theory, as 50 of 71 (70 percent) were described as religious as young men.

Occupation

The popular wisdom on terrorists suggests that they were desperate people, with little economic opportunity or without a decent occupation. In this sample, I collected occupational information on 134 people (Table 5). At the time they joined the jihad, 57 were professionals (physicians, architect, preachers, teachers), 44 had semiskilled occupations (police, military, mechanics, civil service, small business, and students), and 33 were considered unskilled. So only a quarter of the whole sample could be considered unskilled workers with few prospects before them. These unskilled terrorists were heavily concentrated in the Maghreb Arab cluster (20 out of 40) and most were involved in petty crime (false documents traffic, thefts, credit card fraud) in support of the jihad. The rest of the sample showed the same type of upward mobility found in terms of educational levels. An argument can be made that, far from being a product of falling expectations, the jihad was more a result of rising expectations among its members.

Family Status

The final social stereotype about terrorists is that they are single men, lacking any attachment to society as a whole, which allows them to per-

Table 5. Occupation

	Professional	Semiskilled	Unskilled	Total
Central Staff	17	9	1	27
Southeast Asian	14	3	1	18
Maghreb Arab	4	16	20	40
Core Arab	22	16	11	49
Total	**57**	**44**	**33**	**134**

form terrorist acts without being weighed down by their respons
or fears of reprisals on their families.

In the sample, marital status information was available for 114 pec
83 (73 percent) were married and 31 single, including one who was a h
mosexual. Again, there seems to be a cluster factor in play. Of the Centra
Staff and Southeast Asian clusters, all 37 terrorists in these samples were
married. Most had children. The two Arab clusters also showed a married majority, but some mujahedin were still too young to be able to afford to marry.

This high rate of marriage is consistent with the tenets of Salafi Islam,
which encourages its faithful to marry and have children. Most of the single men in the last two clusters were single because of age, student status,
and financial inability to support a family. Those who were full-time mujahedin living with other mujahedin were encouraged to marry their comrades' sisters and daughters. Indeed, these mutual marriages sealed their
religious and political relationships.

The nature of the marriages varied immensely. Although some wives
helped their husbands in their mission, most of these were not marriages
in the Western sense. The wife was segregated according to Salafi rites and
often kept in the dark about her husband's activities. A prototypical il-
lustration is Mira Augustina, the Indonesian wife of Omar al-Faruq. She
had been at an Islamic boarding school when she got a call from her father to come home because there was someone who wanted to marry her.
She arrived the next day after a twelve-hour bus ride and married al-Faruq
that day. She later said that her father must have trusted her future husband completely, otherwise he would not have allowed him to marry her.
She never knew that al-Faruq came from Kuwait or what he did. He left
the house early in the morning and returned late. She never asked what
he did all day and al-Faruq never told her (Murphy, 2003). They had two
children together. He was arrested in June 2002 on his way to the mosque.
She did not hear from him again and did not search for him. She later
said, "When we got married, he made me promise that if he disappeared
one day, I would not go looking for him. So I kept my commitment and
didn't search" (Ratnesar, 2002).

This marital status profile is unique to the global Salafi jihad. Studies
on other types of terrorism report that most terrorists are unmarried and

that those who are married tend to sever family ties upon embarking on a terrorist career.

Psychological Explanations

A second set of explanations for the global jihad focuses on individual factors, especially psychological explanations. Such popular explanations are based on the belief that "normal" people do not kill civilians indiscriminately. Such killing, especially when combined with suicide, is viewed as irrational, based on widespread faith in the general goodness of man. This faith is best relegated to philosophical religious debates about human nature, for it is not amenable to empirical testing. But the hypothesis that this aberrant behavior is the result of some mental abnormality or pathology can be tested. Such explanations focus on the search for some special inner attribute of terrorists that distinguishes them from normal people and explains their behavior. Many proponents of psychological explanations of terrorism are themselves mental health professionals, who know little about terrorism in general and even less about the global Salafi jihad.

Lack of empirical data is the plague of overt psychological research on terrorists and leaves this field open to wild speculations. In this section, I will stay on solid empirical ground and test some of the more fashionable psychological theories of terrorism. The detailed biographical data necessary for such testing was not available for the entire sample, therefore selective biographical fragments on some individuals will be used. I have focused on ten mujahedin on whom more biographical information is available either from court testimony or extensive investigative reporting. Arranged chronologically from the time they joined the jihad, they are Osama bin Laden, Ayman al-Zawahiri, Mahmud Abouhalima, Khaled Kelkal, Ahmed Omar Sheikh, Ahmed Ressam, Kamel Daoudi, Mohamed Atta, Ziad Jarrah, and Habib Moussaoui.

Mental Illness

The mental illness thesis provides a quick and comforting explanation for terrorism. In terms of major mental disorders, as defined by the American Psychiatric Association's *Diagnostic and Statistical Manual of Men-*

tal Disorders (DSM-IV), the data confirm the absence of major mental disorders among the terrorists in the entire sample. One had probable mild mental retardation or borderline intellectual functioning (Stephane Ait Iddir) and two others had some form of psychotic disorder in early adulthood (Wail Mohammed al-Shehri and Othman al-Omari). This is about the incidence of these disorders in the general population.

A variant of the mental illness thesis is the argument that terrorists suffer from overvalued ideas, like people with body dysmorphic disorder, who have anorexia nervosa (McHugh, 2001). This is another way of saying that the global Salafi mujahedin are fanatic. But this is not a mental disorder, but a defining and guiding principle of their lives. Otherwise, we would have to include in the mental disorders any strong beliefs, whether they be religious, political, vocational, or recreational.

Another variant of the abnormality thesis is that terrorists are sociopaths, psychopaths (Cleckley, 1941), or people with antisocial personality disorder (DSM-IV). These terms are generally used to mean that terrorists are recidivist criminals, due to some defect of personality. By definition, the modern concept of antisocial personality disorder has its antecedents in childhood and requires the evidence of conduct disorder before the age of fifteen. Out of sixty-one people on whom I had some fragment of childhood data, only four had evidence of a conduct disorder (Amrozi, Mouloud Bouguelane, and two of the Christian converts, Richard Reid and Jose Padilla). The rest of the sample seem to have had normal childhoods without any evidence of getting into trouble with the law.

On a logical basis, although antisocial people might become *individual* terrorists, they would not do well in a terrorist *organization*. Because of their personalities, they would not get along with others or fit well in an organization, whether in the business world, the army, or a terrorist cell. They lack dedication, perseverance, and ability to sacrifice for the cause, as most spectacularly required in martyrdom. In group activities, they cannot coordinate with others and are disruptive and incapable of discipline. They are least likely to join any organization that makes great demands on them and would be weeded out early if they attempted to join. An example might be Moussaoui, who at his hearings has shown himself to be unruly. The same qualities were apparent to Riduan Isamuddin (a.k.a. Hambali) and Sufaat, his hosts in Malaysia, who asked Khalid Sheikh Mohammed to recall him. In England and the United States before his arrest, he demonstrated the same pattern of behavior. There is evidence that Mohammed and Ramzi bin al-Shibh congratulated themselves for not including him in the 9/11 plot for fear that his antics might have jeopardized the operation. The perpetrators of the hijackings on September 11 did not show the slightest sign of belligerence. They were not hostile, violent, or macho throughout their yearlong stay in the United States. Yet, when the moment came, they killed enthusiastically. Perhaps the argument can be made that in an organized operation demanding great personal sacrifice, those least likely to do any harm *individually* are best able to do so *collectively*.

A more common popular meaning of the various antisocial labels is that terrorists are simply criminals. This removes terrorism from the realm of politics to the realm of crime and law enforcement. Are terrorists just people who break the law?

About one quarter of the sample were involved in petty criminal activities, such as forgery, document trafficking, credit card fraud, and marijuana dealing. They were exclusively the Maghreb Arabs in Europe and North America who acted in logistical support of the global jihad. Some had prior petty criminal activities and joined the jihad specifically to abandon this unclean lifestyle, which was often combined with drug abuse. This was the appeal of Salafi Islam for many of the converts. However, after joining the jihad, they returned to petty crime—without the drug abuse—in support of the cause but not as a source of personal profit, which is the common criminal motive. This small-scale criminal activity is formally sanctioned by fatwas and is consistent with the notion of takfir. Therefore, it appears that terrorists are not just criminals in the usual sense; they break the law in the path of God and not for personal benefit.

One specific characteristic of terrorist activity, their suicide in the process of killing, immediately raises the possibility of mental illness. Most people can conceive of killing for a cause, as police and military are called to do. But for most, suicide is simply beyond the call of duty and therefore must be indicative of some sort of underlying pathology. Yet the type of self-sacrifice called for in the jihad, *shahada*, is the highest form of altruistic sacrifice for the cause. Like the Japanese kamikaze (Morris, 1975; Ohnuki-Tierney, 2002) and the Shi'ite martyr, the Salafi shahada takes place in a specific social, historical, religious, and cultural context that rejects suicide but legitimizes and encourages the nobility of martyrdom. Far from being mentally ill, the global Salafi *shahid* views it as an honor to sacrifice his life for God and is viewed accordingly by his companions and friends. Even the Christian Bible recognizes the value of such sacrifice: "Greater love hath no man than this, that a man lay down his life for his friends" (John 16:13). The desire for martyrdom in the latest phase of the global Salafi jihad is indicated by the now common remark directed at the United States: "We love death more than you love life."

This failure of mental illness as an explanation for terrorism is consistent with three decades of research that has been unable to detect any significant pattern of mental illness in terrorists. Indeed, these studies have indicated that terrorists are surprisingly normal in terms of mental health.

Terrorist Personality

Despite the above consensus, some versions of the mental illness thesis still survive among mental health professionals, who seek an explanation for terrorism in terms of pathological personality dynamics. Such personality disorders involve an enduring pattern of inner experience and behavior, including cognitive, affective, interpersonal, and impulse control elements, which deviates markedly from the expectations of the individual's culture, is pervasive and inflexible, has an onset in adolescence or early adulthood, is stable over time, and leads to distress or impairment. At present, the most fashionable versions of this thesis stem from neo-Freudian theories (Post, 1984, 1986a, 1986b, 1990/1998). While acknowledging the lack of *major* psychopathology in terrorists and *substantially* acknowledging their normality, these sophisticated versions claim that terrorists suffer from some form of personality pathology due to childhood trauma. That is, psychological forces compel them to commit acts of violence. These arguments take three forms.

PATHOLOGICAL NARCISSISM

All versions of the personality pathology thesis confidently assert that terrorists share common personality characteristics without providing any supporting data. They are action-oriented, aggressive people, who are stimulus-hungry and seek excitement. Their common psychological defense mechanisms are "externalization" and "splitting." These last two characteristics are often found in individuals with narcissistic personality disorder, as defined by neo-Freudian theorists like Otto Kernberg and Heinz Kohut, who argued that the characteristics are the result of childhood narcissistic wounds.

The essence of the theory is that narcissistic wounds at an early age split the self into a grandiose "me" and a hated and devalued "not me" projected onto outside specific targets, which are blamed and transformed into scapegoats. Unable to face his own inadequacies, the potential terrorist needs a target to blame and attack. Acknowledging the "paucity of data to satisfy even the minimal requirement of social scientists" and "the lack of a control group," the champion of this thesis, Jerrold Post, cites the descriptive studies of the 1970s German terrorists to show that "a great deal has gone wrong in the lives of people who are drawn to the path of terrorism," namely the loss, at an early age, of one or both parents (25 percent), severe conflicts with authorities, and frequent episodes of school and work failure (Post, 1990/1998: 28). Two types of inner dynamics might heal a fragmented identity, resolve the split, and enable the individual to be at one with himself and society. The "nationalist-separatist" terrorists are loyal to their parents, who reject the regime: they are carrying on the mission of their parents, who were wounded by the regime. The "anarchic-ideologues" are disloyal to their parents' generation, which is identified with the regime. Through terrorism, they are striking at their parents, seeking to heal their inner wounds by attacking the outside enemy. Post's followers (Pearlstein, 1991; Gilmartin, 1996; Volkan, 1997; Akhtar, 1999) are mental health professionals with little experience with terrorism. Their speculations about childhood victimization leading to "pathological" or "malignant" narcissism (or pathological anger or rage) and terrorism lack Post's careful statements about the absence of empirical evidence for this theory.

Post's twin dynamics of disloyalty to parents or the state fails, however, to explain the global Salafi jihad. By definition, this jihad is not directed at the state (near enemy) where the mujahedin grew up but at the United States or the West (far enemy). So they could not avenge their parents against their native state or strike out against their parents in the symbol of their native state. The West or the United States did not "wound" their parents in the "nationalistic-separatist" logic, and their parents are often hostile to the West rather than identifying with it, in the "anarchic-ideologue" logic. The logic of the global Salafi jihad is altogether different.

I was able to gather some short descriptions of the childhoods of sixty-nine mujahedin. The vast majority were positive or neutral labels; shy, introverted, serious, quiet, bright, excellent student, loner, pleasant, easygoing, happy, gentle were recurrent descriptors. They were not indicative of any antecedents of a narcissistic personality disorder. On the contrary, the data suggest that these were good kids who liked to go to school and were often overprotected by their parents. It seems that the loners slightly outnumbered the outgoing children.

Searching childhood information on sixty-one people, I found no evidence of "childhood trauma" described by self, friends, or relatives. Of course, psychological trauma and humiliation might not leave any outside trace that could be noticed by family or friends. But if the trauma was significant, someone was likely to have known about it. There were three whose fathers died before they were ten, two who lost their fathers as adolescents, and one whose father suffered a debilitating stroke when he was ten. In terms of family integrity, six witnessed a divorce or final separation of their parents when they were young. One of them suffered the double misfortune of the father leaving the family to its own means and the mother developing polio. Two others were abandoned by their parents and grew up in foster care; they both had troubled childhoods (Bouguelane and Richard Reid). A few had fathers working abroad while their mothers stayed in their original countries with their own families. Two suffered physical abuse by their fathers. In terms of personal hardship, one became blind as an infant; another had a right-hand birth defect; a third had an ulcer as an adolescent requiring convalescence away from home.

As a group, they had surprisingly little personal trauma in their lives, given their origin (third world with higher mortality rate than the Western world or excluded segment of the Western world). Another form of collective experience that might be construed as a "trauma" leading to long-term resentment is the humiliation of discrimination experienced while growing up in a foreign country. Out of 158 people, 43 (27 percent) grew up in a country as refugees, second generation, or "guest workers." The vast majority of these were sons of Maghreb Arabs in France, Palestinians in the Middle East, and Pakistanis in Kuwait or England. But even in these cases, their hostility should have been directed to the host country rather than the United States or the West in general, according to the pathological narcissism theory.

In terms of the ten more detailed biographies, there is no evidence of pathological narcissism. If anyone had it, it should have been the leader, Osama bin Laden. Yet, one of the most attractive features about him is specifically his lack of narcissism, his humility, which impresses his followers and admirers—especially because he had the means to live luxuriously and chose to give up that lifestyle to live simply, among his mujahedin. His statements are also self-deprecating rather than grandiose. The only trauma in his childhood is the fact that his father died when he was around ten. Otherwise, he lived the privileged life of a prince. Although al-Zawahiri does not share bin Laden's humility, there is no evidence of trauma in his childhood. He does not mention any in his autobiography (al-Zawahiri, 2001). Abouhalima mentioned no childhood trauma in his interviews with the press and researchers. Kelkal also suffered no trauma in his childhood, which he described as happy. His first possible trauma was his arrest at the age of nineteen, too late to cause the type of narcissistic wound described by Kernberg and Kohut. Ahmed Omar Sheikh had a rather idyllic childhood in prestigious private schools. His interest in politics came at the age of nineteen. Ressam's childhood did not include any trauma, except for the development of a stomach ulcer at the age of sixteen, for which he traveled to Paris and convalesced alone for a few months. He was not yet political when he left Algeria at the age of twenty-five in search of a decent job. Kamel Daoudi did suffer at the hands of his father, who beat him with a wooden paddle when he got poor grades. Fortunately for him, he was an excellent student, who was described as the very model of integration in school. His rebellion came in early adulthood after a relatively apolitical and normal childhood. Mohamed Atta suffered no childhood trauma. If anything, he was overprotected by his mother. Ziad Jarrah was a very happy child without any hint of trauma.

Habib Zacarias Moussaoui may be the only one with a traumatized childhood. His father physically abused his family, but not the boys. His mother left her husband when Moussaoui was four and put him in an orphanage for a year. When he was twelve, they moved to the south of France, where finances were tight for two or three years. Moussaoui, however, seemed to have weathered the storm well, was a popular child, and dated a blonde girl. He liked to party, but reported some racism at school. He did well until he moved to London in his early twenties. There he grew more distant from his family and friends and got involved with a Salafi crowd.

Unlike many political organizations, Salafi groups are careful to avoid a cult of personality, for they believe that everything belongs to God. Indeed, they take seriously the notion of Islam as submission, and this is not compatible with a narcissistic cult of personality, which often degenerates into a pyramidal organization, with all the controls lying with the leader. Al Qaeda's structure is quite opposite, with a large degree of local autonomy and initiative.

A variant of the childhood trauma thesis is the argument that early exposure to terrorism can lead to the development of terrorism in the adult. This variant may or may not be combined with the notion of relative deprivation. The sample does not support this thesis. While such an argument can be advanced for regions with intractable conflicts and refugee camps, such as Palestine, it is not relevant for the global jihad. These terrorists were not exposed to terrorism as young people, and they came from relatively well-off social backgrounds on the average.

PARANOIA

A second variant of the personality pathology thesis reformulates the above dynamics to claim that terrorists suffer from paranoid personality disorder, defined according to the DSM-IV. Specifically, they exhibit a pervasive distrust and suspicion of others such that their motives are interpreted as malevolent (Robins and Post, 1997). But this clinical definition is quickly watered down to include a broader definition of a personality style and outlook characterized by guardedness, suspiciousness, hypersensitivity, isolation, and especially the defense mechanism of projection. They warned that they would use these terms interchangeably (5). The DSM-IV atheoretical perspective is further left behind in a flurry of theoretical speculation.

The core dynamic of the paranoid personality is surprisingly similar to that of malignant narcissism. Ideas of persecution and grandeur are a shield against uncomfortable feelings of depletion, inadequacy, shame, and vulnerability. The dynamic consists of a triad of insatiable narcissistic entitlement, inevitably leading to disappointment, disillusionment, and frustration when the narcissistic needs are not satisfied, and producing narcissistic rage due to the rejection of the entitlement and a sense of betrayal. This rage is projected onto scapegoats—hence the need to have enemies (Volkan, 1994)--and results in violence. This is the core of the "psychopolitics of hatred" (Robins and Post, 1997). The origin of this dynamic is the "paranoid-schizoid position," a phase of normal childhood development as postulated by Melanie Klein. This primitive psychological state is characterized by a split between the idealized good, pleasurable, loving object (the good mother) and the bad, uncomfortable, persecuting object (the bad mother). Indeed, these theorists consider religious concepts of God and the devil as projected representation of these early fantasy objects. In this stage, a child's distress concerning the aggressive hatred within himself is relieved by splitting off and projecting the bad part (the internal persecutor) outward onto others and retaining the good parts inside, idealizing them. Paranoid people never mature beyond this stage or they revert to it under stress, channeling aggression to the scapegoat.

Group paranoia is viewed simply as a manifestation of the leader's pathology. The followers suffer from a deprecation of their blemished personalities and demonstrate a readiness to hate, to imitate, to uncritically believe, and to attempt the impossible. Religious ideology provides a rationale for followers who yearn for a calling, a group to join, a leader to follow, in order to flee from the self (Robins and Post, 1997: 100). Their sense of self rests upon the integrity of their belief system, which protects them against painful psychological disintegration. From this perspective, their actions are defensive aggression against an enemy challenging their belief systems, which thereby threatens their psychological integrity. But it is not the beliefs that generate the passion of their striking out. These beliefs are like a container for powerful dangerous feelings. Attacks upon such beliefs threaten to break this container and overwhelm the follower with these feelings. Such attacks therefore provoke a passionate, often violent response.

This account, which depends on mysterious internal forces that cannot be formally surveyed, is of course not refutable. None of the ten biographies of mujahedin made any mention of a painful split self, using violence as a form of self-healing. The deprecation of religion implied in this account would greatly offend any subject in the sample, and not for the reasons suggested in the account.

Every religious or political ideology provides a way to interpret the world. It is easy to label any such interpretation a conspiracy. Demonstrations that many political and religious movements contained elements of a conspiracy theory are trivial and not analytically useful. What needs to be shown is that the leaders and followers in these movements either suffer from paranoid personality disorder or paranoid dynamic triad, rooted in arrested psychological development at the "paranoid-schizoid" position. Granted, such a demonstration would be difficult without access to "inner" data, but until then, this thesis remains a speculation not backed by any empirical evidence.

In the larger sample under study, I did not detect a pattern of paranoid personality disorder or lifestyle before joining the jihad. The nature of a clandestine organization implies some concern with security and secrecy for mere survival. This is realistic, not paranoid. Any politically violent group, whatever its ideology, would also demonize its opponent and stockpile weapons for the fight. This again is in the nature of the organization and does not imply paranoia. The only meaningful way to detect clinical or lifestyle paranoia in terrorists is to look at their psychological adjustment before they joined the jihad. Since this adjustment is by definition of long duration with roots in adolescence, this personality trait or disorder must have preceded joining the jihad.

In the ten detailed biographies, only al-Zawahiri's history gives some hint of paranoia preceding his joining the jihad. He formed his own clandestine group with his friends and brother during adolescence, more than twenty years before founding al Qaeda. While he exhibited some of the behaviors delineated in the preceding paragraph, it is difficult to know whether to attribute them to his innate personality or to the necessity of surviving in a hostile environment. Unlike bin Laden's leadership style, however, which was to promote cooperation among disparate terrorist groups and discourage internal Islamist rivalries, al-Zawahiri's style in the Egyptian Islamic Jihad was far more confrontational and led to many splits and challenges. Leaders of al Qaeda and Jemaah Islamiyah never resorted to frequent purging of the inner circle, a symptom of paranoia according to the above thesis (Post, Ruby and Shaw, 2002a and 2002b). Indeed, infighting among Muslims (*fitna*) is a great sin and specifically proscribed by the Quran. Such infighting is a source of discomfort among many mujahedin, who prefer to strike at the true infidel.

One would be hard pressed to find elements of paranoia in the pre-Afghanistan bin Laden. Abouhalima, Sheikh, Ressam, Jarrah, and Moussaoui were happy young men, devoid of any hints of paranoia. Daoudi and Atta were introverts who did not seem paranoid. Kelkal was embittered by his imprisonment due to being caught in a stolen car, but he did not seem paranoid before his conversion to terrorism.

AUTHORITARIAN PERSONALITY

A more recent publication (Post, Ruby, and Shaw, 2002a and 2002b) tried to revive the Authoritarian Personality project of the 1950s (Adorno, Frenkel-Brunswik, Levinson, and Sanford, 1950). This thesis postulated that punitive child raising results in a personality style characterized by conformity, submission to authority, and aggression toward outsiders. In the ten mujahedin biographies, harsh child raising is present in only two cases. For the majority, it seems that the opposite might be true; the children were overprotected in very caring families with often doting parents, as illustrated by bin Laden, Sheikh, Atta, and Jarrah.

The revived Authoritarian Personality formulation results in a series of propositions characterizing charismatic leader-follower relationships. It postulates that the group uncritically follows the leader's directives and that the leader has a history of violence. Neither is true of the global Salafi jihad, which prominently features local initiative and decentralized decision-making. Bin Laden had no history of violence before joining the jihad.

Authoritarianism is contrary to the tenets of Salafism, which preaches that only God is superior to men, who should relate to each other as equals. Qutb stressed that all authority belongs to God. Intentionally or not, the leadership style in al Qaeda is not an authoritarian one. There is no consolidation of decision-making in its leader. Its structure is not hierarchical or modeled after a military organization, and there has been no split as a result of leadership decisions. All these factors are assumed to have high relevance in predicting terrorism. They do not apply to the global Salafi jihad, which is characterized by decentralization in decision-making, a horizontal fluid structure, and a surprising absence of periodic purges of leadership that are so common in other terrorist organizations.

The main problem with the personality pathology explanation of terrorism is the lack of relevant data. The hypothesis is based on outdated theories, which did not survive the empirical scrutiny of psychiatric concepts following the publication of the DSM-III in 1980 and are no longer relevant to psychiatric or psychological research and practice. All of these core concepts predate this empirical revolution in the field. The survival of such now quaint theories might be due to the insularity of this research, which is sheltered from peer scrutiny and criticism. When these Freudian or neo-Freudian arguments are published in the terrorism literature, political scientists do not believe they have the expertise to challenge them. When they are published in the psychological literature, the references to mysterious "secret" data supporting these theories intimidate psychologists.

The personality pathology thesis suffers from the fundamental problem of specificity. Concepts are stretched to be all-inclusive and lose their analytic usefulness. Such accounts become post-hoc stories that have no practical value. Conspiracy theories are a ubiquitous feature of human life, not particularly indicative of mental pathology and definitely not specific to terrorists. Experts on terrorism have tried in vain for three decades to identify a common predisposition for terrorism. The most extensive research projects focused on former German and Italian terrorists from the 1970s. These studies concluded that there was no psychological profile for terrorism. In addition, recent comprehensive reviews of the evidentiary basis of this thesis have found it to be completely unfounded (Silke, 1998; Horgan, 2003). The personality pathology thesis is not relevant to the global Salafi jihad.

Circumstances of Joining the Jihad

These social and psychological approaches to terrorism neglect the social context around the decision to join the jihad. Joining the jihad is actually a process and not a single decision. The formal induction into al Qaeda often took place in Afghanistan, when the novice pledged *baya*, a formal oath of loyalty, to Osama bin Laden and al Qaeda. That there are no captured records of who joined and who did not presents a problem for this study. "Joining the jihad" is understood here as the decision to go somewhere for training, whether Afghanistan (the most common destination), Bosnia, the Philippines, Malaysia, or Indonesia. Formal recruitment took place at these training sites. It is important to note that not everyone who participated in the training joined the jihad. Indeed, only a minority of the trainees, perhaps 10 to 30 percent, were invited to join.

Age

Some analysts claim that terrorists join as immature naïve young men, vulnerable to indoctrination (Merari, 1990 and 1991). In my sample, the average age for joining the jihad was 25.69 years. In terms of clusters, the Southeast Asians were older as a rule and averaged 29.35 years. Much of the leadership of the Jemaah Islamiyah had been exiled to Malaysia in the 1980s and constituted the core of mujahedin who were still directly involved in operations. The Central Staff cluster, however, was also older than the average at 27.9 years. The two Arab clusters were younger, with the Core Arab being the youngest of all (23.75 years). This last group's average age might be lowered by the 9/11 group from Saudi Arabia, who tended to be younger and had joined the jihad a few months before the operation.

The above does not support the immaturity thesis. Most people joined the jihad well past adolescence when they were responsible young men in their mid-twenties and should have been able to resist any mysterious brainwashing.

Place of Recruitment

Out of 165 mujahedin on whom there is information, 115 (70 percent) joined the jihad in a country where they had not grown up. They were expatriates—students, workers, refugees, fighters (in the jihad against the Soviets)—away from home and family. Another 14 were second generation in France, Britain, and the United States, where they might have felt a strong pull for the country of their parents and not been completely embedded in the host society. In France, they were part of the "excluded" generation. Therefore, a remarkable 78 percent were cut off from their cultural and social origins, far from their families and friends. The remaining 36 (22 percent) included Saudis who participated in the 9/11 attacks and the May 2003 Riyadh bombings, and Moroccans who were too poor to travel anywhere and were involved in May 2003 Casablanca bombings.

For the Central Staff, the most common place where the conversion to the global jihad took place was the Sudan. For later cohorts, with the exceptions of the Saudis from the 9/11 group and the the majority of Southeast Asians, conversions to the global jihad took place in the West, mostly in France, Germany, and England. The Indonesians had joined the global jihad in Malaysia, where the eventual leadership of the Jemaah Islamiyah had been exiled.

Faith

There was a definite shift in degree of devotion to Islam in adulthood by the mujahedin, preceding their recruitment into the jihad. This is not surprising given the fact that the global Salafi jihad is a Muslim revivalist organization. Of the 155 mujahedin on whom I could find relevant information, all but one were considerably more devout right before joining the jihad than they had been as children. More than 99 percent were very religious at that time, often donning Afghan, Pakistani, or traditional Arabic garb and growing beards, as opposed to the 49 percent who were devout as children. The largest shift was in the Maghreb Arab cluster, which went from 8 percent to 100 percent in terms of their commitment to Islam. This new faith was the Salafi version of Islam for 97 percent of the terrorists.

Lonely people look for companionship. In an expatriate community, especially in an unwelcoming non-Muslim Western country, the most available source for companionship with people of similar background is the mosque. Disillusioned with the society that excluded them and the empty promises of the Left in France, second-generation or expatriate Maghreb Arabs went to the mosque and met new friends. Islam was a way to restore their dignity, gain a sense of spiritual calling, and promote their values.

We should be careful not to ascribe a causal relationship to this increased devotion on the part of future mujahedin. This shift in faith may very well be a reflection of a more general process of engagement in the jihad. In this case, it would be more indicative of an effect rather than a cause of this process. At this point, the evidence is still descriptive and does not yet justify conclusions about the contribution of this increased faith to the process of joining the global jihad.

Much has been made in the media of some of the behavior of the September 11 hijackers that seems to be inconsistent with their devotion. The behaviors referred to include going out to some topless bars in Las Vegas and Florida, drinking alcohol, and even hiring an escort service, right before the 9/11 operation. This evidence does not disprove their devotion. First, one can be a sinner and still be devout. Second, as entry to paradise is guaranteed to martyrs, there is little cost to sinning one last time. Third, these were not serious violations of the central tenets of Islam. From the accounts I read, I have no doubts that the mujahedin were sincerely devout Salafists. However, this behavior might have a more ominous meaning, namely the impending immediacy of an operation, and be a cause for alarm for authorities.

Employment

Although most of the mujahedin had strong occupational skills (see above), few were employed full-time. The members of the Central Staff cluster were full-time fighters in the jihad against the Soviets at the time they decided to join the global jihad. They remained full-time mujahedin. The Southeast Asians taught at their Islamic boarding school in Malaysia while waiting for the jihad to unfold in Indonesia. The Maghreb Arabs were likely to be either students or unemployed, involved in petty crimes and living on welfare (32 of 46, or 70 percent). The Core Arabs were either students at home or involved in full-time terrorist activities abroad (30 of 55, or 55 percent), and few had full-time jobs. The discrepancy between their actual jobs and their capability is best illustrated by Wadih el-Hage. When he returned to the United States from fighting in the jihad against the Soviets, he found only two part-time marginal jobs, in a fast-food restaurant and as a janitor for the city. He later joined the global jihad by becoming the personal secretary to Osama bin Laden, which was the equivalent of a vice president for corporate development in a large corporation. His job included a large office and controlling access to his boss, with frequent travel and great responsibilities (Swartz, 2002).

Relative Deprivation

The mujahedin's lack of full-time jobs integrating them into their communities compounded their loneliness while away from home. This underemployment must have been a definite grievance and a source of frustration in these generally gifted individuals. This supports the relative deprivation thesis of the origin of terrorism (Gurr, 1970). These were, however, temporary circumstances leading to their joining the jihad, rather than structural relative deprivation in their original backgrounds. These individuals had rising expectations compared to their families of origin.

The relative deprivation thesis should not be limited to the material dimension of life. Just before embarking on the process of joining, the future mujahedin suffered from social isolation, spiritual emptiness (the impetus for their increase in devotion), and underemployment. But the relative deprivation thesis also runs into the fundamental problem of specificity. Many people are underemployed, but very few of them become terrorists. Relative deprivation would certainly increase the pool of potential mujahedin, but cannot by itself explain the association with the jihad.

Although relative deprivation (perhaps in the context of rising expectation) is not specific to terrorism, it is probably a necessary condition. People who are satisfied with life are unlikely to join a religious revivalist terrorist movement. They will continue to do what they are doing and not subject themselves to the upfront costs, social sanctions, and sacrifices involved in such a movement.

As a gloss, the immediate circumstances leading to their joining the jihad might be supportive of the frustration-aggression hypothesis. This proposed that frustration leads to aggression and aggression is the result of frustration. Again, the validity of this apparent truism depends on how frustration and aggression are defined. Further, this hypothesis is not helpful in prediction of terrorism. Many people have frustration and very few become terrorists. Its value is questionable for it consists of post hoc accounts rather than prospective ones. A variant of this hypothesis is that frustration results in rage, which leads to aggression. Although this might fit our preconception of terrorism, and it was widely broadcast in the news accounts of the 9/11 attacks, there is little evidence to indicate that global Salafi mujahedin were consumed with rage. Certainly the instructions for the preparation and the execution of the attacks left behind by al-Omari (and wrongly attributed to Atta in the media) do not mention anger or rage directed at the targets.

The frustration-aggression hypothesis not only suffers from vagueness; it also implies a certain reflexive element: aggression inevitably follows frustration. The global jihad operations are long premeditated and often well planned, as demonstrated by the 9/11 attacks, which were planned over two and a half years. The 1998 U.S. embassy bombings in East Africa took about five years to plan. This was no reflex action. This practice of long and deliberate planning seems to undermine the frustration-aggression hypothesis. How long does the frustration last? Does it ever fade away? This long duration is not consistent with the known flexibility of people's emotions, which can change quickly. A general state of frustration may eventually lead to aggression, but any nonreflexive aggression is difficult to specifically explain in terms of frustration.

Conclusion

This chapter empirically tested some of the traditional theories of terrorist behavior, namely social, psychological, and situational. The findings seem to reject much of the conventional wisdom about terrorists.

Members of the global Salafi jihad were generally middle-class, educated young men from caring and religious families, who grew up with strong positive values of religion, spirituality, and concern for their communities. There were four general patterns detected. The Central Staff consisted of Islamist militants who met and bonded together during the Soviet-Afghan war and went on to become full-time terrorists. The Southeast Asians, who went on to become members of Jemaah Islamiyah, were mostly the disciples of the two leaders of this organization. The Maghreb Arabs, either first- or second-generation in France, grew up feeling excluded from French society and were generally not religious as young people. They were still upwardly mobile compared to their parents, but in the process of moving up became isolated and sought friendships in local mosques. The Core Arabs, who grew up in core Arab lands, came from a communal society and belonged to one of the most communal of all religions. They were isolated when they moved away from their families and friends and became particularly lonely and emotionally alienated in this new individualistic environment. The lack of spiritualism in a utilitarian culture was keenly felt. Underemployed and discriminated against by the local society, they felt a personal sense of grievance and humiliation. They sought a cause that would give them emotional relief, social community, spiritual comfort, and cause for self-sacrifice. Although they did not start out particularly religious, there was a shift in their devotion before they joined the global jihad, which gave them both a cause and comrades.

Although nothing in the data challenges the rational actor theory, I will postpone a discussion of it to Chapter 5. In terms of the social explanations, the members studied did not come from poor backgrounds leading to grievances against the West. Their education was modern (except for the Indonesians) and they were not "brainwashed" into fanaticism through a madrassa education. Most became more devout before joining the jihad. Contrary to most writing on terrorists, the large majority of the individuals examined were married and most had children. Yet they were willing to sacrifice themselves for the cause. Except for the Western converts and the Maghreb Arabs, who indulged in petty crime, there is no evidence that the terrorists were hardened criminals.

In terms of psychological explanations for their participation, they did not seem to display any psychiatric pathology. There was no pattern of emotional trauma in their past nor was there any evidence of any pathological hatred or paranoia when the facts are analyzed. This "pathological hatred" much talked about in the press cannot be found in the accounts studied. From all the evidence, many participants joined in search of a larger cause worthy of sacrifice.

In terms of social psychology, the frustration-aggression hypothesis is so vague that it cannot be completely tested or refuted. Judging from their backgrounds, the members did not suffer from long-term relative deprivation or from pathological prejudice. Most were from very well-to-do backgrounds and led lives more consistent with rising expectations than relative deprivation. The Core Arabs were so well-off that their families sent them to study abroad, where their radicalization began. In their host countries, they were alienated, underemployed, and perhaps discriminated against, and therefore in a situation of relative deprivation.

In terms of generating a common profile of the global Salafi mujahed, there are as many profiles as they are clusters of mujahedin. The Southeast Asians are different from the Core Arabs, who are distinct from the Maghreb Arabs. The leaders of the movement, organized in the Central Staff, are unlike their followers. Nevertheless, there are patterns.

Just before they joined the jihad, the prospective mujahedin were socially and spiritually alienated and probably in some form of distress. They would not have been the best candidates to form a tightly cohesive group, whose members were willing to perform the ultimate sacrifice in the name of what the group stood for. Yet, this is exactly what happened. This transformation from isolated individuals to a community of fanatics is the subject of the next chapter.

FOUR

Joining the Jihad

ECAUSE ANY attempt to find a common social factor or personality predisposition for terrorism runs into the fundamental problem of specificity, profiles based on such personal characteristics as age, sex, national origin, religion, education, and socioeconomic background are of very little value in identifying true terrorists. In the case of global Salafi mujahedin, however, there is one common element that is specific to them and to no one else, and that is the fact that they have made a link to the jihad. These links are key to the dynamics of terror networks. To further our understanding of these networks, it is critical to understand how these links are formed. How does one go about joining the global Salafi jihad? To explore this question, let us examine the case histories of two terrorist cells, the plotters of the unsuccessful millennial bombing of the Los Angeles airport and the Hamburg cell responsible for the 9/11 attacks.

The U.S. Millennial Plot

Ahmed Ressam was born on May 9, 1967, at Bou Islamil, Algeria. His father, Belkacem Ressam, a hero from the Algerian War of Liberation, owned a coffee shop and a six-bedroom house. He was a devout Muslim but did not demand that his family follow his practice, and his children were not religious. Ahmed, the oldest child, was a shy, skinny boy and a decent student. At sixteen, he developed a stomach ulcer and went to Paris for a lengthy course of treatment. This set him back in his studies, and he failed his final baccalaureate examinations, ending his opportunity for further studies at university. He worked at his father's coffee shop and lived a secular life. He wore designer jeans, drank wine, smoked hashish, frequented nightclubs, went out with girls, and had nothing to do with Islam. He was aloof from the nascent political storms brewing over Algeria in the late 1980s and early 1990s. On September 5, 1992, he boarded the ferry for Marseille, in search of a better life (Ressam, 2001; Bernton et al., 2002).

Lacking proper papers, Ressam drifted to Corsica, where he found work picking grapes and painting houses and got involved in the underground market in false documents. He was arrested on November 8, 1993, for an immigration violation and was released awaiting his hearing in March, 1994. Not wanting to return to Algeria, he flew to Montreal on February 20, 1994, with false documents identifying him as Tahar Medjadi. On arrival at the airport, he admitted that his documents were faked but invented a story about militant engagement and false imprisonment in Algeria and asked for political asylum. He was released on bond, given welfare benefits (for three years) and scheduled to come back for a hearing.

Alone in Montreal, Ressam drifted to places where he could meet compatriots. One of the most popular was the Assuna Annabawiyah Mosque, which attracted about 1,500 worshippers on Fridays, mostly from the expatriate Algerian community. A significant portion of this community was involved in small-scale crime, such as trafficking in false documents, credit card fraud, and petty theft. The mosque was one of the centers where people involved in these crimes met in order to fence their stolen goods. Young men congregated around the mosque and its connected bookstore, which sold Salafi books and tapes. Ressam, who still liked to dress well and go to nightclubs, befriended several of them and got involved in petty crime as well. He met Mustapha Labsi, who had come to Canada on April 30, 1994, also asking for refugee status on the basis of a made-up story. The two became best friends and accomplices in crime. They were first arrested in August 1994 when they tried to grab an elderly woman's handbag. Ressam pled guilty and was sentenced to pay a fine to a charity. He and Labsi continued their careers in crime and specialized in stealing tourists' suitcases from hotel lobbies, taking money, passports, and credit cards. Ressam was arrested four times in four years. He was convicted, fined $100 to $500, put on probation, and ordered to leave Canada. He never appeared at his deportation hearing. In October 1996, he was arrested again for pickpocketing, fined $500, and released on probation. He maintained his lifestyle of dressing well and going to nightclubs.

In early 1996, Labsi and Ressam moved into an apartment rented by Adel Boumezbeur and were joined by Said Atmani. The four were now part of a small group of thieves, organized by Mustapha Kamel, who used the proceeds to support the global jihad. Atmani, also known as Karim, was of Moroccan origin and had fought in Bosnia as part of the al-Mujahedin Brigade in Zenica, where he had met Kamel. After the brigade disbanded in compliance with the Dayton Accords, Kamel invited Atmani to come to Canada. He arrived as a stowaway on September 26, 1995, and reconnected with Kamel. He became a skilled forger and was eventually described as Kamel's right-hand man in Montreal.

When they were not robbing tourists, Ressam and his roommates spent their days idly. They played soccer, smoked cigarettes, and decried the corrupt culture of Canada and the West, especially its immoral dress, music, and godless pursuit of wealth. Their apartment on Place de la Malicorne became the central meeting place of Kamel's group. Regular visitors included Boumezbeur's brother and their childhood friends from Algeria, the Ikhlef brothers, Kamel, and Mokhtar Haouari, who bought Kamel's trinket shop and sold the stolen goods. Sometimes strangers, such as Laifa Khabou, who was connected to the French Roubaix gang and acting as a courier to transport false passports to colleagues in trouble in other countries, stayed at the apartment. Unbeknownst to the occupants, the Canadian federal authorities had placed listening devices in the apartment and were monitoring their conversations, which consisted largely of anti-Western fantasies and plots. The police referred to the group as BOG, "bunch of guys," more pathetic than dangerous—unemployed, no girlfriends, living on welfare or thievery, and crammed into an apartment reeking of cigarette smoke.

Although the authorities did not take them seriously, they would talk about Muslim affairs. The most respected members of their circle were men who had undergone military training in Afghan camps and had actually fought the jihad in Bosnia, like Kamel, Atmani, and Abderrauf Hannachi. Hannachi was a Tunisian of little education, who had also arrived in Canada in 1994. He was a regular at the Assuna Mosque, where he liked to entertain with stories and jokes. He would loudly proclaim his hatred for Western and U.S. culture. In the summer of 1997, he returned from military training in al Qaeda's Camp Khalden in Afghanistan, bragged about what he had learned and declared that he had found meaning as a "warrior." Labsi and Ressam decided to try it out for themselves and asked Hannachi to arrange for their training. Hannachi did so via Hussein (abu Zubaydah) in Pakistan.

Ressam and his friend left for Afghanistan on March 17, 1998. They stayed there for eleven months, during which they learned small caliber weapons tactics at Camp Khalden and took an advanced course in explosives at Camp Toranta. They formed a small five-member cell with Fodail, abu Ahmed, and Hakim. Atmani was to be the sixth member of the cell. Fodail was to be in charge in the field. They discussed several operations with the camp commandant, Makhlulif (abu Doha), Hussein, and abu Jaffar, his deputy for Algerian mujahedin. The plan was for them to meet in Canada and conduct operations against the United States from there. Ressam received $12,000 from abu Jaffar and returned safely to Canada via the Pacific, landing at Los Angeles International Airport on February 7, 1999. He took the opportunity to scout the airport, the objective of an attack planned to coincide with the millennium celebration. Meanwhile Atmani had been arrested in late October 1998 in Niagara Falls in possession of stolen credit cards. He was deported to Bosnia, which deported him to France, where he was facing charges connected with the the 1996 wave of bombings in France carried out by the Roubaix gang. Labsi planned to return to Montreal via Europe, but was prevented from going on to Canada at Heathrow Airport. Labsi stayed in London with Makhlulif, who had been sent to London to oversee al Qaeda's operations in the Western world. Fodail was likewise detained in Europe and unable to fly to Canada. Nor could Ressam turn to Kamel for help; Kamel had been arrested in Jordan in April 1999 and deported to France for charges in connection with Roubaix gang bombings.

The unraveling of his network did not discourage Ressam. He decided to carry out the operation on his own. People who knew him before his trip to Afghanistan noticed a change. He seemed more confident, a man willing to risk his freedom or his life for God. He elicited the help of his friends. Mourad Ikhlef, one of the regulars at the Montreal apartment, had been implicated in a 1992 bombing at Algiers airport, which killed eleven and injured more than one hundred. Ikhlef helped Ressam with the planning of the Los Angeles airport bombing. Haouari provided some money, false credit cards, and logistical support. Samir Ait Mohamed helped as well. Abdel Majid Dahoumane, a friend since his first days in Montreal, promised help in building the bomb. He asked Ressam for help in joining the jihad and getting to Afghanistan for military training. Haouari also had a childhood friend, Abdel Ghani Meskini, who wanted to join the jihad and train in Afghanistan. Meskini might help Ressam deliver the bomb, for he was already living in Brooklyn, New York. Ressam had never met Meskini but Haouari vouched for his trustworthiness, as they had grown up together. Ressam called Makhlulif, who apprised him of the others' inability to come to Canada. Ressam brought him up to date on his plan to bomb the airport and asked for two visas for Pakistan for Meskini and Dahoumane, for training at an al Qaeda base. Abu Jaffar, from Peshawar, sent the visas to London, and Labsi forwarded them to Ressam. Ressam gathered up the necessary material, and in November 1999 he and Dahoumane flew to Vancouver to rent a car and mix some of the explosives. On December 11, 1999, Meskini flew to Seattle to meet Ressam.

On December 14, 1999, Ressam put the material in a rented car and tried to cross the U.S. border at Port Angeles, Washington. An alert customs inspector, Diana Dean, noticed that he was sweating profusely and nervous and asked him to pull over. The chemicals were soon discovered and Ressam was arrested. Two days later, Canadian authorities identified Ressam, who was still resisting under interrogation. Meskini, after waiting for a few days, flew back to New York. From the phone numbers in Ressam's papers, the FBI was able to trace back the network, and eventually Meskini and Haouari were arrested in New York and Montreal, respectively. Dahoumane fled to Algeria, where he was arrested. Mourad Ikhlef was deported to Algeria.

The Hamburg Cell

Meanwhile, in Europe, a strikingly similar process of affiliation with al Qaeda was taking place, involving those who would be responsible for the 9/11 operations. The Hamburg cell emerged from a convergence of nine people in an upper-middle-class expatriate student community. The nucleus of the group formed around Mohammad Belfas, a middle-aged immigrant from Indonesia, Yemen, and Egypt, who had lived in Germany illegally for almost twenty years before being given legal status. He worked for the post office and conducted a study group at al-Quds Mosque in Hamburg. Around 1996, three students from the Technical University of Hamburg-Harburg (TUHH) began attending his study group. Mohamed al-Amir Awad al-Sayed Atta had come to Germany in 1992 to study architecture at TUHH. He moved into the dorm and befriended German students. After a trip back to the Middle East, which included a pilgrimage to Mecca in 1995, he began to change and probably joined Belfas's study group around that time. Mounir Motassadeq and Abdelghani Mzoudi, friends from Marrakech, came to Germany in 1993 and started an electrical engineering program at TUHH in 1995.

It is not clear who first connected with Belfas's study group at al-Quds Mosque. Motassadeq at his trial claimed that Mzoudi introduced him to Atta in early 1996 because he was looking for a place to stay and Atta knew a lot of people at the mosque. A German student who shared Mzoudi's apartment in late 1995 said that Mzoudi was a lonely and private man, who did not utter any radical comment. Motassadeq moved in with them in December 1995 for a few months, and their conversation began to show adherence to radical Islam. On April 11, 1996, the two Moroccan friends witnessed Atta's will. Motassadeq moved into an apartment in the student-housing complex that spring and stayed there three years. It became the center where militant Muslim students congregated when on campus, eating meals together from the common kitchen, and discussing religion and politics in the living room. They also prayed together at al-Quds Mosque.

They were soon joined by Ramzi bin al-Shibh, a student from Yemen, who had come to Germany under false papers, asking for political asylum. Bin al-Shibh was religious, learned in the Quran, charismatic, and charming. He became the most recognizable member of the Belfas study group at al-Quds Mosque. He was learning German in order to later study economics and politics. The group grew with the addition of Said Bahaji, who was of German Moroccan origin and had grown up in Morocco. He had started at TUHH in 1996 and met Motassadeq, who took him to a mosque for the first time. Bahaji, who had grown up in a secular household—his father had owned a discotheque and his mother was a Prussian Protestant—quickly adopted the Salafi ideology of his friends. He publicly aired his extreme views and even started lecturing his German Christian aunt about proper conduct for women.

In 1997, the group expanded again with the addition of Ziad Amir Jarrah, who had come to Germany in April 1996 and moved to Hamburg to study aeronautical engineering at the University of Applied Sciences (UAS) in the fall of 1997. Jarrah's girlfriend later testified that he had grown homesick and began to attend conservative mosques. He met bin al-Shibh at al-Quds Mosque in late 1997 and grew closer to the circle of friends around Belfas's study group. In late 1997, Atta quit his job and seemed to have disappeared for a few months. The authorities later suspected that he might have gone to Afghanistan for training. At the end of the year, Mzoudi dropped out of TUHH and switched to the UAS, where Jarrah was studying. In early 1998, Marwan al-Shehhi joined the group. He came from the United Arab Emirates, which paid for his studies. After a stay in Bonn, Germany, he came in early 1998 to Hamburg, where he met the group at al-Quds Mosque. He went home for his father's funeral and returned to Hamburg, where he grew very close to Atta. The two would become almost inseparable. Bin al-Shibh moved in with Belfas. During the summer of 1998, Atta, Belfas, al-Shehhi, and bin al-Shibh all worked in a computer warehouse, packing boxes. Jarrah had an internship at the Wolfsburg Volkswagen plant, where he met Zakarya Essabar, a Moroccan student who had come to Germany the year before. Jarrah introduced him to the group and Essabar moved to Hamburg that fall to study medical technology at the UAS.

In November 1998, Atta, bin al-Shibh, and Bahaji moved into an apartment on Marienstrasse, which they named Bait al-Ansar, the House of the Supporters (of the Prophet), the same name as al Qaeda's guest house in Peshawar, Pakistan, where prospective recruits transited on their way to training camps. Bait al-Ansar became the place where the group of friends met and talked politics. However virulent and extreme its discourse, a spirit of easy brotherhood prevailed within the group. The men shared apartments, bank accounts, and cars. The group members strictly observed the tenets of their religion; they prayed five times a day, maintained strict Islamic diets, and even debated the proper length of their beards. They talked endlessly about the damage done by the Jews. For entertainment, they watched battlefield videos and sang songs about martyrdom (Laabs and McDermot, 2003). Visitors to Bait al-Ansar included

Mohamed Heidar Zammar, a naturalized German, originally from Syria, who had fought in the Afghan civil war and in Bosnia. He was loud and radical about his views and did not make a secret of his past. German authorities put him under surveillance, but dropped it within a few months for lack of evidence of any criminal planning. He met the group at al-Quds Mosque and became close to Bahaji. They were unaware that the German police had put in a microphone and monitored some of their discussions, which became increasingly virulent with focused hatred against "world Jewry" and the United States. Talk about defeating them through jihad and entry into paradise became more prominent with time.

In early 1999, Bahaji, as a German citizen, did his military service. The group seemed on a mission. Atta finished his dissertation. Jarrah married his girlfriend at al-Quds Mosque. Al-Shehhi gained admission to TUHH. Motassadeq married a fellow student from Belorussia, who converted to Islam. Bahaji married an eighteen-year-old religious Muslim Turkish girl, who had dropped out of high school because it taught un-Islamic subjects like evolution. At Bahaji's wedding in October 1999, the group demonstrated their fervor by loudly proclaiming their devotion to God and the jihad, to the shock of Bahaji's family and relatives. When Bahaji moved out of Bait al-Ansar, Essabar and Mzoudi moved in with Atta and bin al-Shibh.

The eight friends were ready to join the jihad. Originally, they had planned to go to Chechnya to fight the Russians. Russian atrocities against Muslims in Chechnya motivated Muslim militants to join the jihad. Mohamadou Ould Slahi, the brother-in-law of a close lieutenant of Osama bin Laden and who was living in Germany, discouraged them from going to Grozny and suggested instead that they go to Afghanistan for training. In November 1999, Atta, bin al-Shibh, al-Shehhi, and Jarrah went separately in the first wave and regrouped at an al Qaeda guesthouse near Qandahar, Afghanistan. There they were selected for the 9/11 operation, which had been in the planning stages for a few years. What was missing were volunteers familiar with Western countries, able to solve complex problems and work independently. Ideally, they would have studied in a Western country, be technically skilled, and speak perfect English (Fouda and Fielding, 2003; Mascolo and Stark, 2003). The four friends from Hamburg fit the bill. Khalid Sheikh Mohammed, who had conceived the operation, approached them, and they enthusiastically accepted the assignment. They met fellow conspirators Hani Hanjour, Khalid al-Midhar, and Nawaf al-Hazmi there and planned the operation. They returned to Germany and the second wave of Mzoudi, Motassadeq, Essabar, and Bahaji went to Afghanistan in the spring of 2000. Al-Shehhi moved into Bait al-Ansar for a few months. The first-wave members applied for their U.S. visas to go to flight school. Only bin al-Shibh was frustrated in his attempts to obtain a visa to enter the United States. After the fourth refusal, Essabar tried to replace him and get a U.S. visa but was refused twice as well. Bin al-Shibh was the liaison between Khalid Sheikh Mohammed and the team in the field. Atta was in charge in the field and al-Hazmi was his deputy.

With Atta, Jarrah, and al-Shehhi in the U.S. training and preparing for their operation and bin al-Shibh traveling around coordinating it with Khalid Sheikh Mohammed and the Saudi "muscle" group, Mzoudi, Motassadeq, Essabar, and Bahaji played supporting roles, providing their friends with money and taking care of their affairs back in Germany. On August 29, 2001, Atta called bin al-Shibh to tell him the date of the operation in code. Within days, bin al-Shibh, Essabar, and Bahaji disappeared from Hamburg. Motassadeq and Mzoudi stayed in Hamburg and were eventually arrested and tried. It is unclear how much Belfas and Zammar knew about the plot. Belfas became a German citizen in 2000 and immediately took a trip to the U.S., where he might have been casing potential targets. Zammar was probably shut out of the plans because of his big mouth. He was arrested in Morocco and disappeared. It is suspected that he is incarcerated in Syria.

Social Affiliation
Friendship

A striking element in both of these accounts is the absence of both top-down recruitment and brainwashing of the plotters, concepts which have been the mainstay of conventional explanations of al Qaeda terrorism. In the millennial plot, three of the main plotters had not attended training camps in Afghanistan and were not even formally affiliated with al Qaeda. (Two were scheduled to go after the plot.) Nor were they particularly religious. Meskini drank beer, loved movies, and dated women he met in dance clubs. The Hamburg plotters were far more devout in their beliefs and practices. A theme in both accounts is the formation of a network of friendships that solidified and preceded formal induction into the terrorist organization. The size of the networks was similar, with eight members in each group: Ressam, Labsi, Atamani, Kamel, the Boumezbeur and Ikhlef brothers in Canada; Atta, bin al-Shibh, al-Shehhi, Jarrah, Motassadeq, Mzoudi, Essabar, and Bahaji in Hamburg. Some, such as the Boumezbeur and Ikhlef brothers (also Haouari and Meskini) in Canada and Mzoudi and Motassadeq in Hamburg, knew each other from the old country. They had grown up together and trusted each other. Around them were some peripheral members: Haouari and Hannachi in one case, and Belfas and Zammar in the other.

During an incubation period of almost two years, the intensity of their beliefs spiraled upward in an apparent game of oneupsmanship. This took place in what they hoped was the privacy of a refuge, but it was monitored by the police. The Canadian police label of "bunch of guys" is appropriate. Kay Nehm, the German federal prosecutor, commented, "All the members of this cell shared the same religious convictions, an Islamic lifestyle, a feeling of being out of place in unfamiliar cultural surroundings that they weren't used to. At the center of this stood a hatred of world Jewry and the United States" (Williams, 2002). Nor were the friends particularly discreet about their views. Yazir Mukla, a Moroccan student who was occasionally part of the group, testified at Motassadeq's trial that when his father came to visit him, he was so alarmed at the radical atmosphere at al-Quds Mosque that he forbade his son to have any further contact with the group. He eventually forced his son to return to Morocco in 1999 (Notz, Steinborn, and Williamson, 2003).

This escalation of rhetorical militancy and condemnation of the West within a group of close friends was also noted in Milan, where the Italian authorities had wiretapped the apartment of al Qaeda's Varenese network and monitored their conversations for years. The Italian prosecutor Stefano Dambruoso speculated that their "chatter" about destroying the world was essential for keeping up their morale and egging each other on. "These are people with a lot of problems. Adapting to this country is devastating to them. In radical religious activity they found rules, a structure. It's not just religious, it's psychological and personal. The talk helps them stay fanaticized, to maintain their mind and never relent" (Rotella, 2002b).

At some point, the friends were ready to join the global Salafi jihad. As the Canadian example demonstrates, it was not simply because of piety and devotion. Although the Montreal group was somewhat religious, it was not seriously so, like the Hamburg group. I suspect that there was a strong desire for adventure mixed with the religious and political beliefs. But more interesting is the fact that the group of friends seemed to have initiated contact with the jihad. I detected only one instance of any reluctance to join the jihad in all the accounts I read. This exception is instructive.

Abdul Basit Karim (Ramzi Yousef) tried to recruit Ishtiaque Parker, a South African student at Islamabad Islamic University. Karim's brother-in-law, a student at the same university, met Parker by chance and took an interest in his South African citizenship. Two days later, he introduced Parker to Karim, who poured on the charm and expressed an interest in marrying a South African girl in order to get a South African passport. Karim met him again two or three times and carried on innocuous conversations. In December 1994, Karim broke cover and told him about his involvement with the 1993 World Trade Center bombing and several other bombings. He asked Parker to take a bag overseas for him in return for $10,000 and told him he would provide specific instructions later. Karim left for the Philippines and returned precipitously after the fire in Manila ruined his plans for the Bojinka plot. He called Parker, who by this time was terrified of Karim. They both flew to Bangkok, where Karim packed explosives in suitcases and dispatched Parker to the airport to send them as cargo with a U.S. carrier. Parker went and returned but lied that the security was too tight to carry out the plan. They both returned to Islamabad. After their return, Karim told Parker that his computer had fallen into the hands of the police in Manila and that Parker's name was in it. This terrified Parker even more. The next day Karim told Parker to take a small package to a Shiite mosque the following day. Instead, Parker telephoned the U.S. embassy and revealed what he knew. On the basis of this information, a mixed U.S.-Pakistani force arrested Karim on February 7, 1995 (Reeve, 1999).

The above account shows the danger of attempting to prematurely recruit a stranger. Karim was in many ways a loose cannon. He did well when he relied on childhood friends and kinsmen, but his luck ran out when he expanded his operations to strangers. Friends or kinsmen who know each other for a long time can vouch for their loyalty. Usually, the

109

prospective mujahed took the initiative rather than waiting for someone to ask him to join the jihad. Instead of a top-down process of the terrorist organization trying to recruit new members, it was a bottom-up process of young people volunteering to join the organization. Many wanted to join, but didn't know how to get in touch with the jihad organization. Often it was a chance phenomenon.

Meskini's experience in the millennial plot is probably typical. After a few years of a life of petty crime, Meskini asked his childhood friend Haouari to help him join the jihad and fight with Muslim men in Chechnya or Afghanistan (Adams, 2001). Haouari introduced him to Ressam, who asked Makhlulif for a visa. Haouari vouched for his childhood friend and Ressam vouched for Haouari (Ressam, 2001: 565).

Neither of the two accounts has a "recruiter" in the traditional sense of the term. The closest are Hannachi and allegedly Zammar. In Ressam's testimony, Hannachi arranged for Labsi and Ressam to go to an al Qaeda training camp in Afghanistan by getting a message to Hussein (abu Zubaydah) in Peshawar. Zammar has been widely reported in the world press as the "recruiter" of the Hamburg cell, the one who facilitated their affiliation with al Qaeda. People familiar with him, however, ridicule this hypothesis because of his limited intellect and tendency to talk too much. "For people to say that Zammar recruited Atta is like saying a first grader recruited a professor" (Hendawi, 2002). The president of the Al-Muhadjerin Mosque in Hamburg described him as "a little boy who talked too much" (McDermott, 2002b). Ramzi bin al-Shibh, who seems not to have taken his studies seriously and appears to have been devoted to the jihad full-time even before he went to Afghanistan with the Hamburg first wave, may have already been linked to the jihad. He was a cousin of Khalid al-Midhar's wife. But assuming that Zammar did indeed make the connection between al Qaeda and the Hamburg cell, it appears that, like Hannachi, he played a passive role, rather than that of an active recruiter. Furthermore, neither was a core member of the respective group.

Formal affiliation with the jihad also seems to have been a group phenomenon. Friends decided to join the jihad as a group rather than as isolated individuals. The founders of al Qaeda had of course met each other on the fields of Afghanistan and forged strong bonds in the fight against the Soviets. At the end of the war, they decided to create al Qaeda. This group phenomenon may be a strong factor in the formation of the global Salafi mujahedin in general. Abdul Basit Karim (Ramzi Yousef) plotted and executed many terrorist acts with his uncle Khalid Sheikh Mohammed and his childhood friends Abdul Hakim Murad and Abdul Shakur. At the East African embassy bombings trial L'Houssaine Kherchtou testified that he had joined the jihad with four friends from Milan (Kherchtou, 2001: 1107). The Kelkal group consisted of friends who had grown up together and participated together in the bombings of the summer 1995. The members of the Roubaix group had met around the mosque and had gone to Bosnia as a group to fight. The members of the 2001 failed Paris embassy plot also joined as a group of friends. There are hints that the Saudi mujahedin involved in the 9/11 operations also came as groups. Although it is difficult to obtain information from Saudi Arabia, which has been closed to investigative journalists, it has been reported that four friends (Wail al-Shehri, Waleed al-Shehri, Ahmed al-Nami, and Saeed al-Ghamdi), who went on to become hijackers, met at al-Seqley Mosque in the town of Khamis Mushayt in Assir Province, and swore to commit to jihad in the spring of 2000 (Sennott, 2002b; Lamb, 2002; "The Highway of Death," 2002). They went together to al Qaeda's al-Farooq camp in Afghanistan and eventually became part of the 9/11 operation. Even the Lackawanna Six, close Yemeni American childhood friends who underwent training at an al Qaeda camp, did so as a group. The May 16, 2003, Casablanca bombings were carried out by friends who lived within two blocks of each other.

From an empirical perspective, it is difficult to make a statement about friendship bonds preceding affiliation with the global jihad. People who provide an account of how they joined a revivalist group have a tendency to privilege ideological factors as an explanation for their conversion or affiliation. They seldom mention the critical role of friendship in this process. Only prospective participant observation studies show the importance of interpersonal bonds in recruitment into cults and sects (Lofland and Stark, 1965; Stark and Bainbridge, 1980). This difficulty is compounded by the fact that the sample data is derived from court testimony or journalists' interviews, neither of which usually investigates the importance of social bonds in the subject's personal history.

My sample includes 150 subjects on whom I had some information about social bonds preexisting formal affiliation with the jihad or with people who went on to join the global jihad. Preexisting friendship bonds

played an important role in the formal affiliation of 68 percent of mujahedin on whom there was adequate information. Most of them joined
the jihad in small clusters of friends. Al Qaeda's founders had forged such
bonds through their common fight against the Soviets. For many, like
Ahmed al-Kalaylah (a.k.a. abu Musab al-Zarqawi) and Waleed Tawfiq bin
Attash (a.k.a. Khallad), there was just not enough information. Two provided accounts of religious conversions without mentioning friends. Only
in the case of Ahmed Omar Sheikh was there no hint of friends, family,
or religious reaffiliation that might explain his joining the jihad.

Kinship

Friendship is only one type of social bond that might foster affiliation to
the global jihad. Kinship is another. In my sample, kinship played a role
in the affiliation of 14 percent of mujahedin. Some families seemed dedicated to the jihad. Khalid Sheikh Mohammed and Abdul Basit Karim
(a.k.a. Ramzi Yousef, who is Mohammed's nephew) belonged to an extended jihad family. Ahmed Said Khadr, of the Canadian Khadr family,
worked with Mohammed's brother in Peshawar in 1984, fought with
Osama bin Laden at Ali Kheyl (Jaji) in 1987, and financed the Egyptian
embassy bombing in Islamabad in 1995 for al-Zawahiri's EIJ. His three
sons Abdallah, Abdel Rahman, and Omar were also involved in the global jihad. Ali Ghufron and three of his younger brothers (Amrozi, Ali Imron, and Ali Fauzi) were involved in the Bali nightclub bombing in October 2002, as was their next-door neighbor Mubarak. These are the
green-diaper mujahedin. In the millennial plot, two sets of brothers belonged to the Montreal group of friends. The 9/11 perpetrators included
two sets of brothers (al-Hazmi and al-Shehri) and three cousins (Hamza,
Ahmed, and Ahmed al-Haznawi al-Ghamdi).

Kinship bonds also extend to in-laws. Yazid Sufaat became more religious through his wife's urging. He studied with senior members of the
Jemaah Islamiyah, who were exiled in Malaysia, ended up joining that organization, and was the host for the Kuala Lumpur al Qaeda conference
leading to the USS *Cole* bombing and the 9/11 operations. Sufaat eventually personally participated in the Christmas Eve 2000 wave of church
bombings throughout Indonesia. Spouses also played an important role
in convincing Christian converts to join the jihad. Jack Thomas, an Aus-

tralian, was married to an Indonesian woman from the troubled Sulawe-si Province. Luis José Galan Gonzalez, a Spaniard, converted to Islam and took the name of Yusuf Galan when he married a Muslim woman. He joined the jihad as part of Yarkas's (a.k.a. abu Dahdah) logistics group in Madrid. Marriage exposes people to new kinship and friendship networks, which may inspire affiliation with the jihad. For example, el-Hage brought his wife, mother-in-law, and her new husband to Pakistan to fight the So-viets in the 1980s.

In-laws also provided links for prospective mujahedin to join the jihad. Ramzi bin al-Shibh was a cousin of Khalid al-Midhar's wife. In turn, Khalid al-Midhar was the son-in-law of the Yemeni leader of al Qaeda. Marriages commonly cemented mujahedin into kinship relationships. Mujahedin and their families lived in exile because of their clandestine activities, limiting their choice of marriage partners. The most prominent of such bonds was the marriage of bin Laden's son to the daughter of abu Sittah. Marriages were also the ideal way of forging permanent alliances between mujahedin families. Many of the accounts tell of intermarriages in the Sudan, Pakistan, and Afghanistan. Typical was Ahmed Said Khadr's attempt to convince his eldest daughter, Zaynab, to marry a Sudanese ter-rorist in Peshawar in 1995 (Vincent, 2002). In Indonesia, Haris Fadillah, a Muslim militia leader, arranged the marriage of his daughter to Omar al-Faruq, an al Qaeda representative in Southeast Asia, in one day (Mur-phy, 2003).

Combining the friendship and kinship statistics and eliminating the overlap, about 75 percent of mujahedin had preexisting social bonds to members already involved in the global jihad or decided to join the jihad as a group with friends or relatives.

Discipleship

A third type of affiliation for the jihad, discipleship, is unique to the South-east Asian cluster and accounts for about 8 percent of mujahedin who joined the jihad. The Southeast Asian cluster centers around two Islamic boarding schools founded by Abu Bakar Baasyir and Abdullah Sungkar, who later founded and led the Jemaah Islamiyah terrorist group. At Pon-dok Ngruki, in Indonesia, they taught a brand of militant Salafi Islam that made them run afoul of the Indonesian authorities. Rather than face a second term of prison, they fled to Malaysia where they founded the second school, Pesentren Luqmanul Hakiem, and continued their work. It is unclear exactly when the Jemaah Islamiyah was founded and what its actual link with al Qaeda may be. Jemaah Islamiyah is still shrouded in mystery; most arrested members are not cooperating with authorities and have recanted whatever confessions they have made. They are protecting their leader, as a manual discovered in the possession of one prescribes them to do. Some of those arrested in Singapore are fully cooperating with authorities, however, and they date the creation of the Jemaah Islamiyah to 1993.

In Southeast Asia, teachers command strong personal loyalty from their students. This loyalty may be lifelong, as illustrated by the three Jemaah Islamiyah convicts incarcerated in Singapore, who testified against their former teacher Abu Bakar Baasyir in June 2003. Despite their damning testimony, two spontaneously started to cry at the sight of their teacher. They repeated that they loved him but urged him to tell the truth about his activities.

Worship

A common popular belief is that the global Salafi mujahedin were recruited at mosques, where they underwent some sort of brainwashing. Places of worship do figure prominently in the affiliation to the global Salafi jihad, as it is part of a Muslim revivalist movement. Indeed, several mosques became prominent in the process of affiliation to the jihad: in London, the Finsbury Park and the Baker Street Mosques under Mustafa Kamel (a.k.a. abu Hamza al-Masri) and Omar Mahmud Othman (a.k.a. abu Qatada), respectively; the Islamic Cultural Center in Milan, first under Anwar Shaban and then under Abdel Qader Es Sayed; abu Bakr Mosque under Imad Eddin Barakat Yarkas in Madrid; al-Quds Mosque in Hamburg; al-Dawah Mosque in Roubaix, France; Assuna Annabawiyah Mosque in Montreal; al-Seqley Mosque in Khamis Mushayt, Saudi Arabia; and al-Faruq Mosque in Brooklyn, New York.

These mosques served many functions in the transformation of young alienated Muslims into global Salafi mujahedin. A mosque was an ideal place to meet familiar people, namely fellow Muslims—an important desire in upwardly and geographically mobile young men who missed the

114

community of their friends and family. Friendship groups formed around the mosques, as we saw in the millennial plot and Hamburg cell accounts. Each new group became a "bunch of guys," transforming its members into potential mujahedin, actively seeking to join the global jihad. In the sample of one hundred mujahedin with adequate background information, thirteen provided an account of affiliation to the jihad inspired only by their religious beliefs and without the intervention of friends. This may actually overestimate this group, since the mujahedin traditionally account for joining the jihad as a religious revelation without acknowledging the importance of friends, kin, or teachers.

So far I have focused on the process of association with the jihad, and I have argued that social bonds predating formal recruitment into the jihad seem to be the crucial element of this process. However, the global Salafi jihad is not simply a political movement. It is also a religious revivalist movement, and the mosques are where the intensification of religious sentiment takes place, transforming potential mujahedin into dedicated fanatics. The "bunch of guys" incubation goes only so far; it might be enough to make a dedicated political militant or a gang member (see Jankowski, 1991). But it will not produce a religious fanatic, ready to sacrifice himself for the glory of God. This requires a religious dimension, acquired only in places of worship.

Not everyone is responsive to religious appeal. Atheists would not be attracted to a rigorous religious ideology, nor would they go to the mosque to meet friends. Those receptive to a religious appeal accept the notion of an active supernatural dimension. Such belief is facilitated by an intimate familiarity with concepts of faith, as in a person raised in a religious household. Present deep commitment to a religion, however, would bar the development of a new commitment. All things being equal, people who are satisfied with their religion will not seek a new more demanding sect. Those who are already committed to a particular sectarian outlook may simply choose to pursue it in a new setting. Therefore, the Muslims most receptive to global Salafi ideology grew up with religion but either were no longer committed to it or already embraced Salafism. Most Core Arabs were committed to a Wahhabi or Salafi version of Islam as children, whereas the Maghreb Arabs were essentially uncommitted to religion (see Chapter 3). Individuals in both clusters were familiar enough with Islam to seek people sharing this generic background. When shown pictures of

Muslims suffering because of wars, they began to feel a common bond of victimhood based on Islam. Usually, people will not seek new religious or social affiliations except after some significant change that disrupts their social networks. Examples of such changes could be upward or geographical mobility, a new school, marriage, or imprisonment. The last one may account for various "born-again" experiences or conversions in prison. I touched on marriages in the section on kinship. But most of the sample experienced such disruptions due to social or geographical mobility or admission to a new school, often abroad.

Religion is about one's relationship with God. Contrary to some popular beliefs about solitary faith, this relationship is strongly grounded in social processes. Islam is one of the most communal of all religions, with many orchestrated shared rituals. Besides the obvious conviviality of fellowship, religion also entails a commitment involving affective, behavioral, and cognitive components that mutually reinforce each other. Emotions are important in religion and are usually ordinary, natural and positive emotions directed to God and the community of worshippers. Islam prescribes regular behavioral practices such as praying, often in groups, five times daily. It also proscribes many practices, depending on the interpretations one accepts. Salafi Islam is very strict in its code of conduct and prescribes various codes of appearance, dress, diet, and conduct, especially vis-à-vis gender roles. Salafists believe in a literal interpretation of the Quran and the life of the Prophet, and in the necessity of imposing Sharia in the state and protecting the faithful from corruption by Western values. The elegance and simplicity of its interpretations attract many who seek a single solution devoid of ambiguity. Very often these persons have already chosen such unambiguous technical fields as engineering, architecture, computer science, or medicine. Students of the humanities and social sciences were few and far between in my sample.

Like many religions, Islam demands commitment to God in terms of faith and trust. Adherents view their sacrifices in terms of that commitment. Faith and religious explanations are nourished socially, by others' proclamations of faith. To the extent that people trust significant others, they rely on their wisdom, experience, and testimony and accept their expressions of faith. They also place greater trust on the testimony of people who have sacrificed in the service of God. The Arabic word for witness, *shahid*, is also the word for martyr. Martyrdom is a profession of

116

faith, *shahada*. A testimonial from one who has little to gain from his faith on this earth is most credible. So, by his actions and lifestyle, Osama bin Laden demonstrated the strength of his faith by living in poverty and humility, and giving up a more luxurious and leisurely life in the name of God. Likewise, Mustafa Kamel (abu Hamza al-Masri), who lost limbs and sight during the jihad, and Sheikh Omar Abdel Rahman, who is blind, are also credible witnesses because their personal tragedies do not deter them from proclaiming their faith in God.

Participation in rituals builds faith and generates group solidarity and integration. Rituals reinforce religious explanations and faith in God and in the community of believers. Prayers are acts of faith that build bonds of affection and confidence with God and the community of believers. In Islam, they are communal acts involving a sense of sharing and bonding. They bring spiritual phenomena to life, especially when people feel the presence of God during prayers. Each act reinforces the reality of the message, the bond with God and the community. Perceived miracles, such as the defeat of a superpower through faith alone (the Soviet-Afghan war), also increase confidence in the righteousness of the cause. Mystical experiences during prayers or dreams demonstrate the existence of God and reinforce faith. In a videotape in the fall of 2001 Osama bin Laden said that he had banned the reporting of dreams of airplanes flying into buildings prior to September 11 for fear of revealing the plot.

Ideology also played a central role in sustaining commitment to this version of Islam. Although affiliation is a social phenomenon, intensification of faith and beliefs is a stage characterized by active personal learning about the new faith. New adherents listen carefully to preachers and friends, question them, and eventually reach some form of synthetic understanding of their new faith, which they finally choose to embrace. This period involves a reappraisal of life, values, beliefs, and goals. The seekers do not simply succumb to preaching. They progressively accept the new faith because it makes sense in their new interpretation of the world and their role in it. This learning process involves intense social interactions, but it also requires intense introspection. Past biographical experiences are reinterpreted in accordance with the new faith and provide vivid proof of its superiority. This discovery of a strong fit of past events with the new interpretation is critical to the acceptance of and fosters long-term commitment to the new faith. In this ongoing process, new events are made to fit with the new ideology. Social support and interpretation also help this process.

This progressive participation in a strict and rigorous interpretation of Islam brought about a shift in devotion in most of our sample through the various processes described in this section. This intensification of religious feelings and conversion to Salafi Islam took place in a strong social context. It made the prospective mujahed's religious affect, behavior, and thinking conform to that of his friends and kin. This made him even closer to his social group.

Salafi behavioral prescriptions demand sacrifices for the sake of the group. Becoming a Salafist involves great personal costs, often including rejection by one's former friends, family, or even employer, if they do not approve of the group or its attitudes. Furthermore, Salafi behavior is all highly visible for all to see. It is a proclamation of one's faith in God. Growing one's beard, dressing like a traditional Muslim, and giving up some of one's pleasures are sacrifices for God and the true community. This distances new devotees from their original network of friends and family but draws them closer to other Salafists, whose good opinion becomes their only reference. Only the most motivated and dedicated will be willing to bear the social, personal, and economic costs of becoming a Salafist. Those who feel that society as a whole has the least to offer them are the most likely to join. This points to the importance of relative or subjective deprivation in combination with the social isolation thesis developed in Chapter 3. Disappointment with one's social and economic condition combined with the relative lack of social attachment to the world encourages participation in sectarian practices, especially in the presence of unopposed strong bonding to people already in the sect. The more active one's participation in the sect, the stronger will be the bonds with other members as well as one's faith and commitment to the new sect. Only individuals with serious, albeit temporary distress, who feel that they have little to lose, would accept such severe upfront costs of joining and tolerate the strict regimentation and state of high tension with society that participation in the sect involves. This hardship, in turn, increases the emotional commitment to fellow members and fosters a sense of serenity, relieving the previous distress, from spiritual acceptance of sectarian beliefs.

The process of becoming a member of a religious community has traditionally been explained by mass movement theories. The argument is that religious organizations, like other social movements, gather a following through the strength of direct ideological appeals to atomized and alienated masses of people. Autobiographical accounts of members tell stories of revelation and progressive acceptance of the specific ideology. But such retrospective self-reports are biased, as previously mentioned. A variant of this ideological appeal thesis is a version of the Marxist "religion is the opiate of the masses" argument. It claims that religion provides ideological and emotional compensation for the masses' real social and economic deprivation. It therefore appeals to those most open to such compensation, especially those believing in otherworldly rewards for present worldly deprivation. Such ideologies, with their promises of heavenly compensation, make deprivation more bearable. There may be some truth in this thesis for some people. But again, it runs aground on the fundamental problem of specificity. It does not explain the formation of a global Salafi mujahed, except perhaps in the statistical sense that at least a very small random number of individuals might be motivated to carry this ideological commitment to its extreme.

The ideological appeal thesis implies that people would randomly join the movement simply by being exposed to its ideology. The stronger the exposure, the greater the recruitment would be. Historically, joining al Qaeda was definitely not a random process. One of its surprising features was its complete failure to recruit members where its headquarters and training camps were located. In its short history, its headquarters were located in Afghanistan, Pakistan, the Sudan, and Afghanistan again. Yet, no Afghans or Sudanese joined the organization when it was located in these countries. Wali Khan Amin Shah, the only significant Afghan to join the global jihad (although not formally, for he was part of Abdul Basit Karim's group), was a personal friend of bin Laden from the 1980s, before al Qaeda was formed. The Sudanese, Jamal al-Fadl, had joined the organization before the move to the Sudan. Therefore, the bonds of terror did not form spontaneously by mere exposure as implied in the mass ideological appeal thesis.

The flaw in this thesis is its individualistic perspective that cannot capture the sectarian phenomenon. Revivalist social movements like the global Salafi jihad are vigorous social enterprises. They provide immediate social and emotional rewards of close community and a sense of totality

119

and meaning. Religious faith and beliefs are grounded in social interactions. With few exceptions, which by their rarity attract attention, loners or even pairs of individuals are seldom able to sustain strong otherworldly commitments without strong social support. In the absence of such support, beliefs and faith fade. During the wait for heavenly rewards, a religious revivalist community sustains its members with strong social and emotional benefits, which give a general sense of direction to their lives and opportunities for involvement in a cause.

Formal Acceptance

The processes of social affiliation with potential members of the jihad and intensification of beliefs and faith are necessary, but not sufficient conditions for joining the jihad. The critical and specific element to joining the jihad is the accessibility of a link to the jihad. Without it, the group of friends, kin, pupils, and worshippers will undergo a process of progressive isolation. They may try to participate in the jihad, but without know-how or resources. Although lethal, their operations do not constitute a serious threat to society. Only the global jihad, with its organization, resources, and skills, poses such a danger.

These patterns show that the pool of potential mujahedin is composed of small clusters of close friends, relatives, worshippers, and disciples, who are connected through strong bonds. As such they all know each other's close friends, who would also be part of this group. This promotes intense social cohesion in terms of views and loyalty and a strong sense of community with mutual emotional support. The group becomes self-sufficient and closed in on itself. This social isolation protects the group, but prevents it from linking with other movements in the outside world. This becomes a weakness if the group wants to join a larger social movement, like the global Salafi jihad. Not possessing any independent bridge to the jihad (under the ideal conditions, all the friends are strongly bonded to each other and no one else), they will not know how to join. Acquaintances, who are weakly connected to one or another of the friends but do not really belong to the circle, provide access to other groups in the world, for they are linked to others with whom the original friends have no ties. Hannachi and Zammar are good illustrations of such bridges to the outside world. So was Kamal Derwish, who made the arrangement for the Afghan training of the Lackawanna Six. The "strength of weak ties" (Granovetter, 1973 and 1983) plays an important role in a social movement like the global jihad that links multiple independent clusters of closely connected friends who want to join but do not know how.

This perhaps chance encounter with a formal member of the global Salafi jihad is the critical element leading to enrollment into the jihad. Without someone able to make arrangements to send him to Afghanistan, where senior members of the jihad could further evaluate him, a prospective candidate would remain a sympathizer rather than become a full-fledged mujahed. Formal acceptance into the jihad took place in Afghanistan, Malaysia, the Philippines, or the Sudan, after evaluation of the trainee in a jihad training camp. From the available information, al Qaeda offered the opportunity to join its ranks to only 10 to 30 percent of the trainees. The formal ceremony was the oath of loyalty, *baya*, to al Qaeda and Osama bin Laden. The Jemaah Islamiyah had a similar ceremony in Malaysia. This formal acceptance marks the end of the three-prong process that had started with social affiliation to a group of like-minded friends or family and the twin intensification of militancy and faith that took place in small, densely connected groups.

Training in Afghanistan not only taught terroristic skills, but also built confidence and forged an esprit de corps among friends, cementing their identities as global mujahedin. This confidence was visible in Ressam after his return from Afghanistan.

Recruitment

The concepts of recruitment and brainwashing have not surfaced in the argument so far, partly because I have taken the perspective of the potential mujahedin. From this point of view, becoming a member of the global jihad is a process of joining. Recruitment is the same process, from the organization's perspective. The notion of recruitment implies an active process through which an organizational insider gets a new person to work for the organization. The account usually shows the "recruiter" in a heroic light, overcoming reluctance on the part of the target. The popularity of such accounts probably comes from the fact that many commentators on terrorism have an intelligence background. Here recruitment means agent acquisition to provide clandestine foreign intelligence. This is dangerous work, for if discovered, the agent will face years in prison if he is not killed outright. Most people are reluctant to do it. The main themes of an agent acquisition cycle are clandestine spotting, assessing, developing, and formally pitching the agent. For an intelligence officer, recruitment leads to promotion. I am skeptical of this type of account of agent acquisition. I suspect that the majority of agents are volunteers, "walk-ins" in the jargon. But such facts would not advance the career of a case officer. So the difficulty of agent acquisition is emphasized as a self-serving claim for promotion within the organization. By now, it has attained mythical status.

It is a small jump to generalize agent acquisition from intelligence organizations to the global jihad. The process of joining the jihad, however, is more of a bottom-up than a top-down activity. A lot of Muslim young men want to join the jihad but do not know how. Joining the jihad is more akin to the process of applying to a highly selective college. Many try to get in but only a few succeed, and the college's role is evaluation and selection rather than marketing. Candidates are enthusiastic rather than reluctant. So far, I have read no accounts of sinister al Qaeda "recruiters" lurking in mosques, ready to subvert naïve and passive worshippers, although I have looked for them. Ressam twice described the process of joining al Qaeda. For his own formal affiliation, he asked Hannachi, who had just returned from training. When he himself returned from training, two people asked him to facilitate their joining the jihad. One of them, Meskini, described the frustrations of his past failures to join the jihad to his childhood friend Haouari (Adams, 2001). Personal acquaintances vouched for the candidate to maintain the security of the organization. The problem was that this process, which favored personal friends, acquaintances, relatives, and fellow worshippers, was not selective enough. It required a period of observation in training camp to evaluate whether the potential candidate was worthy of being offered a spot. Zuhair Hilal al-Tbaiti, who was convicted in Morocco for his plot against U.S. ships in the Straits of Gibraltar in 2002, admitted that he had first been rejected because of his poor performance in military and religious training. He was also rejected for a suicide mission to the United

States, which he believed might have been the 9/11 operation. Only the dispersal of al Qaeda as a result of U.S. bombing and the overthrow of the Taliban government gave him the opportunity to participate in an operation (Ilhami, 2002).

One of the surprising aspects of the global Salafi movement, given its notoriety and ubiquity, is the relative lack of resources invested in any recruitment drive. I did not detect any active top-down organizational push to increase al Qaeda's membership. The pressure came from the bottom up. Prospective mujahedin were eager to join the movement. The proselytizing arm of Salafi Islam is the peaceful Tablighi group, which actively seeks to convert young Muslims to its version of Islam. Tablighi students come to Pakistan to study. Perhaps some al Qaeda "recruiters" came to the Tablighi schools to inspire some students to join the jihad and succeeded in convincing some students to take military training at al Qaeda camps in neighboring Afghanistan. After assessment at the camp, the prospective candidate might have been formally invited to join the jihad. But generally, these activities took place only in Pakistan, Afghanistan, or perhaps Saudi Arabia. They were not part of a worldwide top-down campaign to increase membership. No aggressive "publicity" campaigns targeted potential recruits; no dedicated recruitment committee had full-time staff at al Qaeda headquarters (except a reception committee in Peshawar for people already on their way to the camps), and no powerful recruitment program drew on a budget dedicated to these activities.

This is surprising because Sheikh Abdullah Azzam had established such a successful campaign to recruit mujahedin against the Soviets in the 1980s. Indeed, the organization he created, the Mekhtab al-Khidemat (the Service Bureau), a forerunner of al Qaeda, was in essence the institutionalization of a permanent recruitment campaign. Nothing comparable to Azzam's work exists in the present global Salafi jihad. Some audiotapes, videotapes, books, and magazines can be found in selected Salafi mosque bookstores. These mosques were listed above and are led by imams sympathetic to the jihad if not outright members of it. The groups of friends spontaneously assembling in such mosques constitute the main venue for joining the jihad. Their intense interactions facilitate the process of conversion, culminating in their readiness to join the jihad. But there is no evidence that this was an intentional process, conceived, planned, and executed by al Qaeda. The movement invested a surprisingly small amount of resources in its expansion. So far, the concept of recruitment as an active organizational process is not relevant for the global Salafi jihad.

Brainwashing

Brainwashing is the second concept dominating the public discourse on joining the jihad. The brainwashing thesis is the counterpart of the ideological appeal thesis. The charge of brainwashing is a value judgment about an ideology couched in a pseudo-scientific argument. An appealing ideology is considered intrinsically attractive to anyone and able, by its persuasive force, to motivate someone to join its organization. In contrast, a singularly unappealing ideology would never attract anyone in his right mind, and only some form of coercion could explain its adoption. Brainwashing is this forcible indoctrination to induce someone to abandon his basic beliefs and adopt less desirable ones instead. The argument implies deception and powerful techniques to overwhelm victims' minds. It is the twentieth-century form of mind control, like the Middle Ages' demonic possession, the eighteenth century's mesmerism, and the nineteenth century's hypnotism.

The notion of brainwashing originated in the sense of betrayal the American public felt during the Korean War when some American prisoners of war apparently proclaimed Communist doctrines, confessed to false crimes, and repudiated their own political system. Technically, it described the brutal techniques of indoctrination involving torture, death threats, and deprivation of water, food, and sleep. While the brutal techniques were all too real, their alleged results triggered a self-flagellating panic in the United States. Even the very few who succumbed to these techniques might not have really believed the doctrines their captors tried to pound into them (Biderman, 1963). The scientific rationale was that intolerable stress overwhelmed one's ordinary equilibrium and forced the collapse of the nervous system to produce bizarre behavior and sudden changes in personality and beliefs in suggestible people. This theory was later extended to suggest a "physiology of faith," where intense religion can assault the mind and weaken it to the point of madness (Sargant, 1971). This argument exculpates the deviant, who later claims to have been a victim of such mind control. This argument, now used mostly by relatives and friends of cult members, is the basis of an entire new industry to deprogram "victims" back to their original state (Singer, 1996; Hassan, 2000).

Many problems surface when the notion of brainwashing is applied to the global Salafi jihad. First, from a scientific perspective, five decades of research have failed to provide any empirical support for this thesis. Second, the biographical accounts of those explaining their embrace of the ideology fail to describe any coercive techniques leading to their final acceptance of the ideology. Third, like its ideological appeal counterpart, it is vulnerable to the fundamental problem of specificity. If so many people are exposed to the global Salafi jihad ideology, why do only a few succumb to it? Fourth, some incarcerated members now see the errors of their ways in pursuing violence in the name of God. If brainwashing is so powerful that only deprogrammers could restore victims, why can some do it on their own without apparent help, except for books supplied by their families? Fifth, no visitor to Salafi mosques has ever reported the use of coercive techniques. Sixth, people who were part of the "bunch of guys" groups also do not report coercive techniques. Finally, my arguments have explained the transformation of potential candidates into dedicated global Salafi mujahedin without recourse to this mysterious brainwashing process. There is no need for an additional and suspect concept to explain this transformation.

Evidence for the Importance of Social Bonds

Before concluding this chapter, let me present three lines of evidence for the importance of social bonds in joining the jihad. One set of evidence will be a review of the in-depth research done on a religious revivalist movement, the Unification Church, from three independent teams of researchers, who came to surprisingly similar conclusions that strongly support my previous arguments. The second is a review of the comprehensive social and psychological investigation of captured German and Italian terrorists from the troubled 1970s. Again, these independent projects concluded with arguments similar to mine. The last set of evidence deals with the Egyptian Salafi groups that were the forerunners of the global Salafi jihad.

The Unification Church

Al Qaeda is not only a terrorist political organization; it is also a revivalist religious social movement. Recruitment and conversion by these organizations have been the focus of intense research based on careful prospective participant observations. This empirical project challenges the conventional mass movement theses of direct ideological appeals and supports the importance of social bonds in recruitment and conversion. It has led to a new paradigm in the sociology of religion (Bainbridge, 1997; Stark and Bainbridge, 1985 and 1996; Stark and Finke, 2000). The most extensive field work on this issue was done on Reverend Sun Myung Moon's Unification Church. Three independent teams investigated the Moonies, as the members of this organization are called: John Lofland (1981) and Rodney Stark (Lofland and Stark, 1965) from 1962 to 1963 in California and Oregon; Eileen Barker (1984) from 1977 to 1983 in Britain, California, New York, and some Scandinavian countries; and Marc Galanter (1989) from 1977 to 1985 in New York, Boston, California, and Washington, D.C. They came up with consistent findings and similar conclusions.

Lofland's careful participant observations refuted converts' retrospective accounts, which stress their own self-conscious search for the truth culminating in their experience of revelation with the new theology. Such retrospective accounts fall prey to the distortions of memory, allowing people to reinterpret the past in light of the present (Schachter, 1996 and 2001). When asked why they converted, Moonies invariably reported the irresistible appeal of the church's Divine Principle, implying that only the ignorant could reject such obvious and powerful truths. But the empirical evidence did not support their statements. The researchers had met the members at a time well before they had accepted this doctrine and when they regarded it as quite odd. On the basis of their observations, Lofland and Stark proposed the following seven-step theory of conversion: "(1) Experience enduring, acutely felt tensions (2) within a religious problem-solving perspective, (3) which leads him to define himself as a religious seeker; (4) encountering the D.P. [Divine Principle] at a turning point in his life, (5) wherein an affective bond is formed (or pre-exists) with one or more converts; (6) where extra-cult attachments are absent or neutralized; (7) and, where, if he is to become a deployable agent, he is exposed to intensive interaction" (Lofland and Stark, 1965: 874).

The first three elements are general background conditions, creating a pool of potential converts. Reversing the first two facts, prospective converts generally are "religious" in the sense of imposing religious meanings on events. They might have been raised in a religious tradition but were unaffiliated with a specific congregation at the time. They experienced considerable tension, "a felt discrepancy between some imaginary, ideal state of affairs and the circumstances in which they actually saw themselves" (Lofland, 1981: 34). The prospective converts sought the solution of this tension in religion, becoming religious seekers.

The next four elements in the Lofland-Stark theory are situational factors, where timing becomes significant. The first of these is that shortly before and concurrently with their encounter with members of the new cult, all pre-converts had reached what they perceived as a turning point in their lives. Recent migration, loss of employment, loss of a partner, or the start or end of schooling were usually the cause. "The significance of these various turning points is that they increased the pre-convert's awareness of and desire to take some action about his problems, at the same time giving him a new opportunity to do so" (Lofland and Stark, 1965: 870). Again reversing the next two steps, the prospective converts were "social atoms" in the sense that they were distant from previous attachments that might have prevented affiliation with the new group. For many the tension they experienced was precisely this lack of social ties. Moving away from home reduced the influence of former friends and family to restrain them from joining a cult. The next step is the crucial one in the process of conversion: the development of a strong emotional bond bridging the gap between first exposure to and final and full acceptance of the doctrine. "That is, persons developed affective ties with the group or some of its members while they still regarded the D.P. perspective as problematic, or even 'way out.' In a manner of speaking, final conversion was coming to accept the opinions of one's friends" (Lofland and Stark, 1965: 871). This step involved a chance encounter with someone involved with the movement, which escalated quickly into strong affective bonds, despite the fact that the prospective converts had strong reservations about the group's doctrines. In the absence of strong countervailing outside ties, when such bonds developed, the prospective convert joined the group; when they failed to develop, he did not join. Doctrine played a negligible role at this stage; many moved into the Moonie commune because of their attachment to group members while still openly expressing rejection of the Moon ideology.

The last step is the true total conversion. Prospective converts who go through the first six steps become sympathetic to the doctrine of their friends. The mastering of their friends' beliefs came after a long period of intense day-to-day interactions with them, which often required living with them. This group living intensified their bonds, which began to take on a depth and uniqueness beyond their ties to outsiders, even their girl-friends (like Jarrah of the Hamburg group) or wives (in the traditional Muslim sense). Their marathon discussions inculcated them with the religious doctrines, trained them to adopt the practices of the group, and instilled commitment. The resulting social, emotional, and spiritual benefits eliminated the previously experienced tension. At the end of this process, the prospect was a full-fledged totally committed convert, loyal to his new faith and his new friends.

Subsequent work on other revivalist movements has slightly modified this model. The notion of preexisting tensions—somewhat vague and subjective—has come under question. Everyone experiences some frustration in his life. Some people may be attracted to a new doctrine just because of its novelty. However experienced, distress motivates people to look for help. In later works, Stark distanced himself from the notion that prospective converts sought relief from distress in religion. He argued instead that converts were very seldom religious seekers; they did not so much find a new faith as the new faith found them (Stark and Finke, 2000: 122). But all subsequent work confirmed that interpersonal relationships are the one essential element in all realistic models of revivalist religious recruitment. Membership spreads through social networks, and faith constitutes conformity to the religious outlook of one's intimates (Stark and Bainbridge, 1980; Bainbridge, 1997: 177).

While Lofland and Stark conducted their intensive research on a small group of individuals during the birth of a movement, Barker (1984) and Galanter (1989) independently studied the same, now mature, movement twenty years later. They found that people joined for a variety of positive rather than negative reasons. Only 8 to 9 percent of those approached eventually joined the group, and fewer than 5 percent were still members after two years. Most joiners were from middle-class families, with few outside social ties. They were spiritual and concerned about the world. Barker noted that the people in her sample had experienced a relative dip in happiness or "droop" in spirituality right before joining. They had had happy normal childhoods and had come from happy, slightly overprotective, religious, and caring middle-class families, which had inculcated them with strong values of decency, duty, and service to the community. These children in early adulthood were ill prepared to cope with life on their own. When confronted with this adversity, the Unification Church provided them with the emotional support and spiritual security of a "family." It also provided them with the feeling of being special and being part of a movement working according to God's principle and seeking to improve the world.

Marc Galanter (1989), a psychiatrist who studied the mental health of the members of the Unification Church, found no evidence of increased incidence of mental illness. On the contrary, membership conferred an emotional relief effect. There was an inverse relationship between feelings of emotional distress (alienation) and of closeness to the group. The distress was usually generated in dealing with outsiders, such as family and former friends, who disapproved of their group. This distress was relieved when members returned to the group. They interpreted this relief effect as dependent on loyalty to the group. Full involvement in church activities also coincided with relief from distress. This led to further commitment to the community and self-sacrifice. Social cohesiveness and shared beliefs also resulted in a feeling of well-being. This helped maintain strong group loyalty even in conditions of isolation. Everything became interpreted through these shared beliefs, creating a selective and biased perception of the real world, a fantasy world. Only a lack of social ties to outsiders—social alienation—distinguished those who joined from those who did not.

Singer (1996) and Hassan (2000) challenge these empirical analyses and claim that these cults "brainwash" members. They present only anecdotal evidence based on their clinical work with hostile former members of such cults. As argued earlier, retrospective accounts are of questionable validity. Neither Barker nor Galanter found any evidence of brainwashing in their extensive experience as participant observers. Galanter and Barker even interviewed former members who voluntarily left the

Unification Church, who denied any evidence of brainwashing. The findings of other participant researchers studying multiple religious organizations in various countries provide no empirical evidence of possible brainwashing in the entire religious revivalist literature. On the contrary, these two studies of recruitment and conversion seem to confirm the Lofland-Stark model.

West European Terrorism

The global Salafi jihad is not just a religious revivalist movement; it is also a terrorist movement. The most extensive social psychological studies of terrorism came from the German and Italian experiences with terrorism in the 1970s. Although these movements were secular and directed against their own governments, the findings of these two research projects can be evaluated against the arguments proposed here.

GERMAN RED ARMY FACTION

At the end of the 1970s, the German Federal Ministry of Domestic Affairs commissioned a large social psychological study of 227 left-wing terrorists who had been arrested. They came from the upper middle class, and their parents had high social and occupational hopes for their children. But there seemed to be a lot of friction with their families and absent parents in their childhoods. The terrorists' level of education was above average, as most attended university, but then the majority dropped out. Prior to becoming terrorists, only 35 percent had held full-time jobs at any time of their lives.

Before joining a terrorist organization, the prospective member underwent a process of social isolation. "In the course of this early phase, the decisive processes of disassociation with existing social links, such as the parental home, family, partner, place of residence, and habitual milieu, took place. This process of disassociation consists of several stages: first, the hitherto existing social and emotional ties are generally called into question; then a phase follows in which these ties are loosened and a process of alienation sets in; and, finally, there is a total negation of everything that existed earlier in life. Ultimately, there follows a total break with the existing social milieu" (Wasmund, 1986: 204). This void was filled with new ties to groups in sympathy with terrorists. "Most terrorists, in fact, have ultimately become members of terrorist organizations through personal connections with people or relatives associated with appropriate political initiatives, communes, self-supporting organizations, or committees—the number of couples, and brothers and sisters is astonishingly high" (204).

Their emotional longing for a community that would act as a substitute for their families was satisfied by these new countercultural groups or communes. Wasmund described these communities as "total groups" (205), for they were intense, tightly knit social groups that satisfied their members' social, emotional, and spiritual needs. This further isolated them from the outside social world, which in turn rejected them. Originally apolitical, some of these groups gradually became involved in politics. They sympathized with imprisoned terrorists, who shared their lifestyle and ideas, and formed support groups for the prisoners. Soon, they identified with their new friends and felt a sense of social injustice, inspiring them to become more engaged politically. Their activities gradually moved them from a support role to more central activities, crossing over to illegality. At some point, they formally broke with the legal world through an illegal act. The result was a clandestine life, which further increased their material and emotional dependence on the group. The ideology of the group became a rationalization for action and put them "at war" with society. Social involvement preceded ideology; many of the captured terrorists started reading Marx only in prison (Wasmund, 1986; Merkl, 1995; della Porta, 1992b).

ITALIAN RED BRIGADES

Italy also underwent a serious terrorist threat around the same time. From a data bank based on court records of twelve hundred left-wing militants and twenty-eight in-depth interviews, della Porta (1988) indicated that, unlike their German counterparts, captured Italian terrorists had happy and serene childhoods and came from generally left-wing families (confirmed in Passerini, 1992). In della Porta's large sample, 70 percent of the recruits had at least one friend already involved in a terrorist organization. Three-fourths of these had two or more friends involved, and 42 percent had eight or more friends involved.

Decisions to join underground organizations were taken by clusters or cliques of people connected to each other by joint involvements in more than one activity. For example, quite frequently new recruits were next-door neighbors who worked in the same department of a big factory; school friends who used to spend their vacation together; cousins who belonged to the same voluntary association. Moreover, the intensity of the relations is also shown by the high frequency of kinship ties: in 298 cases of my quantitative sample, militants in underground organizations had at least one relative—usually a husband/wife or brother/sister—who shared their commitment. . . . Participation in clandestine groups is more likely when it is strengthened by previous affective ties. (della Porta, 1988: 158)

Della Porta turned to her in-depth interviews to interpret this data.

Membership in the small legal political group was of great importance in their daily lives. Even where friendship ties external to the political milieu did exist, their importance tended to diminish as political socialization developed. In a spiraling series of interrelationships, as the amount of time a member spent in political activities increased, so did his contacts with political companions. At the same time, the strengthening of friendship ties inside the political environment increased the value attached to political involvement and encouraged people to dedicate more and more time to political activities. In this way, other ties lost their power to exert countervailing effects on the formation of the personality. (163)

This strong affective network implied that there was already a built-in solidarity and loyalty toward the group. This was carried forth during membership and helped maintain the group during adversity. This social network also became the main source of information about issues relevant to the member. It allowed for escalation toward terrorism, as violence on the street led to verbal escalation, with military metaphors replacing a discourse of grievance. These affective ties also prompted activists to make the transition from nonmilitant groups to the underground. Clandestine living involved danger and isolation, which intensified the social bonds of the members. This led to a spiral of further isolation from the outside world, the development of a collective identity, and total commitment to the group (della Porta, 1988, 1992a, 1992b).

Both the German and Italian cases independently demonstrate the importance of social bonds in joining a terrorist organization. In both cases, social bonds came first, and ideology followed.

Egyptian Islamic Groups

A third line of evidence supporting the importance of social bonds to joining the global Salafi jihad comes from independent research on the Egyptian Salafi militant organizations that were the forerunners of al Qaeda. Earlier, we looked at their ideology and their evolution. Here, I want to look at the process of recruitment.

Before the assassination of Egyptian President Anwar al-Sadat in 1981, Ibrahim (1980 and 1982) studied two Egyptian Islamic militant groups that had been heavily influenced by Qutb's ideas, the Islamic Liberation Organization (ILO) (the Technical Military Academy Group, see Chapter 2) and the Jamaat al-Muslimin (the Muslim Group, or MG, labeled by the press al-Takfir wa'l-Hijra, see Chapter 2). In terms of recruitment, Ibrahim stated that both movements recruited among students or recent university graduates. "Three recruitment mechanisms were employed: kinship, friendship, and worship." The ILO relied on friendship and worship. The MG relied heavily on kinship and friendship. Its leader, Shukri Mustafa, began with close friends from prison days and relatives, including his brother and a nephew. These in turn enlisted their close friends and relatives as members of the group (Ibrahim, 1980: 438).

The profile of the members was "young (early twenties), of rural or small-town background, from middle and lower middle class, with high achievement motivation, upwardly mobile, with science or engineering education, and from a normally cohesive family. . . . Most of those we investigated would be considered model young Egyptians" (Ibrahim, 1982: 11). Their mobility had distanced them from their original families or friends and, when they were socially isolated in a big university city, they found a family substitute in the MG. There was a progressive insulation from society at large and complete absorption and commitment to the new group. This total commitment was carried out with zeal and joy and included personal sacrifice for Islam. Ibrahim commented on the superior attractiveness of a religious revivalist organization over a secular political one, namely the strong sense of communion that Muslim groups

133

provided for their members. "The typical recruit is usually of recent rural background, a newcomer to a huge impersonal city. . . . The militant Islamic groups with their emphasis on brotherhood, mutual sharing, and spiritual support become the functional equivalent of the extended family to the youngster who has left his behind. In other words, the Islamic group fulfills a de-alienating function for its members in ways that are not matched by other rival political movements" (Ibrahim, 1980: 448). In this religious context, the interviewed militants viewed their prison sentences as an integral part of their struggle (jihad), as God's test of their faith and perseverance. "There was deep joy in defying society and its physical means of coercion. Several who claimed to have been severely tortured reported having images and dreams of prophets and saints welcoming them to the Garden of Eden, or images of the just Islamic society being established upon their martyrdom" (Ibrahim, 1982: 12).

The Tanzim al-Jihad, which carried out Sadat's assassination, was created by the 1980 merger of two clusters of Islamist groups: a Cairo branch, under Mohammed Abd al-Salam Faraj, and a Saidi (Upper Egypt) branch, under Karam Zuhdi. The composition of these groups was similar to that of the MG, and at first they were mistaken for the remnant of the MG. Their recruitment patterns were slightly different. Faraj used to deliver Friday sermons in a private mosque that had been built by his in-laws. During the ensuing discussions with his listeners, he managed to convince some to join in a clandestine organization to eventually wage violent jihad. They in turn introduced him to their friends and relatives, who became additional recruits. The Cairo branch was composed of five or six groups, loosely connected and each with its own amir (one of whom was Ayman al-Zawahiri). They had autonomy but met weekly to work out a general strategy. The Saidi branch was composed of several groups, based in provincial university towns. They recruited heavily according to kinship and tribal bonds, similar to the above MG recruitment pattern. While the Cairo branch was not organically linked to the population of the city, the Saidi branch was still embedded in its social context. This enabled the Saidi branch, but not the Cairo branch, to stage an uprising in Asyut in the aftermath of Sadat's assassination (Kepel, 1993).

Kinship bonds also played a large role in the motivation and composition of the four conspirators who killed Sadat. All evidence indicates that the plot originated as an unanticipated opportunity just a few days before the operation. It was first suggested by Khaled al-Islambuli, who was very upset that his brother Mohammed, a leader of the Saidi branch, had just been arrested. Al-Islambuli, a military officer, had just found out about his participation in the upcoming October Victory Parade before President Anwar al-Sadat. To round up the necessary conspirators, al-Islambuli brought a friend and kinsman from home, a retired army man. Faraj enlisted the support of two active duty soldiers: one was a childhood friend from home and the other was the brother-in-law of a close friend and senior member of the organization, who had recently been arrested. Anger at the arrests of their kinsmen figured prominently in the motivation of at least two of the conspirators (Ansari, 1984: 128; Guenena, 1986).

* * *

In this chapter, I have described the process of joining the jihad, rejecting the common notions of recruitment and brainwashing to account for the process. Instead, I argue for a three-prong process: social affiliation with the jihad accomplished through friendship, kinship, and discipleship; progressive intensification of beliefs and faith leading to acceptance of the global Salafi jihad ideology; and formal acceptance to the jihad through the encounter of a link to the jihad. Relative deprivation, religious predisposition, and ideological appeal are necessary but not sufficient to account for the decision to become a mujahed. Social bonds are the critical element in this process and precede ideological commitment. These bonds facilitate the process of joining the jihad through mutual emotional and social support, development of a common identity, and encouragement to adopt a new faith. All these factors are internal to the group. They are more important and relevant to the transformation of potential candidates into global mujahedin than postulated external factors, such as common hatred for an outside group. To an outsider, these invectives stand out. But for an insider, they are not what keeps the group together. As in all intimate relationships, this glue, in-group love, is found inside the group. It may be more accurate to blame global Salafi terrorist activity on in-group love than out-group hate.

FIVE

Social Networks and the Jihad

THE ACCOUNT of the global Salafi jihad provided so far tries to capture its empirical nature. It is not a specific organization, but a social movement consisting of a set of more or less formal organizations, linked in patterns of interaction ranging from the fairly
centralized (the East Africa embassy bombings) to the more decentralized (the two millennial plots) and with various degrees of cooperation
(the Egyptian Islamic Jihad versus the Egyptian Islamic Group), resulting in more or less connected terrorist operations. Participants in the
global jihad are not atomized individuals but actors linked to each other
through complex webs of direct or mediated exchanges. In this chapter,
I derive some practical insights from analyzing the data in light of social
network analysis.

Social Network Analysis

A group of people can be viewed as a network, a collection of nodes connected through links. Some nodes are more popular and are attached to
more links, connecting them to other more isolated nodes. These more
connected nodes, called hubs, are important components of a terrorist
network. A few highly connected hubs dominate the architecture of the
global Salafi jihad. The Central Staff, Core Arab, Maghreb Arab, and Southeast Asian are large clusters built around hubs: Osama bin Laden, Khalid
Sheikh Mohammed, Zein al-Abidin Mohamed Hussein (a.k.a. abu Zubay-

dah), and Abu Bakar Baasyir (a.k.a. Ustaz abu Somad), respectively. After 1996, the Central Staff was no longer directly involved in terrorist operations, but the other three major clusters were connected to their Central Staff contacts by their lieutenants in the field: Ramzi bin al-Shibh, Waleed Mohamed Tawfiq bin Attash (a.k.a. Khallad) and Abd al-Rahim al-Nashiri (a.k.a. Abul Bilal al-Makki) for the Core Arabs; Fateh Kamel then Amar Makhlulif (a.k.a. abu Doha) for the Maghreb Arabs; and Riduan Isamuddin (a.k.a. Hambali) and later Ali Ghufron (a.k.a. Mukhlas) for the Southeast Asians. Each of these field lieutenant hubs was then connected to the operational field commanders in charge of specific operations. For the Los Angeles airport millennial plot, Ressam assumed the command of his operation when the appointed field commander Fodail was unable to come to Canada. He reported to Makhlulif, who facilitated logistic support and kept al Qaeda aware of new developments. Atta, the operational commander for the 9/11 operations, reported to bin al-Shibh, who also facilitated logistic support in the field and kept the leadership apprised of new developments. For the Bali operation, Isamuddin was the link from the Central Staff that provided funding for the opera-

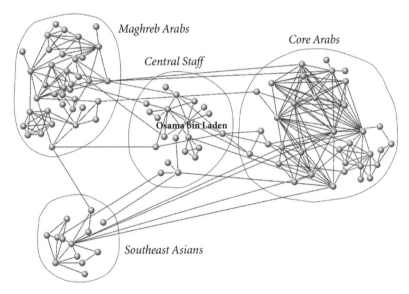

Figure 2. The Global Salafi Network

tion; Ali Ghufron was the field lieutenant; and Abdul Aziz (a.k.a. Imam Samudra) was the operational commander.

Network Characteristics
The Small-World Network

Terrorist networks are not static; they evolve over time. Fateh Kamel was the hub around which the network responsible for the millennial plot grew. He was originally from Algeria and immigrated to Canada in 1987. He obtained Canadian citizenship and frequented the Assuna Mosque in Montreal, where apparently everyone knew him. Under the cover of an international business, he traveled extensively on behalf of the jihad. He underwent training in an Afghan camp in the early 1990s and fought in Bosnia several times. In Canada, he set up a network of supporters for the Bosnian jihad with Mohamed Omary. Ressam, Labsi, and Boumezbeur became part of this network. During his eight trips to Bosnia, Kamel met Said Atmani, Abdullah Ouzghar, Christophe Caze, Lionel Dumont, and Safé Bourada. In Milan, he helped set up a logistic support network around the Islamic Cultural Institute. After the Dayton Accords, the Mujahedin Brigade in Bosnia was disbanded. Kamel invited Atmani and Ouzghar to Canada and suggested to Caze and Dumont that they set up their own logistic cells in Roubaix. In Canada, he sold his business to Haouari and resumed his worldwide organizing activities on behalf of the jihad. He sold stolen cars in Turkey and organized operations in Jordan, where he was arrested in 1999 and extradited to France for his role in the 1996 Roubaix violence. His phone number kept surfacing on captured mujahedin all over Europe.

Kamel was a typical hub, a charming and handsome man with a knack for making friends and acquaintances. Everyone in the Maghreb community of Montreal seems to have known him and his beautiful Canadian wife, who had converted to Islam. In network language, he was a hub with lots of links. The better known he became, the easier it was for newcomers to find him and the more people he met. Given his attractive personality, it became likely that new people sharing his beliefs connected with him. Through Kamel, the Maghreb Arab network grew.

In more formal language, growth of this network was not a random process but one of preferential attachment, meaning that the probability that a new node will connect to any given node is proportional to the number of its existing links. A network growing through this process of preferential attachment evolves into a "small-world" network structure, similar to that of traffic on the Internet, in which gigantic hubs like Google, Yahoo, and CNN receive far more hits than most other web sites. This approximates the structure of the two Arab clusters of the global Salafi jihad.

The structure of the Southeast Asian network is more hierarchical than that of the other parts of the global jihad. From the evidence, it appears that Abdullah Sungkar and Abu Bakar Baasyir intentionally created the Jemaah Islamiyah from above and structured it along hierarchical lines. At the top were the amir and the consultative council. The Jemaah Islamiyah was divided into four mantiqis or regions: Singapore and Malaysia; Indonesia; Sabah, Sulawesi, and the Southern Philippines; and Australia. Below the mantiqi were several wakalah (branches). The head of the branch was supported by a branch consultative council to which reported several staff units. One of these units was the operations unit, which further subdivided into operational cells of four to five people. Initiatives for the operations, as well as plans for their organization and execution, came from the top (see Ministry of Home Affairs, 2003; International Crisis Group, 2002b and 2003). The Jemaah Islamiyah in this sense is a fairly traditional terrorist organization in contrast to the rest of the global Salafi jihad.

Robustness of the Network

Small-world networks have interesting properties. Unlike a hierarchical network that can be eliminated through decapitation of its leadership, a small-world network resists fragmentation because of its dense interconnectivity. A significant fraction of nodes can be randomly removed without much impact on its integrity (Barabasi, 2003). Random attacks, such as stopping terrorists arbitrarily at our borders, will not affect the network's structure. These actions may stop individual terrorists from coming and operating here, but they will leave the network largely undisturbed. Where a small-world network is vulnerable to targeted attack is at its hubs. If enough hubs are destroyed, the network breaks down into isolated, noncommunicating islands of nodes. Were the jihad to sustain such damage, it would be incapable of mounting sophisticated large-scale operations like the 9/11 attacks and would be reduced to small attacks by singletons. It is possible for such nodes to try to spontaneously regenerate some semblance of a network around them to carry out operations. Ahmed Ressam tried to recruit new untrained collaborators in the millennial plot after his original coconspirators were unable to travel to the Canada. The evidence so far is that such short-term improvised operations have failed. But the survival of potential brokers to the jihad may in the longer term allow the rebuilding of a network on the site of an incompletely destroyed one.

Hubs in a social network are vulnerable because most communications go through them. By tracing messages through good police work, law enforcement authorities should be able to identify and arrest these human hubs. This strategy has already shown considerable success. The arrests of Baasyir, Isamuddin, and Ali Ghufron have seriously disrupted the Southeast Asian cluster. The arrests of Zain al-Abidin Hussein (abu Zubaydah), Fateh Kamel, and Amar Makhlulif (abu Doha) have broken up the Maghreb Arab cluster. Less is known about the structure of the Central Staff and Core Arab clusters. No doubt the arrests of Khalid Sheikh Mohammed and his nephew Abdul Basit Karim (Ramzi Yousef) and the death of Subhi Mohammed abu Sittah (Mohamed Atef) have significantly weakened it. But the survival of many central staffers, such as Osama bin Laden and his son Saad, Ayman al-Zawahiri, and Mohammed Makkawi (Sayf al-Adl) still makes the global jihad a potent threat. Future terrorist operations are most likely to come from the Core Arab cluster (more or less sponsored by the Central Staff) or from spontaneous local Maghreb Arab clusters under less direct control by the Central Staff but still under its inspiration.

The jihad is resilient to random arrests of its members but fragile in terms of targeted attacks on its hubs. Because of the network's ability to spontaneously grow and self-organize, attacks against the large hubs must be undertaken simultaneously to break up the network. Given that many hubs are linked to each other, degradation of the system into small unconnected islands of nodes often requires taking out as many as 5 to 15 percent of all hubs at once. Otherwise, with time, new hubs will take the role of the eliminated ones and restore the network's ability to function. The price of its robustness is its extreme exposure to targeted attacks.

In contrast, the Jemaah Islamiyah is not so robust and is vulnerable to conventional decapitation of its leadership. As the local cells are not used to operating on their own without specific orders from the top, the elimination of the leadership or even the intermediary will have strong effects on the organization as a whole. The 2002-2003 arrests of much of the Jemaah Islamiyah leadership, including its emir Baasyir and most of the mantiqi leaders, have seriously degraded its ability to conduct large-scale terrorist operations. As of late 2003, only the central technical bomb experts are still at large and in hiding, and it is unclear whether they can rebuild the network by themselves in the near future. The Jemaah Islamiyah, therefore, could be eradicated.

Geographical Distribution

One significant aspect of a small-world topology is its suggestion of a spontaneous process of self-organization rather than intentional construction from above. I have already mentioned the absence of a formal overall recruitment program in the global jihad, except perhaps for the Jemaah Islamiyah portion of it. This lack of a comprehensive recruitment drive left the global jihad at the mercy of self-recruits, establishing clusters of mujahedin who built upon preexisting linkages to the jihad. This "natural" growth of the jihad took place within particular social niches that were susceptible to its message. These niches included the expatriate and excluded Muslim communities in Europe, bored middle-class Arab youths, and more recently, local disenfranchised youths in the Maghreb.

The exact structure of the jihad is not randomly distributed within this niche. For instance, Abdel Ghani Meskini's efforts to join the jihad failed because he had no bridge to it. Living in Brooklyn, he asked his childhood friend Mokhtar Haouari, who lived in Montreal and had boasted about some connection to the jihad, to help him. Haouari was unable to do so until he met Ahmed Ressam, who promised to help (Adams, 2001). Potential mujahedin have a hard time joining the jihad if they do not know how to link up with the movement. The jihad must build on preexisting nodes. Locales where the jihad has already established a foothold thus disproportionately contribute to the jihad. For example, Montreal, London, Milan, Madrid, Hamburg, and the Saudi province of Asir have contributed heavily to the global jihad because of the presence of mujahedin who might act as brokers for potential members of the jihad. In contrast, similarly prominent cities like Berlin, Rome, Barcelona, and Paris have not harbored many mujahedin owing to the absence of such brokers there. The robustness of the network and the fuzziness of the boundary condition of what is a node make it difficult to completely eradicate the jihad once it has set root in a place. People who have not actively participated in the jihad may still help potential candidates establish new links to the jihad through their acquaintances among the mujahedin. I will say more later about the importance of these weak bonds. So, centers that have traditionally sent people to the jihad will continue to contribute new mujahedin unless they are severed from brokering connections to the jihad.

Salafi mosques in Brooklyn, Milan, London, Montreal, Madrid, Hamburg, Roubaix, and Khamis Mushayt in Saudi Arabia have produced large numbers of mujahedin in the past decade. Traditional institutional settings have been the locus of emergence of social movements, and the prominence of these mosques has to do with the fact that the global jihad is foremost a Muslim revivalist movement. Muslims engage in the jihad because they share certain norms, values, and worldviews. The creation and shaping of these social identities occur through a process of socialization at these mosques, under the guidance of a Salafi imam preaching the benefits of the global jihad. Social interactions at these mosques build and reinforce ideological commitment to a particularly salient cause and in the process foster a common sectarian identity. The mosques offer opportunities for people to meet new friends, foster the development of an ideological commitment to the jihad (which these ever-closer new friends further encourage), and provide links to the jihad through already-connected members.

Although a few Salafi mosques are sites of emergent terrorism, most fundamentalist mosques are not. Mosques are as apt to constrain as to facilitate the global jihad. Mosques are generally conservative institutions with a strong emphasis on the status quo, not on "propaganda by deed" or "outrage for God" (Ibrahim, 1980: 437), but on submission to God's will and realization of rewards in the afterlife. Salafi mujahedin reject the interpretations of the traditional Muslim clergy, whom they accuse of being "pulpit parrots" (434) in the pay of the state. The Salafi jihad flourished in private mosques, unregulated by the state, where their brand of Islam was the only acceptable one. Mosques, even fundamentalist ones,

143

are generally *not* supportive of the global jihad even if the imam and the congregation sympathize with some of the grievances motivating the jihad—presence of U.S. troops in the Arabian Peninsula, persecution of Palestinians, and former harsh sanctions against Iraqi children.

The prominence of certain Salafi mosques comes from the retrospective analysis of mujahedin trajectories. Their paths to the jihad started at specific mosques. It is important not to generalize from retrospective accounts, which cannot estimate prospective risks of a future event. For instance, if the great majority of serial killers are male, it does not mean that being male predisposes one to serial murder. The key issue here is not to condemn Muslim fundamentalism in general but to try to understand how the very few mosques that facilitate the global jihad do so. They are sites where a pro-jihad discourse takes place. Specifically, they provide a view of the world where Islam is in grave danger and the jihad is the only opportunity to fight this urgent threat. This grand narrative fosters the development of an Islamic collective identity. These mosques contain some brokers to the jihad, who may be the imam himself or another member of the congregation. Examples of such imams were Abu Bakar Baasyir, Sheikh Omar Abdel Rahman, Sheikh Anwar Shaban, and the notorious London preachers. There were quite a few in Saudi Arabia, as the Saudi government suspended one thousand individuals from preaching after the May 12, 2003, bombings in Riyadh.

The presence of the jihad in these places may be due to either chance or specific characteristics of the location. The evolution of Montreal, Milan, and Madrid as early contributors to the jihad was probably due to the chance migration of Fateh Kamel, Imad Eddin Barakat Yarkas (a.k.a. abu Dahdah), and Sheikh Anwar Shaban to these respective cities. These individuals' presence became a kernel around which the jihad grew. A few years later, only Yarkas was still in Madrid, but the other two sites continued to flourish as strongholds of the jihad despite the departures of their founders. In Montreal, Ressam tried to recruit new members after Kamel had been arrested in Jordan. In Milan, Abdel Qader Mahmoud Es Sayed, and Essid Sami ben Khemais built on the work of Shaban.

The rise of London as the main center of the jihad in Europe was probably due to its tolerant laws allowing for sanctuary and its large pool of potential mujahedin. It is close enough to Algeria to have attracted a large number of Algerian mujahedin fleeing persecution in their country after protesting the cancellation of the 1992 election. France no longer provided a sanctuary when the violence spilled over to its territory. The arrival of the Salafi preachers Omar Mahmoud Othman (a.k.a. abu Qatada) and Mustafa Kamel (a.k.a. abu Hamza al-Masri) attracted French people of Maghreb origins who were searching for a more militant form of Islam. London is also a center for world media, through which the teaching of these preachers is easily propagated to the Muslim world. The shift of the center of influence from Montreal to "Londonistan" was formally recognized with the arrival of Makhlulif (a.k.a. abu Doha) to take field command of that cluster. This shift shows the dynamic topology of the global jihad responding to a changing environment.

This distribution of the global jihad has implications for its ability to accomplish its mission. As its network depends on bottom-up self-selection in places where specific mosques and existing brokers are located, there are many areas where the global jihad has no presence. As long as its mission was to repel an invading infidel enemy or overthrow the "near enemy," a location adjacent to its target facilitated its mission. Having its headquarters in Peshawar was quite convenient during the Afghan-Soviet war. Likewise, being in the Sudan assisted its mission against Egypt. The move back to Afghanistan, however, seriously hampered Egyptian operations.

The distribution of the global Salafi jihad assets seriously affects its mission against the United States "far enemy." The self-organizing evolution of the jihad, contingent on random encounters with local hubs or availability of bridges to the jihad, leaves large gaps in its geographical coverage. The absence of proselytism and recruitment program kept its profile low enough (despite its size) to avoid raising the alarm in the U.S. government. At this juncture, the global jihad's main weakness is the inability of most of the mujahedin to get close to its preferred target, the United States. Specifically, it does not have a large pool of members able to operate clandestinely in the United States, and thus is limited in its ability to wage war on U.S. soil. Its only effort to remedy this weakness was to identify the few trainees already in Afghan training camps who could enter the United States with valid travel documents and operate there without raising suspicion (Mascolo and Stark, 2003). I found no evidence of any comprehensive recruitment drive in the United States.

The lack of a recruitment program prevented the global Salafi jihad from developing native U.S. assets upon which it could build its operations on American soil. This gap in coverage could be filled with temporary foreign visitors who were able to blend into American society and operate on American soil. As long as the U.S. authorities did not take this danger seriously, this was a viable strategy. After the success of the 9/11 operations, however, increased vigilance made it more difficult for global mujahedin to get a visa to the U.S. or, if already in place, to operate without raising suspicion. Most global mujahedin are from Muslim countries, physically distinguishable and requiring a visa to come to the U.S. I am surprised that the jihad has not used people from Indonesia or the Philippines to conduct operations in the United States. European converts to the global jihad might also be a potential pool of global mujahedin operating here, but I suspect that most are known to European intelligence services that might have alerted the U.S. authorities. Muslims born in the United States who might be attracted to the global jihad against enemies of the umma in the periphery of the Muslim world, may hesitate to perpetrate large terrorist operations against their own country. The Lackawanna Six might have volunteered to drive the Russians out of Chechnya, but there is no indication that they were ready to strike at their own country. On the contrary, they may have been surprised and repelled by the anti-American messages at the training camps in Afghanistan (Purdy and Bergman, 2003).

Embeddedness

The term embeddedness refers to the rich nexus of social and economic linkages between members of an organization and its environment. Being embedded in society encourages trust in ongoing interactions (Granovetter, 1985). It makes people sensitive to local criticism. If grievances are aired, they are anchored in concerns that are close to home. Being embedded in a segment of society promotes local collective behavior on behalf of this segment. Social bonds also imply some sort of sensitivity and responsiveness to maintain them. The lack of such bonds frees people from these responsibilities and local concerns. In Chapter 3, I argued that prior to joining the global jihad, future mujahedin were socially alienated, or temporarily disembedded, from their societies of origin. Here, I will argue that this absence of connection is a necessary condition for a network of people to join the global jihad by contrasting the two rival Egyptian Salafi jihadist organizations: the Egyptian Islamic Jihad (EIJ), which embraced the global jihad, and the Egyptian Islamic Group (EIG), which rejected it.

In Chapter 4, I showed that the EIG originated in the Islamic groups of upwardly mobile students in provincial university cities of the Said. Although they had moved out of their original homes, they did not go far and maintained their tribal, kinship, and friendship ties. Corruption, lack of meaningful employment, and disillusionment with secular socialist nationalism led them to militant Salafi Islam. Although their strategy for instituting the Islamist state was a mass uprising modeled on the Iranian Revolution, their immediate concerns were still local, especially the apparent prominence of the Copts. Up to the Asyut uprising shortly after the assassination of President Sadat, violent outbursts against Copts dominated their illegal activities. The Asyut uprising, which lasted several days, was possible because the Saidis were embedded in the social fabric of their society, and got help from their tribes and friends to carry out the uprising.

The EIJ, which had its origins in Cairo and later Alexandria, was composed of students, professionals, and government officials (leaders) and the urban poor coming to worship at private Salafi mosques (the rank and file). They were mostly young people who had migrated to the large, impersonal cities where they lacked strong social bonds. They advocated a military coup that, they hoped, would trigger a popular uprising. After the assassination of President Sadat, the Egyptian government threw the whole bunch into prison, but was rather lenient in the ensuing trial. Only the four direct perpetrators and Faraj, the leader of the Cairene branch, were condemned to death. In prison, sharp lines of rivalry surfaced between the Cairenes, who later became the EIJ, and the Saidis, who later formed the EIG. Since most of the Tanzim al-Jihad leadership was Saidi, they got longer prison sentences than the middle-rank members, who were discharged after three years. Most of these Islamist militants fled to Pakistan and Afghanistan when official persecution continued after their release.

Exile distanced both sets of expatriates from their original social bonds and further disembedded them from their original society. The Cairenes

147

lost any remnant of social connection with the distance, as they had not grown roots in the cities. They reconstituted themselves in Peshawar as the EIJ, with very loose ties to their nominal imprisoned leader, Abud al-Zumur. The real power seems to have been Ayman al-Zawahiri, whose leadership style was autocratic. The complete break with al-Zumur occurred around 1991 after al-Zawahiri grabbed the reins of power in the EIJ. At this point, the EIJ became a free-floating network without any real ties to its original society or to its surrounding society. It welcomed other urban expatriates as new members, and similarly disembedded Alexandrians flocked to its ranks.

The Saidis also reconstituted themselves in Peshawar as the EIG, but with strong ties to the imprisoned collective leadership (the *shura*) and their mufti. They retained some remnants of the social bonds to their society of origin despite their distance and were able to muster a strong following in the Said. The distance created a gap, however, between the imprisoned and expatriate leaders of the EIG. The imprisoned leaders in Egypt maintained their closeness to the Said. While in prison they married relatives of other members and even fathered children. They received frequent visits from family and friends. The expatriates were farther from their roots and closer to other exiled militants. As such, they got to know these other militant Salafi exiles and toyed with their ideas, strategy, and tactics. From neighboring Sudan, the EIG launched a wave of violence on Egyptian society and tourism in the first half of the 1990s, culminating in the attempt on the life of President Mubarak in Addis Ababa. The effect of this wave of violence on Egyptian society was the opposite of what they intended. Instead of further polarizing society in preparation for a mass mobilization and uprising, it alienated the Egyptian masses from the EIG. Recognizing the failure of their strategy of violence because of their embeddedness in this society, the imprisoned EIG shura initiated a ceasefire in 1997 to restore its closeness with the Saidi population. The expatriate leadership at first rejected this new initiative and even tried to force the hand of the imprisoned leader with the 1997 Luxor massacre, killing about sixty people. After their mufti endorsed the initiative, however, the expatriate leaders closed ranks with their imprisoned colleagues and even resigned from the shura to leave room for proponents of this new strategy.

In contrast, no strong bonds bound the EIJ leadership—all exiles—to

the Egyptian population. Nor was their strategy dependent on mass mobilization. Therefore, it was detached from the demands of its presumed
constituency and free to pursue any strategy dictated by its ideology. The
EIJ was more representative of the rest of the global Salafi jihad. The Sudanese exile played a crucial role in the evolution of the global jihad ideology. The assembled mujahedin, who were from various countries and
backgrounds, had lost their common enemy when the Soviets withdrew
from Afghanistan in 1989 and its puppet regime collapsed in 1992. They
were on the brink of separation and breaking up into smaller local jihads,
albeit under the umbrella of a loose supporting organization, al Qaeda.
A great deal of discussion during the Sudanese exile concerned what to
do next. Mamdouh Mahmud Salim from Iraq and Osama bin Laden from
Saudi Arabia, both of whom had lost their attachments to their respective countries, were the strongest advocates for the shift to a global jihad
(al-Fadl, 2001). The creation of a common enemy, the U.S. "far enemy"—
the "head of the snake"—redefined the jihad and revitalized al Qaeda.
Such a shift to a new mission helps prolong the existence of an organization that has accomplished its goal.

The progressive loss of bonds to society transformed the jihad into a
truly global movement, based on virtual bonds to abstractions such as
God and the umma. Although the network as a whole was disembedded
from an earthly constituency, its members, or nodes, were more tightly
linked with each other as they abandoned their bonds to the outside world.
They became members of an "imagined community," not on the basis of
a nation (a challenge to Anderson, 1991) but on a "virtual," sectarian basis. Their operations did not have to be responsive to any earthly constituency and were unrestrained by social bonds found in embedded networks.

This ideal virtual community has strong appeal to alienated youths ex-
patriated in the West, bored youths without any economic or social
prospects in Core Arab countries, and disenfranchised youths without
much hope in Maghreb Arab countries. Many responded to the mass appeal of the call of "Islam in danger" during the U.S. invasions of Afghanistan
in 2001 and Iraq in 2003. This was a spontaneous mass mobilization of
youths to defend Islam, as opposed to a more organized and formal joining of the global jihad. But the virtual character of their motivation became quite apparent once these individuals were in place. Their insular-

ity from the local population and their naïve attraction to the ideal of a virtual jihad blinded them to the reality of the situation. The local population in both instances rejected their self-sacrifice and at times turned on them. Afghan forces from the Northern Alliance and even the Taliban murdered these expatriates or held them for ransom (Abdallah et al., 2002). Iraqi forces left the virtual recruits on the front line to confront U.S. troops (while they melted away into their own societies), and the local population betrayed them (Stalinsky, 2003). Their travails make for somber and sober reading. Because of their inability to connect with the formal jihad movement, they simply became cannon fodder in the cynical posturing of the leaders of the Taliban, Iraqi government, and global jihad to discourage U.S. intervention. Their experience illustrates the fact that being part of a pool of potential mujahedin does not automatically translate into formal participation in the global jihad.

In this section, I have argued that the lack of embeddedness of the networks in any society allowed dramatic shifts in the ideological focus of the jihad movement in response to changing social conditions. The mujahedin's need to stay united and the difficulty of carrying out operations in their respective countries led them to choose a common and more available target, the U.S. "far enemy." They also assumed that this target would be easier to attack owing to its previous weak responses to provocations. Unrestrained by responsibility to any society, this free-floating network was free to follow the logic of its abstract ideology and escalate the scale of terror, culminating in the 9/11 operations. There is evidence that the strong U.S. government response to this qualitatively unprecedented terror attack took them by surprise.

Ironically, this section returned to the now discarded 1950s theories that radical mass protests originated among groups that were atomized, disorganized, deviant, and disoriented (Adorno et al., 1950; and Arendt, 1958). The empirical literature on social protest movements from the past three decades has discredited these arguments. On the contrary, this research project has indicated that mobilization in protest movements was facilitated by embeddedness in networks of friends already involved and in established social settings destined for later involvement (Diani and McAdam, 2003). At first, this appears to contradict my argument. But this view does not take into account the temporal dimension of that argument. Attraction to a violent abstract global movement based on virtual ties to a virtual community is more likely among socially alienated young men because of their lack of embeddedness in their ambient society. At this stage, this supports Arendt's argument of atomization as the precondition for destructive mass movements. It is precisely this *temporary* loss of embeddedness that makes them vulnerable to drift to specific Salafi mosques and become embedded within the nexus of bonds there. At this next stage, my arguments about the importance of social bonds and established social settings are consistent with the empirical evidence of social protest movement studies. They become embedded in a socially disembedded network, which, precisely because of its lack of any anchor to any society, is free to follow abstract and apocalyptic notions of a global war between good and evil.

Nature of the Nodes
Fuzzy Boundaries

The global Salafi jihad has a very fuzzy boundary. The indistinctness of this boundary raises some epistemological issues on a group and individual level: what represents a node, a link, or a network. The jihad is a dynamic social movement that forms and breaks bonds to various Salafi terrorist groups. The nature of this bond may be financial support, logistical support, or common planning for operations. Some of the links have been permanent, such as al Qaeda's relationship with the EIJ and Jemaah Islamiyah. Others have waxed and waned. For instance, after an initial period of enthusiasm, al Qaeda seems to have disavowed its links to the Abu Sayyaf Group in the Philippines when it degenerated into banditry. Likewise, al Qaeda strongly supported the Algerian Groupe Islamique Armé, but let this link fade when the group started to commit widespread atrocities against the civilian population. Al Qaeda switched its support to the breakaway Groupe Salafiste pour la Prédication et le Combat instead. Al-Tawhid, headed by Ahmed al-Kalaylah (abu Musab al-Zarqawi), may not be formally connected to al Qaeda, probably because of personal rivalries. Because it conducts terrorist operations against Western targets in Europe and the Middle East, it is nonetheless solidly part of the global jihad.

On an individual level, membership in the jihad may be difficult to assess at the boundary. For instance, Ahmed Ressam invited Abdel Ghani

151

Meskini to become an important part of the millennial plot before the two ever met. Meskini accepted, but he had no knowledge of what would be asked of him. When he failed to connect with Ressam in Seattle, he returned to Brooklyn and tried to fade away (Adams, 2001). Although he was never formally inducted into the jihad and his only contacts with it were his long-distance friendship bond with Haouari and the few vague phone conversations with Ressam, Meskini must be considered part of the global jihad because of his willingness to carry out an undisclosed terrorist attack against the West. His was clearly an operational link. Other individuals that had stronger links with the jihad and underwent formal terrorist training in Afghanistan chose to disappear from the jihad without any intent to carry out terrorist operations. For example, the Lackawanna Six are not considered part of the global jihad because of their lack of intent. They were offered an operational link but chose to decline it. More ambiguous cases are people in the networks of the Maghreb Arab cluster in Canada and Europe who were supporting themselves and the jihad through small-scale crimes. Were they true mujahedin or just petty criminals? Juries in Detroit and the Netherlands have made this distinction and exonerated them from involvement in the jihad. Other ambiguous cases are financial contributors to Islamic charities, who suspect but do not really know whether the charities also support terrorist operations.

Cliques

Previously, I have shown that people joined the jihad in small groups. Several individuals lived together for a while and had intense discussions about the jihad. When one of the friends was able to find a bridge to the jihad, they often went as a group to train in Afghanistan. Examples abound in my sample: the Montreal group, the Hamburg group, the Khamis Mushayt group, the Lackawanna group. These are dense, small networks of friends who can vouch for each other. In network terminology, they form cliques. In a clique, every node is connected to every other one.

Cliques are often built on human similarities. Friendships reflect common background, education, and beliefs, but the dense networks that members of a clique form are local and based on face-to-face encounters, attraction, and development of long-term bonds. They are not global. Although a common profile can be drawn within a certain clique, it does not generalize to a social movement as a whole. For a movement like the global Salafi jihad, there are as many valid profiles as there are cliques of similar friends. Even a relatively small network carrying out common operations may be composed of a number of cliques, each with its own distinctive profile. For instance, the French Maghreb Arabs who conducted four simultaneous operations in Morocco in August 1994 included at least three cliques. The close friends and relatives who grew up together in adjacent blocks in Orleans, France, were from middle-class, well integrated backgrounds and were university educated. The close friends from La Courneuve were also raised together, but in poverty with little education and were excluded from the formal integrated French economy. The nascent group in Besançon all came from the Faculty of Pharmacy of that city. Despite their different profiles, members of separate cliques were mixed into commandos executing the 1994 attempts (Erhel and La Baume, 1997). This shows the difficulty of generating a common profile of a global Salafi mujahed.

Over time and space, cliques of friends may respond to various systematic sociopolitical appeals, according to world events occurring at the time and in the vicinity. The group who answered Azzam's appeal and went to Afghanistan during the Soviet-Afghan war looks different as a whole from later waves of mujahedin. Likewise, the Maghreb Arab cliques were especially sensitive to events that occurred in Algeria and Morocco in the 1990s. Cliques forming both large Arab clusters were also quite moved by the events in Bosnia and Chechnya in the 1990s. The Jemaah Islamiyah responded to events in Indonesia and the Philippines. But even within these large clusters, cliques provide different profiles. The Saudis involved in the 1995 Riyadh Saudi National Guard training center bombing came from a relatively poor background and had only elementary education. On the other hand, some of the Saudi cliques involved in the 9/11 operations came from the economic and social elite of the country. As cliques become connected to the jihad partly by chance, there can be no overall profile for global Salafi mujahedin, only local profiles.

Cliques play a crucial role in transforming potential contributors into full-fledged mujahedin. Revivalist religious movements, like any large-scale social movements, suffer from Mancur Olson's free-rider paradox. Translated to al Qaeda's case, this argument states that even if terrorism is a rational strategy for the group as a whole, it is not so for each of its members (Olson, 1971). Each would be better off stepping aside and allowing other members bear the necessary costs involved with these activities. If the group succeeds, each member would enjoy the benefits at no cost. A terrorist organization aiming to change society for the good of all is vulnerable to the possibility that each of its members will take a free ride. The free-rider paradox suggests that participation in terrorism may not be based on utilitarian calculations.

Game theorists have tried to rehabilitate the rationalist approach. They acknowledge that people's behavior does not occur in a vacuum, but takes into account other people's behavior. Game theorists show very elegantly that under conditions with a prospect of future interactions, the best strategy for an individual is tit-for-tat cooperation with others. Friends are presumed to join the jihad because of the veiled threat of withdrawal of friendship in case a friend does not join. This is not a convincing argument, however, for two reasons. First, the presumed threat of withdrawal of friendship is simply not credible unless the relationship means very little to the one doing the threatening. Second, and more devastating in this case, suicide undermines the assumption of future interactions. Tit-for-tat modeling shows that if the end of a game is known, the most rational strategy is to defect just before the other does, and take the resulting benefits. Suicide, therefore, seems to undermine the rationalist approach.

Cliques solve this rationalist paradox. They are the social mechanism that puts pressure on prospective participants to join, defines a certain social reality for the ever more intimate friends, and facilitates the development of a shared collective social identity and strong emotional feelings for the in-group. This process, which takes time and intense face-to-face interaction, is not well studied empirically because it would involve long-term observation of groups of friends, as opposed to short-term observations of strangers in psychological laboratories. Cliques literally transform lives and, in doing so, change the meaning and impact of friendship bonds that pave the way to joining the jihad. Selected events that might otherwise be largely independent and disconnected are linked through symbolic means that stress continuity and form a unified worldview. For instance, clique members lump together events such as the U.S. presence in Saudi Arabia and Somalia, cancellation of the election in Algeria in

1992, Serb and Russian invasions of Bosnia and Chechnya, respectively, sanctions imposed on Iraq, discrimination against Palestinians, Christian aggression in Indonesia, and expansion of central government power to Mindanao. They weave a grand narrative that Islam is in danger, implying a common fate that builds a collective identity.

Social or religious activism is born in cliques and changes the value of friendship. Participation in causes transforms the activists' sense of themselves and their relationship with others (Gould, 2003). The horrors of its terrorist operations mask a general fact about the global Salafi jihad, namely that it demands a sacrifice, and often the ultimate sacrifice for the cause. Although outsiders focus on the terrorists' willingness to kill, the insiders focus on their willingness to die. Becoming martyrs, shahidi or witnesses for God, not killers, is what they strive for. Their awareness of their own readiness to transcend their self-interest fosters a special view of themselves and others like them. Ironically, it may be tied to the fact that the jihad is susceptible to Olson's free-rider paradox and the temptation to reap its benefits without actually participating. This flight from egoism symbolized by their conscious rejection of this free ride injects a semblance of virtue into the way they view themselves and their friends who have chosen the same path. Friendships cultivated in the jihad, just as those forged in combat in general, seem more intense and are endowed with special significance. Their actions taken on behalf of God and the umma are experienced as sacred. This added element increases the value of friendships within the clique and the jihad in general and diminishes the value of outside friendships.

To friends hovering on the brink of joining an increasingly activist clique, this promised shift in value may be difficult to resist, especially if one is temporarily alienated from society. This happens progressively and imperceptibly over a period of time. People may not be aware that they are being drawn into the clique. But once they become members, strong bonds of loyalty and emotional intimacy discourage their departure. This process is rarely a fully conscious one, as cliques do not start out as terrorist groups. They evolve in that direction as their mutual relationships deepen, in a spiral of greater loyalty, mutual devotion, self-sacrifice, and intimacy. The best descriptions of this progressive but ultimately intense process are the three independent participant observations of Sun Myung Moon's Unification Church (Barker, 1984; Galanter, 1989; Lofland, 1981).

Friends may join an activated clique not only to contribute to the cause but also to enhance the nature of their friendship. In some cases, such intense emotional feelings may compete with and even be stronger than those of love. At Motassadeq's trial Ayel Senguen testified about her progressive loss of her fiancé and later husband Ziad Jarrah's love to the Hamburg clique (Laabs and McDermott, 2003). Ziad Jarrah piloted the airplane that crashed in Pennsylvania on September 11, 2001. The loss of love to this type of friendship shows the strength of this transformed bond. In many ways such positive emotions may motivate human beings to carry out horrific acts more easily than negative emotions do. People are willing to kill in defense of their families, friends, and countries. Fewer are willing to do so out of hate. Despite the popular accounts of the 9/11 perpetrators in the press, in-group love rather than out-group hate seems a better explanation for their behavior.

The same transformation of friendship that explains the progressive intensification of in-group bonds may explain the weakening of out-group ties so often seen in cliques and in the jihad. An out-group friend who rejects an opportunity to join the clique does not just refuse to sign up for the jihad. He also refuses to become what the mujahed has become: a violent militant with a deep commitment to God and the Salafi interpretation of the Quran, who strives for the establishment of an Islamist state and is eager to become a martyr. This account of the transformation of the nature of friendship brings us back to the rationalist argument, for now the implicit withdrawal of friendship becomes a credible threat. A refusal to join leads to emotional distancing. In this case, spurning a former friendship is less costly than was the case before the commitments diverged. It will hurt the activated clique member less than it will hurt the out-group friend because the in-group member is likely to replace this friendship with stronger ones.

Such intense relationships are bound to strongly affect one's sense of identity. This leads to the development of a social identity, in which the feeling of belonging to the global jihad can be grafted on to the sense of belonging to the now religiously and politically activated clique. The clique becomes closed in on itself and operates like a subculture or counterculture, leading to intense cohesion in both emotional ties to the group and cognitive view of the world. This transformation was clear in the Hamburg group and especially noted at Bahaji's wedding when family guests, who were not part of the clique and knew some of the members prior to their joining the clique, were shocked by the in-group members' utterances and behavior.

Dense networks like cliques commonly produce social cohesion and a collective identity and foster solidarity, trust, community, political inclusion, identity-formation, and other valuable social outcomes. Dense social networks foster intense face-to-face interactions in which collective identities are formed. The "bunch of guys" phenomenon noted in the wiretaps of the Hamburg, Milan, and Montreal apartments illustrated the conversations that shaped the social life of clique members by altering individual and collective perspectives, transforming social ties, collectively processing events and generating specific meanings and interpretations, and forging commitments to the clique and the jihad. This process of transformation from an alienated individual to a committed activist is commonly seen in religious sects and terrorist groups and requires investment in intense lengthy face-to-face interactions. This implies that the fear that vulnerable young Muslims may be recruited to the jihad through Internet messages is overblown. Reading and sending messages about the jihad on the Internet may make these individuals receptive to its appeal, but direct involvement requires face-to-face interaction.

This intense collective identification furthers both commitment to the clique and the integrity and cohesion of the jihad. This cohesion also leads to group conformity in terms of behavior, attitudes, and appearance. Salafists grow their beards and commonly dress in Afghan, Pakistani, or traditional Arabic outfits. Lack of conformity may also lead to intolerance of and sometimes punitive actions against persons not conforming to clique norms and rules. These two elements of authoritarianism—in-group conformity and out-group aggressiveness—may be a product of the intensity of activated clique cohesion, a group phenomenon rather than a dimension of some "authoritarian" personality (Duckitt, 1989).

Let me end this section with a note of caution. I have considered only cliques that further of the goals of the jihad; they may also hinder it. It may be that the clique is united in its desire to join the jihad and that its members travel to Afghanistan, where they are faced with specific statements and demands that they had not anticipated. Individually, they may suffer silently and perhaps succumb to the new vision and demands. But as a group their friends may support them in their resistance to the new

157

ideology and demands. The clique may then be a strong factor in resisting the official ideology and official jihad demands. This may be exactly what happened to the Lackawanna Six, who went as a group to Afghanistan. They gained strength from each other and were able to resist anti-U.S. propaganda, which conflicted with their personal experience of life in the United States. Future research may explore the factors delineating the circumstances under which a clique facilitates or hinders involvement in a social movement.

Nature of the Links

Social networks are complex communicative networks that create shared worlds of meaning and feelings, which in turn shape identity, perceptions, and preferences. In this section, I will examine the impact of dramatic changes in communication and information technology, of network topology on flexibility and performance, and of connected acquaintances on the global Salafi jihad.

New Communication Technology

Traditionally, religious terrorism has been based on face-to-face interactions. These are still necessary for the growth of religious terrorist movements, for the transformation from an outsider to a dedicated insider requires intense intimate exchanges. Once established, however, a terrorist organization may not require such intensity as long as regular two-way communication reinforces the member's dedication with emotional support and general guidance. Older communication technologies did not allow for such interactions, and the more isolated the fanatic, the more likely it was that his fanaticism would fade. Enthusiasm for one's task is difficult to preserve in a vacuum. The revolution in communication technology in the 1990s has dramatically changed this situation.

This revolution coincided with the rise of the global Salafi jihad. When al Qaeda was created on the border of Afghanistan and Pakistan around 1990, its members complained about isolation from their respective countries. Moving to the Sudan brought them closer to their theaters of operations (al-Fadl, 2001). During the Sudanese exile, rapid changes in communication technology spread around the world. The global Salafi jihad was quick to grasp its possibilities. Osama bin Laden bought a new satellite telephone during that time. Al Qaeda operatives started to use laptop computers to store information and send e-mail to each other. Fax transmission was used to release communiqués in London sent from undisclosed sites. Dedicated web sites informed mujahedin and their supporters of new developments in the jihad. By the time the Central Staff of the jihad returned to Afghanistan in 1996, it was fully integrated into the new global network of communication, which in turn made the global jihad possible. Indeed, this was the main difference between the first Afghan phase of the jihad, when global aims were not yet possible, and the second Afghan phase, when technological advances made it possible to contemplate a global strategy. This new technology enabled a global jihad based on a loose, decentralized network of mujahedin transcending the limitations of face-to-face interaction. After the return to Afghanistan, al Qaeda's Central Staff was able to oversee a truly global jihad through the use of satellite telephone, e-mail, fax, and web sites. Its geographical isolation became a source of strength, for it provided a sanctuary and protected the staff from effective retaliation by the West.

Computers have been ubiquitous among the global Salafi mujahedin. The computer captured in Manila in January 1995 belonged to Abdul Basit Karim and provided the outline of the ambitious Bojinka Plot. Data from the hard drives of computers captured in Europe, Asia, Africa, and the Middle East provide a significant portion of what we know about the global Salafi jihad. Yosri Fouda's portrait of Ramzi bin al-Shibh sitting on the floor of a Karachi safe house, surrounded by three laptops and five mobile phones, underscores the importance of this technology to the jihad (Fouda and Fielding, 2003: 36). It allowed bin al-Shibh and his boss Khalid Sheikh Mohammed to support and direct their subordinates scattered around the world. E-mail was routine among the members of the Hamburg clique and helped them sustain emotional closeness and common beliefs despite physical separation by communicating shared meanings, past events, and internal jokes. In the past, letters fulfilled the same function. Through its speed of expression and response, e-mail goes a step further by reducing time spent waiting for the intimate partner's reply.

And yet, too great a reliance on this new technology leaves the jihad vulnerable to sophisticated monitoring of communication and triangulation of its source. Intercepts of cellular telephone calls have figured prominently in the capture of major leaders of the global jihad. When bin Laden found out that his satellite phone conversations were being intercepted, he stopped using this technology. Until the 2001 U.S. offensive denied him the open sanctuary of Afghanistan, his subordinates were able to fill this direct gap and maintain communications with global mujahedin scattered worldwide. Now his reluctance to use this form of communication has greatly hampered his effectiveness as a leader. Documents found in computers have also played a major role in the conviction of terrorists, as in the trials of Abdul Basit Karim and the East Africa embassy bombings defendants in New York and Abdul Aziz (a.k.a. Imam Samudra) in Indonesia.

The new advances in communication technology increase the organization's vulnerability. As use of satellite phones and the like becomes difficult because of monitoring, communications with Central Staff break down and the global jihad may revert to plotting local operations without much support from the staff. The amateurism of the May 16, 2003, Casablanca bombings (when bombers got lost on their way to the targets) may indicate the new state of the global jihad, stripped of much of its communication capability.

Impact of the Internet

The Internet has also dramatically affected the global jihad by making possible a new type of relationship between an individual and a virtual community. Slightly older technology had already shown its potential to effect religious and political changes in Iran, where the dissemination of cheaply replicated audiocassettes brought Ayatollah Khomeini's message to the masses. Videocassettes brought the wars in Bosnia and the horrors of Algeria to Muslim living rooms in Europe. They spread the myth and promise of the jihad to alienated young Muslims in search of a mission. They glamorized military training in Afghanistan and advocated it as a requirement for becoming a good Muslim. The regular appearance and humble demeanor of Osama bin Laden in these videotapes also increased his appeal to young Muslims as a model to emulate, transcending their lack of opportunities and expectations. Videocassettes of popular Salafi preachers, like Omar Mahmoud Othman (a.k.a. abu Qatada), have been commonly found in apartments of arrested mujahedin. This diffusion of the Salafi message bypassed local imams, who are in general far more con-servative and do not approve of the jihad by violent means.

The Internet creates a seemingly concrete bond between the individ-ual and a virtual Muslim community. This virtual community plays the same role that "imagined communities" played in the development of the feeling of nationalism, which made people love and die for their nations as well as hate and kill for them (Anderson, 1991). Because of its virtual nature, the Internet community has no earthly counterpart and becomes idealized in the mind of surfers. This community is just, egalitarian, full of opportunity, unified in an Islam purged of national peculiarities, and devoid of corruption, exploitation, and persecution. The appeal of this approximation of paradise can become irresistible, especially to alienat-ed young Muslims and potential converts suffering from isolation or from ordinary discrimination. The immediate responsiveness of Muslim chat rooms and the relevance of the messages bring concreteness and reality to this virtual community. Without the restraints from real interactions with the social world, this virtual world allows extreme violence against the presumed conspirators against the virtual umma.

The nature of this relationship between individuals and the Internet favors the Salafi message. The Internet both appeals to and fosters dis-embeddedness. On the one hand, it appeals to isolated individuals by eas-ing their loneliness through connections to people sharing some com-monality. On the other hand, it leads them to spend more time with this virtual community at the expense of interaction with the immediate so-cial environment. This encourages a global outlook. The virtual com-munity is no longer tied to any nation, a condition that corresponds to the mythical umma of Salafism, which specifically rejects nationalism and fosters the global Salafi jihad priority of fighting against the "far enemy" rather than the "near enemy." Disembedded from any territory, the vague establishment of an Islamist state must necessarily come into conflict with the only remaining political, economic, cultural, and military superpow-er—the United States. This reduces the project of the umma to a global Manichean fight with the United States in all these arenas for hegemony of the world, a true clash of civilizations.

Communications on Internet chat rooms are egalitarian, recognizing no authority except the texts of the Quran and hadith. Arguments that would appeal to all, regardless of their theological educational background, are bound to be direct and simple. These simplified positions negate the sophistication of fourteen centuries of commentaries on the Quran, which often include past responses to difficulties in applying its teaching to contemporary problems. Again, this plays into the argument of Salafists, who advocate a return to the practices of the salaf and reject any innovations as Western corruption of God's message. In this great contest for the soul of Muslim Internet surfers, the elegant simplicity and clarity of militant Salafism has no real competition from more traditional (and too complicated) Islamic tradition. The mass nature of Internet communication encourages sound bites and other reductionist answers to difficult questions. Drawn to their logical conclusion, these views encourage extreme, abstract, but simplistic solutions, without regard to the reality and complexity of life. The universal availability of these chat rooms tends to reduce the level of discourse to the lowest common denominator of the group. As most potential recruits to the jihad are not Islamic scholars, they are attracted by these simplistic views. At the same time, they believe that they have acquired enough Islamic knowledge to guide important life decisions without having recourse to more traditional scholars. Indeed, Salafists dominate Muslim Internet sites, most of which are created by Muslims who are living in the West, predominantly in the Anglo-Saxon world, and who have immigrated, converted, or are temporarily studying there (Roy, 2002: 165-183). Traditional Islamic schools tend not to sponsor web sites or encourage participation in chat rooms.

Use of the Internet has certain requirements. First, users need to have access to it, which implies some familiarity with a computer in the past. Although they might have had such access in school in a modern education program, most had possessed one of their own. To be able to afford even a used computer with access to the Internet, they could not have come from the poorest social class in the developing world. The impoverished Afghans studying in madrassas on the Afghan-Pakistani border simply could not be connected to the global jihad. Of course, once familiar with their use, the mujahedin can easily go to an Internet café equipped with computers. The anonymity of these places protects the identity of the user, and their proliferation enables communication even in the developing world. The use of the Internet also implies a modern education that relies on computers rather than traditional Islamic studies. Indeed, most mujahedin have a higher technical education rather than a classical one. Finally, they need to have a common language to be able to discuss things and exchange information. The most common language on the Internet is English. Clique members may communicate with one another in their common language; the Hamburg clique exchanged e-mail in German. But for communication with the jihad outside the clique, English or Arabic is most common.

The Internet can help bridge the gap from the isolated potential mujahed to the global jihad. An interested person could find out the address of mosques and some organizations that might eventually make such links to the jihad after an appropriate process of vetting the candidate. However, the Internet does not provide a means to contact the jihad directly nor does it allow the organization to assess the reliability of a potential candidate. There is no friend or kin to vouch for him, and his commitment is uncertain. For the type of allegiance that the jihad demands, there is no evidence that the Internet is persuasive enough by itself. So far, none of the people in the sample joined the jihad solely on the basis of what they had read on the Internet. Many were sensitized to Muslim issues on the Internet and developed a sense of collective social identity through it, but none went straight from interacting on the Internet to an Afghan training camp. So although the Internet may socialize a potential mujahed to the ideology of the global Salafi jihad, it is still uncertain whether he is willing to make the sacrifices for the jihad and can be securely counted on. He still needs to undergo an intense period of face-to-face interaction to check for his commitment and devotion to the cause and generate bonds that will prevent him from betraying the cause. The danger of prematurely bringing an acquaintance into the jihad was illustrated in the circumstances leading to Abdul Basit Karim's arrest.

The mujahedin's experience in Afghan training camps may strengthen their dedication to the jihad. In the artificial setting of the camps, a semblance of equality and fraternity can easily be approximated for the duration of the training. The trainees live in a communal setting, where their normal life responsibilities are suspended and mutual care is encouraged. The camps re-create the ideals of the mythical umma and give concrete life to the virtual community hinted at on the Internet. The camps generate an esprit de corps for this ideal umma, for which the graduate mujahed might be willing to sacrifice himself.

Flexibility and Performance

In this section, I want to address the impact of network topology on its flexibility and performance.

Small-world networks are composed of nodes linked to well-connected hubs. Hubs receive the most communications from the more isolated nodes. Because of their larger numbers, innovations are more likely in nodes. The nodes link to hubs who, in turn, send the information along their numerous other links. If the appropriate hub likes the innovation, he will likely encourage it by communicating to the appropriate nodes.

The genesis of the plan behind the 9/11 operations is a case in point. Abdul Basit Karim's childhood friend Abdul Hakim Murad became a pilot in the United States in the late 1980s. He dreamed of using airplanes as weapons, filling them up with explosives and dive-bombing into the Pentagon or the Central Intelligence Agency headquarters. After Murad became a member of Karim's terrorist cell around 1993, Karim introduced Murad to his uncle Khalid Sheikh Mohammed, who became fascinated with Murad's idea. In late 1994, they all went to Manila to plot operations against the visiting Pope and President Clinton and devised the Bojinka plot of blowing up eleven airliners over the Pacific in a day's time. Karim's computer, captured in Manila in January 1995, contained the outlines of the Bojinka plot. One alternative to this plan was crashing the airliners into the World Trade Center, the White House, the Pentagon, the John Hancock Tower in Boston, the Sears Tower in Chicago, and the Transamerica Tower in San Francisco (Fouda and Fielding, 2003: 99).

In 1996, Mohammed proposed Murad's plan to Osama bin Laden, who allegedly replied: "Why do you use an ax when you can use a bulldozer?" Instead of a single chartered plane filled with explosives targeting CIA headquarters, bin Laden suggested the "bulldozer" approach of hijacking several passenger jets and flying them into their targets as airborne bombs (Mascolo and Stark, 2003). Mohammed expanded his plan to hijacking a dozen aircraft simultaneously on both coasts and even targeting nuclear power plants (Fouda and Fielding, 2003:114). By 1999, the difficulty of coordinating such an ambitious attack forced Mohammed to settle on the simultaneous hijacking of four passenger aircraft to be used as flying bombs. When he passed the baton for the execution of the operation to

Atta and bin al-Shibh, the general outline of the plan was already sanctioned by bin Laden himself. Mohammed functioned as hubs classically do in the diffusion of information. With their numerous links, hubs are among the first to notice and use the experience of innovators, Murad in this case. Their conversion to the new idea is the key to launching it throughout the network. If they resist it, they prevent it from reaching others, and the innovation will fail. If they accept it, they influence a large number of people.

In addition to rapidly diffusing innovations, the topology of a small-world network is also able to adapt to changing circumstances and solve unforeseen obstacles in the execution of general plans. This flexibility is especially useful in terrorist operations. When a terrorist network embarks on a major new operation, the people involved do not know exactly how they are going to do it. No role is specified in advance. Each mujahed starts with a general notion of what is required of him and improvises with other mujahedin as he goes along. Terrorist operations are not so frequent that they become routine, for law enforcement forces would then catch on and be able to prevent them. These operations involve much uncertainty and many unanticipated obstacles. This state of affairs requires communication among mutually dependent mujahedin, in the sense that each possesses information and resources relevant to the other and none has enough to act in isolation. At this local level, the mujahedin form a network of information processors, where the network handles large volumes of information efficiently without overloading any individual processor. The self-organizing hubs and nodes topology of a small-world network or the dense topology of a clique performs this function very well. Communications are possible horizontally among multiple nodes, allowing them to solve their problems locally without having to refer them upward to Central Staff and overwhelming the vertical links of communication.

This flexibility and local initiative of small-world networks and cliques contrast with the rigidity of hierarchies, which do not adapt well to ambiguity but are excellent at exerting control. In an operating terrorist hierarchy, the uneven burden of information processing jams the chain of command. Central staffers who try to micromanage will become overburdened and ineffective in dealing with unanticipated obstacles. Terrorist organizations advocate strict compartmentalization to maintain security in a hostile environment. This implies a hierarchy with slow communications because of the vulnerability to interception of faster ones. Slow communications prevent the network from responding to new developments in a timely fashion and will further degrade its effectiveness.

According to Gunaratna (2002: 76-84), who had an opportunity to examine several versions of the al Qaeda training manuals and the Encyclopedia of the Afghan Jihad, al Qaeda prescribed the traditional strict hierarchical cell structure according to a need-to-know principle with compartmentalization and secure communication. This model was "composed of many cells whose members do not know one another, so that if a cell member is caught the other cells would not be affected and work would proceed normally" (76). Likewise, operations followed three phases. First, target intelligence is obtained by one team and relayed to an attack team in Afghanistan for planning and rehearsing. Next, a third team comes to the area of operations and organizes the logistical support: safe houses, vehicles, weapons, and explosives. Last, the attack team arrives, puts everything together, and conducts the attack. If it is not a martyrdom mission, it withdraws after completion of the operation. Although this strategy ensures secrecy and security, it also encourages failure.

To overcome the inevitable obstacles inherent in any large-scale terrorist organization, the operational network needs good communication at the local level. The 1998 East Africa embassy bombings, the 2000 USS *Cole* bombing, the 9/11 operations, and the 2002 Bali bombings succeeded owing to the fact that unanticipated local problems were resolved. The East African operation was very unusual in that it was five years in the making and the only one that involved the direct on-the-ground participation of the Central Staff, including Ali Amin al-Rashidi (a.k.a. abu Ubaydah al-Banshiri), the head of al Qaeda's military committee. Although it did follow the pattern outlined in the manual, it had enough time to anticipate and resolve most obstacles. The USS *Cole* operation came on the heels of the failed attack on USS *The Sullivans* nine months earlier. The local team's success in escaping detection allowed it to adjust to the circumstances and blow a large hole in the USS *Cole* on the second try. Despite the dramatic success of the 9/11 plan, carried out by the Hamburg clique, the operation itself was characterized by poor tradecraft, allowing investigators to quickly identify the perpetrators. There was little compartmentalization, and each cell mixed freely with the others. Atta had the authority to choose the date of the operation and the targets. The operators met frequently in Las Vegas and Florida and traveled together. Indeed, the operation succeeded because they did not follow their own rules. Because most of the planners, including the field coordinator and principal executors, were from the same clique and informally benefited from the free flow of information, they were able to overcome the myriad obstacles they encountered. Likewise, four of the major participants in the 2002 Bali bombing belonged to the same family and another was their next-door neighbor from childhood. Although the field commander was not part of this tightly knit group, he no doubt benefited from the informal flow of information in the family. The success of these operations may be due to their violations of their own operational guidelines.

Other global jihad operations were failures: the December 1999 Amman and Los Angeles millennial plots, the December 2000 Strasbourg plot, Christmas Eve 2000 Indonesian church and Manila bombings (even though it caused a few deaths, this must be considered a failure due to poor execution), the January 2000 USS *The Sullivans* plot; the fall 2001 Paris U.S. embassy plot; the December 2001 shoe bomber and Singapore bombing plots; and summer 2002 Straits of Gibraltar plot. The perpetrators tried to follow the guidelines in the manual but ran into unanticipated problems. The lack of effective communications led to failures of execution or to discovery of the plot.

A real danger of the global Salafi jihad is its informal, decentralized structure. Osama bin Laden seems to provide some upfront money for various operations and leaves it to the mujahedin to find the rest. Sometimes these activities to raise money through petty crime alert law enforcement officials, who later detect the major operation. This forces the mujahedin to improvise. These last minute strategies often fail, as the Los Angeles millennial and Straits of Gibraltar plot showed. But given a dedicated and methodical field commander who leaves no details to chance and is fully funded from Central Staff so as to avoid detection in raising money, the results of such local improvisation supported by good local communications among the plotters can be devastating.

The Strength of Weak Bonds

So far I have considered the influence of close friendships on the transformation of potential candidates into committed fanatics. The most intense friendships were formed in cliques. In its purest form, a clique is a dense network of nodes, each connected to every other one. The dynamics described seem to point to a process of social implosion, with the clique as a whole folding onto itself, with no connection to the outside world. In this extreme condition such a clique, despite desiring to join the jihad, would have no way of doing so since no node would have access to a link. Yet if a node were to have a strong link to an outside bridge to the jihad, this bridge would be sucked into the clique and progressively give up his link to the jihad since it would be outside the clique. So how does a clique connect to the jihad?

Let us return to the Montreal and Hamburg cliques. In the Montreal case, Ressam asked Hannachi, a peripheral member of that network, to arrange the formal link with the jihad. This in itself is surprising, for Ressam was already well acquainted with Fateh Kamel, the leader of the network. In retrospect, I can only speculate about this reason. Ressam said that he got the desire to undergo military training in Afghanistan only in the summer of 1997 after Hannachi's return from the camps. At the time, Kamel was already traveling extensively, and it is possible that he was no longer available to make the bridge. Alternatively, Hussein (a.k.a. abu Zubaydah) was promoted to his position of welcoming new candidates only in 1996, after Osama bin Laden's return from the Sudan. Kamel, who had undergone training long before then, might not have been part of this new network bringing new members into the jihad. He may then have simply continued as chief of the logistical support for the Maghreb Arab cluster with no role in recruitment. After his arrest, Makhlulif replaced him and held the dual position of logistics support chief and general recruiter for the Maghreb Arab cluster.

In the Hamburg case, Mohamed Heidar Zammar, again a peripheral acquaintance of the clique, is widely credited with being the bridge between the clique and the jihad. Some went so far as to suggest that he recruited them, but this is not plausible. In contrast to the well educated and sophisticated members of the clique, Zammar was loud and boasted of his past exploits on behalf of the jihad, in essence an advertisement of his link to the jihad. Instead, he probably helped the clique make the link.

In both cases, weak ties to the clique were the bridge to the jihad. In many social processes such as getting a job, learning about new information and spreading fads or rumors, weak ties are more important than strong friends (Granovetter, 1973 and 1983). In a social world of cliques, strong friends lump together into separate groups. So far, there is no connection between them and they are in danger of social implosion, totally disconnected from the rest of the world. What keeps these cliques connected to each other are weak ties, linking certain members of one clique to another. These ties are not strong enough to include the outside individuals in the clique. But they play a crucial role in bridging the clique to the rest of the world. As in these two examples, weak ties play this crucial role in bringing enthusiastic new candidates to the jihad. This is a self-generating process from below rather than a recruitment drive from above.

In our two case studies, both Hannachi and Zammar shared characteristics that might be useful to a broker-link into the jihad. They had wide visibility and prestige. They were loudmouths without much regard for operational security. Their prestige came from the fact that both had fought in wars after their training. Such combat experience showed life-risking commitment for the jihad. War is also more acceptable than terrorism because of the fact that civilians are traditionally not intentional targets. They were models that young militant Muslims wanted to emulate. Members of the Montreal and Hamburg cliques gave the names of these two highly voluble but peripheral individuals as their main inspiration to join the jihad rather than the much more important and active members of the jihad they knew, Fateh Kamel and Mohamadou Ould Slahi, respectively. The Hamburg clique wanted to fight in Chechnya rather than train in Afghanistan. Slahi persuaded its members to go to Afghanistan instead.

There seems to be a contrast between the more secretive and brainy types, who go into terrorism and avoid publicity about their exploits, and the less discreet and unsophisticated broker types, who brag about their doings. Because of their lack of discretion, the brokers are unlikely to be trusted for involvement in true clandestine operations. A potential broker must both be highly visible and have superficial contacts with others rather than be discreet with strong commitment to others. Their unintentional but organizationally important roles may be confined to being a passive bridge to the jihad. They were far from the active and persuasive recruiters postulated by most commentators of the jihad.

This process of cliques joining the jihad as groups has strong implications for its rate of growth, which depends on its ability to forge links with the pool of potential members. The structure of this pool affects this rate. If the pool is composed of isolated individuals, its growth will be slow, for each potential member will need his own bridge. If the pool is composed of cliques of friends, families, or worshippers, however, the jihad will experience explosive growth as one link brings clusters of new fighters, each of whom can then serve as an efficient weak tie to new potential members.

The degree of ambient hostility or tolerance to the jihad also affects its rate of growth. In tolerant countries where people like Zammar can publicly "advertise" their connection to the jihad, applicants can reach out to them to make the bridge. This congenial atmosphere of tolerance based on the principles of religious tolerance and free speech characterized Western Europe and the United States prior to September 11, 2001. This was also the case until recently in Saudi Arabia, Yemen, Malaysia, Indonesia, and a bit more subtly in Salafi mosques sympathetic to the cause. Given the worldwide post-9/11 clampdowns on global Salafi mujahedin, with credible threats of incarceration for even peripheral involvement with the jihad, human bridges to the jihad have become reluctant to reveal their affiliation. This slows down considerably the expansion of the jihad.

The bridge to the jihad seems to have determined where the new mujahed would be deployed. If a Maghreb Arab had made the arrangement, the candidate would train with other Maghreb Arabs and eventually be in a cell with other Maghreb Arabs, under the supervision of Abu Zubaydah. If the original link was through a Core Arab, the eventual mujahed would be in the Core Arab cluster, under the supervision of Khalid Sheikh Mohammed. So the Hamburg cell belonged to the Core Arab cluster despite the fact that half the cell consisted of Arabs who were originally from the Maghreb. Likewise, the Jordanians in the Jordan millennial plot made contact through a Maghreb Arab and ended up being a part of the Maghreb Arab cluster. These clusters seemed to be compartmentalized, with their respective operations depending on different logistical support. Although the mujahedin were richly connected within their own cluster, they were separated from those in the other clusters. There were very few exceptions to this rule. The Syrians (Yarkas, Darkazanli, and Zammar) knew each other and spanned the Core and Maghreb Arab clusters. Moussaoui crossed all three clusters. He started out with the Maghreb Arabs in England, got involved with the Core Arab cluster in Afghanistan, who dispatched him for flight training to Malaysia, where he met the Southeast Asians. He was linked to the Core Arab cluster through bin al-Shibh when he was arrested. Khalid Sheikh Mohammed and his protégé Mohammad Jabarah also bridged the Core Arabs and Southeast Asian clusters.

Conclusion

In conclusion, the final shape of the global Salafi jihad consists of four major clusters surrounded by innumerable islands consisting of cliques and singletons of potential candidates. At the top is the Central Staff cluster, which connects to the rest of the clusters. The structure of this cluster is difficult to describe. It is both an informal self-organizing group of friends and acquaintances forged during the Soviet-Afghan war and a hierarchical organization with Osama bin Laden as its emir, supported by a shura composed of about a dozen members and dominated by Egyptians. The staff is divided into four committees, consisting of finances, military affairs, religious affairs, and public relations. There is no mention of personnel, recruitment, intelligence, or logistics. I presume that the first function probably falls under finances, whereas the last two come under the military committee. Recruitment is still a mystery.

The two Arab clusters approximate small-world networks. The Southeast Asian cluster consists of the Jemaah Islamiyah, which is more hierarchically organized. There are multiple alliances among separate organizations in the jihad. Close to the Maghreb Arab cluster are the Groupe Salafiste pour la Prédication et le Combat and former Groupe Islamique Armé, the Moroccan Salafia Jihadia, and various smaller violent jihad organizations. The Core Arab cluster is close to the Egyptian Islamic Jihad (in fact, al Qaeda is now officially merged with this organization), the Egyptian Islamic Group, al-Tawhid, and various smaller Yemeni organizations. The Indonesian Jemaah Islamiyah is closely allied with the Moro Islamic Liberation Front. These organizations are the tip of the iceberg

171

of those who sympathize and may want to participate in the jihad. This much larger disconnected and unorganized network consists of small cliques and singletons who want to join the jihad but have not been able to do so. This pool of potential candidates may increase or decrease according to sociopolitical events in the world. But in order to formally join the jihad, these individuals still need to find a bridge.

This network is the picture emerging from my data. Valdis Krebs (2002a and 2002b) published an early map of the network of the 9/11 terrorists based on preliminary data. The resulting mapping shows inaccurate links and neglects other much more important ones. He was on the right track, but rushed to publish too early. This present picture fits better what we have now learned about the structure and dynamics of the networks.

This informal social network analysis allows us to make statements that no other perspective in the field of terrorism ventures to state. These can be empirically tested. In this chapter, I made statements about the self-organizing evolution of some of the clusters and how they affected structure, robustness to random attacks, vulnerability to targeted attack, distribution and ability to carry on the fight in the United States, and the impact on its operational limits of the lack of social embeddedness of the network. I also made statements about the nature of the participants in the jihad, their frequent organizations in cliques, which have a transformational effect on their members, and the lack of a common profile of the mujahedin. I analyzed the impact of the new communication technology and the Internet on the jihad; argued that the topology of the network affects its flexibility and performance; and concluded with the crucial role played by weak acquaintances that provided the critical bridges to the jihad.

Osama bin Laden's most brilliant stroke may well have been to allow the global Salafi jihad network to evolve spontaneously and naturally, and not interfere too much with its evolution, except to guide it through incentives because of his control of resources. The system developed into a small-world network with robustness and flexibility and became more militant and global for both internal and external reasons. Bin Laden's relatively hands-off policy and repeated pleas for Islamist unity before the "far enemy" is unusual. The common wisdom in the field of terrorism is that terrorist leaders suffer from "malignant narcissism" (Post, Ruby, and Shaw, 2002b: 118). As a practicing psychiatrist, I do not know of any reliable, agreed upon definition of this vague term. But it seems that terrorist leaders thrive on power and control of their organizations. Osama bin Laden seems to be the opposite. He is publicly self-effacing and seems content to relinquish control of an organization (which would have implied a more hierarchical structure) for the sake of efficacy. He shows his disapproval not by killing his potential rivals but simply by withdrawing funds from them until they come back to his fold. This type of leadership is rare and may well account for the robustness of the global Salafi jihad, its ability to respond to changing conditions, and its widespread appeal to Muslim youths.

A more common pattern of leadership is that exercised by Abu Bakar Baasyir. Although the more hierarchical Jemaah Islamiyah escaped detection far longer than al Qaeda, it is now in danger of disappearing. In 2000, the Indonesian government had not reacted against the ambitious Christmas Eve church bombings. The 2002 Bali bombings galvanized them to action. Now most of the Jemaah Islamiyah leadership is in jail. The imprisoned members will be difficult to replace, although some other leaders are still at large and may be capable of rebuilding the network. Likewise, the government of Singapore was able to eliminate the Jemaah Islamiyah threat because its well-ordered structure was created from the top instead of evolving from the bottom. In contrast, the topology of the rest of the global Salafi jihad allowed it to survive a far more devastating blow from a U.S. government mobilized by the horrors of the 9/11 operations.

Conclusion

T HE GLOBAL Salafi jihad is a threat to the world. Its theater of operations spans the globe, and its apocalyptic vision melts away any barriers to its planned atrocities. It will not hesitate to use weapons of mass destruction to further its mission. Elimination of this movement is imperative. The war on this type of terror must be fought on many fronts. Some of the macro-level factors that influenced this Muslim revivalist social movement, such as Western policies toward Muslim countries, social policies of immigration and education in the Western world, lack of occupational opportunities in the Middle East, and state policies toward religious practices are beyond the scope of this book. Several other authors have already and very competently covered the larger social, cultural, economic, and political factors that encourage the jihad (Khosrokhavar, 1997 and 2002; Kepel, 2002; Roy, 2002). In conclusion, I shall confine my remarks to practical recommendations drawn from my empirical findings.

Law Enforcement Issues

In the war on terror, the United States and many other countries are already doing many things right. Many of the following recommendations simply amount to good police work. The social network analysis gives it a theoretical frame.

Nodes

The nature of the networks of the various clusters composing the global Salafi jihad dictates a variety of strategies. The small-world approximation of the Maghreb and Core Arab network implies a coordinated attack targeted against its social hubs. They are particularly vulnerable because most communications and human contacts go through them. Arresting these individuals would degrade these networks into isolated units, singletons or cliques, who would consequently be incapable of mounting complex large-scale operations owing to lack of expertise and logistical and financial support. Small-scale operations would be very hard to eradicate completely, but without spectacular successes to sustain their motivation for terrorism, isolated operators will lose their enthusiasm. These small-scale operations can still be quite deadly, as shown in the Casablanca bombings in 2003. But these should be treated as straightforward law enforcement matters. This will reduce terrorism to simple criminality and not allow terrorists to promote their agenda of jihad, which might further inspire alienated young men to take up the cause. Winning the media war to label terrorists as criminals rather than brave mujahedin is especially important to eliminate the appeal of self-sacrifice for a cause and discourage potential terrorists from engaging in such behaviors.

Random arrests of low-level individuals (nodes) at border points will not degrade the network. Increased vigilance will stop terrorists from coming to the United States and prevent them from conducting operations on American soil. This is a good thing, but this protection comes not from the actual arrests of the terrorists, but from the fear of arrest that discourages others from trying to come here. Nevertheless, it does not eliminate terrorism; it displaces it to soft targets in more accessible countries. The post-9/11 wave of bombings in traditional places of sanctuary, such as Saudi Arabia, Indonesia, Morocco, Yemen, Pakistan, and Afghanistan, seems to be an implicit admission of weakness from terrorists. These operations provoked responses from those countries, which had previously been reluctant to pursue or prosecute terrorists in their territory. This crackdown denies terrorists the refuge they previously enjoyed and further degrades their network. The new enthusiasm of Indonesia, Saudi Arabia, and Morocco for the war on terror is a direct result of the terrorists' violation of these governments' previous implicit policy of live and let live. Britain, which has traditionally acted as a sanctuary for many terrorists who were tried and sentenced in other countries, may be at great risk of terrorist attacks now that access to other targets is denied.

The nature of the Jemaah Islamiyah networks dictates a different strategy. The Jemaah Islamiyah is structured along hierarchical lines, and the network can be degraded through decapitation, the arrest of its leaders. An effort to round them up has been under way since the 2002 Bali bombings, and the Jemaah Islamiyah could be eliminated if the leaders remaining at large cannot rebuild it from the top down. Operational planning and support was always top-down, with little evidence of local initiative. The network was built on the principle of discipleship, with most of its members coming from two Islamic boarding schools, where they were indoctrinated with global Salafi ideology. These schools need to be closed down to prevent further education of terrorists. The Malaysian government has already closed down the Pesentren Luqmanul Hakiem. The Indonesian government needs to do the same for the Pondok Ngruki. Since Jemaah Islamiyah membership was so closely linked to these schools, their faculty and students over the past two decades should be tracked down and investigated. This would narrow down the field considerably in Indonesia.

From a pragmatic law enforcement perspective, a shift in devotion may provide a clue to impending illegal operations. By prescription, Salafists adopt a strict code of behavior, dress, and appearance, and are therefore easily recognizable. They abstain from alcohol and lewdness, grow beards, and dress in a traditional Muslim style. Sudden abandonment of this lifestyle should raise an alarm. Shaving their beards, dressing in a Western way, or using perfume at airports may signal that they are trying to blend with the surrounding society or conceal something from authorities. Indeed, any sudden change from a Salafi to a Western appearance should immediately be investigated. The odds are that it is a false alarm and not grounds for arrest, but it should raise the index of suspicion about the reason for the change. Intelligence "eyes and ears" in the Salafi community should alert the authorities of the change and prompt urgent investigation.

Likewise, the demand for a new passport from a Salafi Muslim should raise the index of suspicion. It was common practice for those who could travel to the West to report their passports lost in order to eliminate any trace of previous travel to Afghanistan or Pakistan that might trigger scrutiny at border points. This attempt to conceal past travel may be an indication of malevolent intentions.

Links

One of the major conclusions of this study is that social bonds play a more important role in the emergence of the global Salafi jihad than ideology. Friends and relatives of identified terrorists need to be pursued and investigated wherever they reside. Especially important are those who were friends of a terrorist just before he started acts in furtherance of the jihad, such as traveling to Afghanistan for training. These friends helped transform him from an alienated Muslim into a dedicated global Salafi mujahed. As they were close friends, probably part of a clique, these friends are probably also mujahedin themselves or strong supporters of the global jihad. Because of the amount of time members of a clique spend together and the dense network of relationships they represent, it should not be very difficult to identify all the members of a clique. Each should be closely investigated for formal links with the jihad. Relatives, including in-laws, especially of converts, should not be overlooked in this process.

Peripheral social acquaintances were crucial to the process of joining the jihad. These need to be identified and investigated as well, as they were the ones who made the introduction. Without these bridges, potential candidates would not have been able to join the jihad. These individuals will be more difficult to identify because they were not part of the dense network of the cliques. However, they are probably where the members of the clique found them, namely around the mosques that traditionally send potential candidates to Afghan training camps. These few mosques need to be closely monitored or shut down. Previous sites where links to the jihad have been made must be investigated, in the event a bridge is lying low in the vicinity. He may also have moved; the search should focus on individuals who were around at the time of the contact with the jihad in addition to any suspicious longtime members of the congregation. The threat of incarceration creates a hostile environment and prevents these human bridges from freely advertising their connection to the jihad and facilitating the enrollment of new members. These human bridges might also be more useful for potential collaboration with intelligence agencies than members of a clique, whose strong emotional bonds discourage betrayal.

The importance of intercepting and monitoring terrorist communications through satellite telephone, landline phone, e-mail, facsimiles, and

Internet chat rooms has already been established. With good international police cooperation, these activities have led to the arrest of many important terrorists. Implanting listening devices in places frequented by terrorists has also provided a window on their interactions. Even when these links are not monitored, the fear that they might be hinders terrorist communications because they revert to slower, more secure means of exchanging information such as letters or face-to-face contact. This degrades their ability to supervise worldwide operations. The failure of the plot to bomb naval vessels in the Straits of Gibraltar in the summer of 2002 was partly a result of such difficulties in communication between the field action commando and the lieutenant overseeing the overall operation.

The elimination of easily accessible training camps prevents potential candidates from learning terrorist skills and finding resources to carry out operations. This has been done in Afghanistan and the Philippines. There may still be some areas where training can take place, outside the reach of international governments, in the Philippines, Pakistan, Afghanistan, Indonesia, Yemen, Palestine, Lebanon, Chechnya, and Central Asian Muslim states. Some failed states that do not exercise control over much of their territories are potential sites for such camps. The remoteness that provides security from effective governmental interference, however, also prevents easy access for potential candidates. Nevertheless, suspicious movements, especially by Muslim fundamentalists, need to be monitored to detect the establishment of new camps. Remote areas of Iraq with easy access to Iran, Turkey, or Syria may be future sites for such camps, as the presence of U.S. troops in Iraq will act as a magnet for global Salafi terrorists, who will naturally target what they see as the infidel invaders of Muslim lands.

The intense international vigilance after September 11, 2001, makes the establishment of such training sites difficult. I suspect that in the future, the training of global Salafi mujahedin will be done locally, where the candidates volunteer. If so, the experience in Morocco may be the wave of the future. The perpetrators of the Casablanca bombings went on weekend or week-long camping trips in caves or forests in the vicinity of large cities, where they followed military discipline and learned about bomb making from local "experts," who had been previously trained in Afghanistan. The quality of the training was poor, but their efforts still resulted in significant carnage.

Penetration of the Global Salafi Jihad

The greatest priority now should be extensive penetration of the jihad. Recruitment of agents in place is a difficult task because of the strong emotional bonds among members of the jihad, making them reluctant to betray their friends and their faith. The best avenue for penetration lies in recruitment from the pool of those who went through the training but decided not to join the jihad. Although there is no evidence that these people are actively involved in terrorist operations, they are being prosecuted for providing material support and resources to the jihad. Before prosecuting them, all efforts should be made to try to turn them around and have them go back and join the jihad. Their ability to operate clandestinely in the United States makes them attractive recruits for the jihad. At present, however, they are unlikely to volunteer the fact that they have undergone training in Afghanistan for fear of prosecution. Perhaps a policy of immunity in exchange for a good-faith effort to help fight the jihad may help convince some to volunteer.

The implication from my examination of the background and circumstances of the mujahedin is that it will be difficult to recruit an agent in place because of his commitment to his faith and strong emotional bonds to his fellow terrorists. There is always the possibility that some mujahedin become disillusioned with their organizations. Most will try to disappear and keep a low profile—the strategy of the Lackawanna Six. Some may be willing to provide information in exchange for consideration in their prosecution. This was the case of al-Fadl and Kherchtou, who testified at the East Africa embassy bombings trial in 2001. The source of disillusionment was lack of support from the organization in one case and discovery of embezzlement in the other. The government should be ready to try to turn them around and convince them to return to the jihad as agents in place, at least for a while if they have not yet burned their bridges. If a terrorist organization goes from failure to failure, disillusionment may set in for at least some members, who could become susceptible to deals with prosecutors. The government should advertise a program of consideration on a case-by-case basis for people wishing to volunteer their services to encourage such defections and desire to work in place. Elimination of the threat of terrorism should take priority over prosecutions aimed at making examples of past terrorists. If, as reported in the press, the Lackawanna Six were not planning any terrorist attacks, the aggressive policy of prosecuting them without exploring ways to use them for penetration of the jihad was a mishandled opportunity in the war on terror. Here, I am arguing for a carrot (generous consideration of one's cooperation and willingness to take risks in fighting terrorism in sentencing) and stick (aggressive prosecution of terrorists, collaborators, and active supporters to eliminate the public bridges to the jihad) approach.

Intelligence agencies are unlikely to recruit an agent in place simply through a cold pitch or through the classical agent acquisition cycle. They are more likely to find success if they identify a terrorist, then go and recruit someone close to him but not part of the jihad. This person may be more likely to cooperate with the government and then approach his relative or friend. These prior social bonds will help the intermediate agent to reach the terrorist, probe for vulnerability, and progressively suggest cooperation with the government if the terrorist is vulnerable and susceptible to this pitch. This indirect approach has a greater likelihood of success than a direct approach.

Imams of conservative or fundamentalist mosques who reject terrorism could be excellent sources of information on their congregations. They would be valuable allies to recruit in the war on terror. They may know which members of their congregations are relatives or former friends of suspected terrorists. Such persons can become intermediary agents who can probe the terrorist. Again, premature arrest may foil the much greater priority of having a penetration of the terrorist organization.

Decreasing the Pool of Potential Terrorists

The war against global Salafi terror also requires active support from American and other Muslim communities. Interacting with them requires skill and cultural sensitivity, as does recruitment and handling of Muslim agents. I would suggest the creation of a special cadre of case officers, with strong backgrounds in Muslim cultures and perhaps language, to handle these populations and agents. This cadre could even be subdivided according to expertise in Southeast Asian, Core Arab, and Maghreb Arab communities. Strong-arm governmental tactics antagonizing Muslim communities in the United States will not earn their support in the fight against the jihad. U.S. government agencies urgently need to implement active measures to restore their previous good relationship with the Muslim community and elicit its support.

Not all Muslim fundamentalists are the same. Just as European socialists acted as a bulwark against Soviet communism in the twentieth century, peaceful fundamentalist Muslim groups such as the Tablighi Jamaat may help to promote a conciliatory message and repudiate terrorist violence. Their help is essential to efforts to neutralize terrorist networks, for they attract the same clusters of alienated young men as the global Salafi jihad and may provide them with a peaceful alternative to terror. Many such organizations have been penetrated by the global jihad and may welcome outside help to regain their purity by unmasking and eliminating those that subvert their message.

The global Salafi jihad feeds on anti-Western and anti-American hate speech. Such virulent discourse is a necessary condition for the jihad and provides a justification for it. It is important to eradicate it and encourage civil discourse in Muslim communities. I believe that it is necessary to establish an international anti-defamation league to monitor such hate speech and work with the respective press, religious organizations, governments, and justice systems to control and condemn it. This should target not only Muslim radicalism, but any form of intolerant extremism that preaches violence instead of dialogue. The U.S. government should show strong support for such a program to promote universal tolerance and peace. Anti-American or anti-Western hate speech is not acceptable. The British have already adopted this position and banned some extremist imams from preaching. There are indications that the Saudi government is starting to reassess the role of extremist Wahhabi preaching in motivating terrorism after the Riyadh bombings in 2003. This policy should be encouraged, but there is a great deal more to do. This campaign for tolerance should enlist the support of many courageous Muslims who challenge the extremist Wahhabi interpretation. The firing of Saudi journalist Jamal Khashoggi shows that there is still strong resistance to such challenge in the kingdom. The U.S. government should strongly protest this dismissal to the Saudis and encourage them to open up their sterile press to more freedom.

Anti-Americanism and anti-Westernism should also be actively countered through the media worldwide. Magazines and newspapers presenting credible news should be made widely available to counter some of the egregious rumors propagated by the extremist press. Television news organizations can provide a more balanced perspective to the Middle Eastern populations and encourage real discussions about their social and economic problems.

The U.S. intervention in Iraq has changed the Middle East landscape, making the United States a direct participant in Middle Eastern politics. Now that U.S. troops are in Iraq, that conflict has become the litmus test of our role in the Middle East and will determine the size of the pool of potential young volunteers for the jihad. If U.S. efforts to rebuild Iraq fail, it will be a boost for the global jihad and the United States must anticipate an increase in terrorist operations. If Iraq can develop a responsive government for its people and allow them to live well in prosperity and regain their past cultural glory, it will be a model for the rest of the Middle East to follow. Iraq is a great opportunity but also a great danger. These developments will take decades. The next few years are critical.

Iraq may also attract all potential anti-Western mujahedin wanting to fight the infidel who has invaded Dar al-Islam. Our presence in Iraq is widely viewed as an occupation now that the liberation from Saddam Hussein is accomplished. The gathering of an international group of mujahedin is reenergizing the global Salafi jihad, which had been fading away in the post-9/11 era. Iraq has the potential of becoming a site, like Peshawar or Khartoum, where the ideology of the global jihad is further developed and the excitement for the jihad is renewed.

Despite some major victories, we have not yet defeated the global Salafi jihad. Given its structure, if we relax our vigilance, it will spontaneously reconstitute itself. We must continue our fight based on an understanding of its network and dynamics. With good police and intelligence work combined with more global measures, international assistance, and an effective policy in Iraq, we can conclusively eliminate it.

Let me end by anticipating an objection to my analysis. My account of the global Salafi jihad is mostly that of a self-generated network with unusual characteristics of robustness and flexibility rather than one created by the intention of bin Laden (the intentionalist argument). This perspective may trouble some people because this weak structuralist account may appear to mitigate his guilt and that of the other terrorists. In my defense, I plead that this structuralist flavor is necessary at present to counter the strong intentionalist bias in the field. I do not reject the intentional-ist argument. The mujahedin were enthusiastic killers, not robots simply responding to social pressures or group dynamics. While their success was largely due to the dynamics of their networks, the level of fervor and com-mitment was their own. Much of the success of the 9/11 plot was due to the dedication of Atta, bin al-Shibh, and Khalid Sheikh Mohammed, and the inspiration of Osama bin Laden. The social forces might have been difficult to resist, but the terrorists must be held accountable for the choice between enthusiasm and reluctance. Beyond a certain point, though, it simply does not matter. Subtle degrees of guilt are lost in the sea of dev-astation. Any subtle differences in criminal responsibility were obliterat-ed by the tidal wave of blood on September 11, 2001. Let there be no doubt that I regard the global Salafi terrorists as maximally guilty of their enormous crime.

Appendix: Names of Terrorists

Names listed by cluster, in chronological order of joining the jihad.

Name	Alias	Date & Place of Birth
Central Staff of al Qaeda		
Osama bin Laden	Abu Abdullah	1957, Saudi Arabia
Ayman al-Zawahiri	Abdel Muiz, Dr. Nur	1951, Egypt
Ali Amin Ali al-Rashidi	Abu Ubaydah al-Banshiri	Egypt
Shubhi Mohammed abu Sittah	Abu Hafs al-Masri, Mohd Atef	1957, Egypt
Sheikh Omar Abdel Rahman		1938, Egypt
Mohammed Shawqi al-Islambuli		1955, Egypt
Zain al-Abidin Mohd Hussein	Abu Zubaydah	1971, Saudi Arabia
Mohammed Ibrahim Makkawi	Sayf al-Adl al-Madani	1945, Egypt
Mustafa Ahmed al-Hawsawi		1968, Saudi Arabia
Rifai Ahmed Taha	Abu Yasir	1954, Egypt
Talat Fuad Qasim		1956, Egypt
Osama Rushdi		1960, Egypt
Mustafa Ahmed Hassan Hamza		1957, Egypt
Khalid Sheikh Mohammed		1965, Kuwait
Khalid Abdel Rahman al-Fawwaz		1962, Kuwait
Ahmed Fadl al-Kalaylah	Abu Musab al-Zarqawi	1966, Jordan
Mohammed al-Zawahiri		1954, Egypt
Omar Mahmoud Othman	Abu Qatada	1960, Jordan
Mamdouh Mahmud Salim	Abu Hajer al-Iraqi	1958, Iraq
Hamid al-Fakhiri	Ibn al-Sheikh al-Libi	1971, Libya
Ahmad Hussein Mustafa Ujayzah		1962, Egypt
Jamal Ahmed Mohd al-Fadl		1963, Sudan
Osama Siddiq Ali Ayyub Muntasir		1966, Egypt
Wadih el-Hage	Abu Abdullah al-Lubnani	1960, Lebanon
Said al-Sayyid Salamah Khalid		1963, Egypt
Ahmed Said Khadr	Abu Abdurrahman al-Kanadi	1948, Egypt
Yasir Tawfiq al-Sirri	Abu Ammar	1962, Egypt

Name	Alias	Date & Place of Birth
Central Staff of al Qaeda (continued)		
Sulayman abu-Ghayth		1965, Kuwait
Mustafa Kamel	Abu Hamza al-Masri	1958, Egypt
Tharwat Salah Shitahih		1960, Egypt
Adil Mohd Abd al-Majid	Abd al-Bari	1959, Egypt
Abd al-Aziz Musa al-Jamal		1955, Egypt
Core Arab Cluster		
Waleed Mohd Tawfiq bin Attash	Khallad	Yemen
Mahmud Abouhalima		1959, Egypt
Ali Abdel Suud Mohd Mustafa	Ali Mohammed, Jeff	1952, Egypt
Khalid al-Sayyid Ali abu al-Dahab	Sheikh Adam	1964, Egypt
Abdul Basit Mahmoud Abdul Karim	Ramzi Yousef	1968, Kuwait
Abdul Hakim Murad		1968, Kuwait
Wali Khan Amin Shah	Osama	1967, Afghanistan
Abdul Shakur		1972, Pakistan
Abdul Aziz Fahd Nasser		1970, Saudi Arabia
Riyad Hajir		1970, Saudi Arabia
Muslih Shamrani		1970, Saudi Arabia
Khaled Ahmed Said		1970, Saudi Arabia
L'Houssaine Kherchtou	Abu Said Maghrebi	1964, Morocco
Mohammed Sadeek Odeh	Abu Yasser	1965, Saudi Arabia
Abdallah Mohammed Fazul	Haroun Fazul	1973, Comoros
Khalfan Khamis Mohamed		1973, Tanzania
Ahmed Omar Sheikh		1973, England
Mohamadou Ould Slahi		1970, Mauritania
Abdal Rahim al-Nashiri	Abu Bilal al-Makki	1966, Saudi Arabia
Mohamed Heidar Zammar		1961, Syria
Mohamed Rashid Daoud al-Owhali		1977, England
Mamoun Darkazanli	Abu Ilyas	1958, Syria
Mohammad bin Nasser Belfas		1946, Indonesia
Mounir al-Motassadeq		1974, Morocco
Abdelghani Mzoudi		1974, Morocco
Said Bahaj		1975, Germany
Mohamed el-Amir Awad el-Sayed Atta	Abu Abdul Rahman al-Masri	1968, Egypt
Ramzi Mohd Abdullah bin al-Shibh		1972, Yemen
Ziad Amir Jarrah	Abu Tareq al-Lubnani	1975, Lebanon
Marwan al-Shehhi	Abu Qaqaa al-Qatari	1978, United Arab Emirates
Zakarya Essabar		1977, Morocco
Hani Hanjour	Orwah al-Taifi	1972, Saudi Arabia

Name	Alias	Date & Place of Birth
Core Arab Cluster (continued)		
Nawaf al-Hazmi	Rabia al-Makki	1975, Saudi Arabia
Khalid al-Midhar	Sinan	1974, Saudi Arabia
Saleem al-Hazmi	Bilal al-Makki	1979, Saudi Arabia
Majed Mishan al-Harbi	Majed, Moqed, al-Ahnaf	1979, Saudi Arabia
Wail Mohd al-Shehri	Abu Mosaeb al-Janoubi	1975, Saudi Arabia
Waleed Mohd al-Shehri	Abu Salman	1980, Saudi Arabia
Hamza al-Ghamdi	Julaibeeb al-Ghamdi	1981, Saudi Arabia
Ahmed Ibrahim al-Ghamdi	Ikrimah al-Ghamdi	1980, Saudi Arabia
Ahmed Ibrahim al-Haznawi al-Ghamdi	Ibn Jarrah al-Ghamdi	1981, Saudi Arabia
Abdul Aziz al-Omari	Abu-l Abas al-Janoubi	1978, UAE
Satam Mohd al-Suqami	Azmi	1976, Saudi Arabia
Fayez Ahmad al-Shehri	Abu Ahmed al-Emarati, Bani Hamr	1977, Saudi Arabia
Muhannad al-Shehri	Omar al-Azdi, Mohand al-Shehri	1977, Saudi Arabia
Saeed al-Ghamdi	Moataz	1980, Saudi Arabia
Ahmed al-Nami	Abu Hashem	1980, Saudi Arabia
Zuher Hilal Mohammed al-Tbaiti		1976, Saudi Arabia
Jose Padilla	Abdullah al-Muhajir	1970, United States
Adnan Gulshair Mohd el-Shukri-Jumah	Jafar al-Tayer	1975, Saudi Arabia
Kamal Derwish	Ahmed Hijazi	1973, United States
Mohammad Mansur Jabarah	Sammy	1982, Kuwait
Abdul Rahman Mansur Jabarah		1980, Kuwait
Shadi Abdullah		1977, Jordan
Omar Khan Sharif		1976, England
Asif Hanif		1981, Pakistan
Jamal Ahmed Mohd al-Badawi	Abu Abed al-Rahman al-Badawi	Yemen
Fahd al-Quso	Abu Hathayfah al-Adani	Yemen
Khaled Mohammed Jehani		1974, Saudi Arabia
Abdallah Khadr		1980, Canada
Abdel Rahman Khadr		1982, Bahrain
Omar Khadr		1986, Canada
Ali Abdal Rahman Said al-Faqasi al-Ghamdi	Abu Bakr al-Azdi	1974, Saudi Arabia
Othman Hadi Makbould al-Mardi al-Omari		1966, Saudi Arabia
Muhammad Othman al-Shehri		1972, Saudi Arabia
Turki Mishal Dandani		1976, Saudi Arabia

187

Name	Alias	Date & Place of Birth
Southeast Asian Cluster		
Abu Bakar Baasyir	Ustaz abu Somad	1938, Indonesia
Abdullah Sungkar		1937, Indonesia
Riduan Isamuddin	Encep Nurjaman, Hambali	1964, Indonesia
Ali Ghufron bin Nurhasym	Mukhlas	1960, Indonesia
Fikiruddin Muqti	Mohammed Iqbal, abu Jibril	1959, Indonesia
Abduragak Abubakar Janjalani	Abu Sayyaf	1961, Philippines
Omar al-Faruq		1971, Kuwait
Yassin Syawal		Indonesia
Fathur Rahman al-Ghozi		1971, Indonesia
Abdul Aziz	Imam Samudra	1970, Indonesia
Enjang Bastaman	Jabir	Indonesia
Amrozi bin Nurhasym		1962, Indonesia
Ali Imron bin Nurhasym		1972, Indonesia
Yazid Sufaat		1965, Malaysia
Agus Dwikarna		1964, Indonesia
Jack Thomas	Jihad Thomas	1974, Australia
Hashim bin Abbas		1961, Singapore
Mohammed Nazir bin Abbas		1969, Malaysia
Faiz bin abu Bakar Bafaba		1962, Malaysia
Jafaar bin Mistooki		1961, Singapore
Saifulla Yunos	Muklis	1972, Philippines
Maghreb Arab Cluster		
Abdillah Ziyad	Rachid	1958, Morocco
Mohamed Zinedine	Said	1959, Morocco
Stephane Ait Iddir	Said	1973, France
Radouane Hammadi		1973, France
Tarek Falah		1974, France
Khader abu Hoshar		1965, Jordan
Rachid Ramda		1970, Algeria
Ali Touchent	Terek	1957, Algeria
Safé Bourada		1970, France
Khaled Kelkal		1971, Algeria
Karim Koussa		1972, France
Nasserdine Slimani		1971, France
Boualem Bensaid	Banabas, Mehdi	1967, Algeria
Smain Ait Ali Belkacem		1969, Algeria
Fateh Kamel		1960, Algeria

Name	Alias	Date & Place of Birth
Maghreb Arab Cluster (continued)		
Christophe Caze	Walid	1969, France
Lionel Dumont	Abou Hamza	1971, France
Rachid Souimdi		1971, France
Omar Zemmiri		1966, France
Hocine Bendaoui		1977, France
Mouloud Bouguelane		1970, France
Karim Said Atmani		1966, Morocco
Abdellah Ouzghar		1964, Morocco
Amar Makhlulif	Doctor, Abu Doha, Haydar	1966, Algeria
Raeed Hijazi	Abu Ahmed al-Amriki	1969, United States
Ahmed Ressam		1967, Algeria
Mustafa Labsi		1969, Algeria
Abderraouf Hannachi		1950, Tunisia
Mohammed Bensakhria	Meliani	1968, Algeria
Aeurobui Beandali		1975, Algeria
Lamine Maroni		1971, Algeria
Fouhad Sabour		1965, France
Abdel Qader Mahmoud Es Sayed		1962, Egypt
Essid Sami Ben Khemais	Saber, Omar the Traveler	1968, Tunisia
Tarek Maaroufi		1965, Tunisia
Imad Eddin Barakat Yarkas	Abu Dahdah	1960, Syria
Habib Zacarias Moussaoui	Sahrawi	1968, France
Djamel Beghal		1965, Algeria
Kamel Daoudi		1974, Algeria
Richard Colvin Reid	Abdul Rauff	1973, England
Nizar Trabelsi		1970, Tunisia
David Courtailler		1976, France
Jérome Courtailler		1974, France
Yacine Akhnouche		1975, Algeria
Hervé Djamel Loiseau		1973, France
Nizar ben Mohd Nasr Nawar	Sayf al-Islam Ettounsi	1978, Tunisia
Mohamed Rafiki	Abu Hafs	1974, Morocco
Mohamed Damir		1972, Morocco
Mehdi Damir		1980, Morocco
Mohamed al-Omari		1979, Morocco
Richard Pierre Antoine Robert	Abu Abderrahmane, Lhaj	1972, France
Mohamed Hassouna		1981, Morocco
Mohamed al-Mehini		1978, Morocco

Glossary of Foreign Terms

baya formal oath of loyalty

bidah innovations (considered non-Islamic corruptions diluting the word of God)

dar al-harb land of conflict

dar al-Islam land of Islam

dar al-kufr land of infidels

dar al-suhl land of treaty

dawa call to Islam

fard ayn individual obligation

fard kifaya collective obligation

fitna temptation or trial; discord within Muslim community

hadith stories recording the words and deeds of the Prophet by people who knew him.

hijra exile; withdrawal

jahiliyya the state of barbarism and ignorance that prevailed in the Arabic Peninsula before Muhammad's revelations. *jahili*, adj.

jihad striving

jihad bis sayf striving through the sword; violent revolt

kufr infidel

Maghreb North African Islamic lands

mantiqi region (Indonesian)

mujahed, pl. *mujahedin* jihad fighter

salaf ancient one; companion of the Prophet

shahada profession of faith; also martyrdom

shahid witness; also martyr

Sharia strict Quranic law

shura council

takfir excommunicated; a lapsed Muslim, from the Arabic root kufr for impiety.

tawhid unity of god

umma Muslim community

wakalah branches (Indonesian)

Bibliography

Abdallah, Issam; Hurayz, Jamal-al-Din; al-Wazzani, Maniyah; and al-Rumayzan, Id. 2002. "Returnees from Afghanistan Cited on Situation of Arab Afghans, Links to al-Qaida." *Al-Majallah* (London), February 24.

Abuza, Zachary. 2000a. "Tentacles of Terror: Al Qaeda's Southeast Asian Network." *Contemporary Southeast Asia,* 24 (3): 427-465.

————. 2002b. "Kuala Lumpur a Vital Hub for al-Qaida Strike plans." *Australian*, December 24.

Acacio, Pereira. 1999a. "Le réseau islamiste responsable des attentats de 1995 est jugé à Paris." *Le Monde*, June 1.

————. 1999b. "Boualem Bensaid se pose en militant pur et dur du GIA qui n'a peur que d'Allah." *Le Monde*, June 5.

————. 1999c. "L'itinéraire de Khaled Kelkal éclaire le procès des attentats islamistes." *Le Monde*, June 9.

————. 1999d. "Karim Koussa, au nom de Dieu et de son frère Khaled Kelkal." *Le Monde*, June 10.

————. 1999e. "Les membres présumés du commando lyonnais se présentent en copains d'enfance unis par l'islam." *Le Monde*, June 12.

————. 1999f. "Smain Ait Ali Belkacem reconnait à l'audience sa participation aux attentats de 1995." *Le Monde*, June 16.

————. 1999g. "Les avocats des islamistes accusés des attentats de 1995 plaident la thèse du terrible engrenage." *Le Monde*, July 1.

Adams, Lorraine. 2001. "The Other Man." *Washington Post*, May 20.

Adorno, T. W.; Frenkel-Brunswik, Else; Levinson, Daniel; and Sanford, Nevitt. 1950. *The Authoritarian Personality*. New York: Harper and Brothers.

Akhtar, Salman. 1999. "The Psychodynamic Dimension of Terrorism." *Psychiatric Annals*, 29(6): 350-355.

Akram, Assem. 1996. *Histoire de la Guerre d'Afghanistan*. Paris: Editions Balland.

Al-Banyan, Hasin. 2001. "Saudi 'Afghan' Talks About Involvement with al-Qaida, Bin-Ladin, Related Topics." *Al-Sharq al-Awsat* (London), November 25.

Al-Fadl, Jamal Ahmed Mohamed. 2001. *United States of America v. Usama bin Laden, et al.* February 6-13: 162-392.

Al-Haruji, Khalid. 2002. "Interview in Sanaa of Ahmad bin al-Shibah." *Al-Majallah* (London), August 4.

Al-Ridi, Essam. 2001. *United States of American v. Usama bin Laden, et al.* February 14: 540-583.

Al-Shafii, Muhammad. 1999a. "UK Crackdown on Fundamentalist Noted." *Al-Sharq al-Awsat* (London), March 22.

———. 1999b. "Returnees from Albania Case Detailed." *Al-Sharq al-Awsat* (London), April 16.

———. 2000. "Report on Bin-Laden's Maronite Christian Secretary." *Al-Sharq al-Awsat* (London), December 24.

———. 2001. "Arab Afghan Says Usama Bin Ladin's Force Strength Overblown." *Al-Sharq al-Awsat* (London), October 6.

———. 2002a. "Former Egyptian Officer Recalls Life with Bin Laden, Al-Zawahiri's Influence." *Al-Sharq al-Awsat* (London), January 17.

———. 2002b. "Report Cites 'Repentant' Member on 'Secrets' of Al-Qaida Leaders, Identities." *Al-Sharq al-Awsat* (London), March 8.

———. 2002c. "British Court Releases Egyptian Fundamentalist Sirri and the Police Re-arrest Him in Response to a U.S. Extradition Request." *Al-Sharq al-Awsat* (London), May 17.

———. 2002d. "U.S. Asks British Court for Time to Prepare Evidence Against Islamist Al-Sirri." *Al-Sharq al-Awsat* (London), June 1.

———. 2002e. "Islamist 'Returning from Afghanistan' Cited on Bin Laden, Ibn al-Shaykh al-Libi." *Al-Sharq al-Awsat* (London), June 3.

———. 2002f. "Islamists Sirri, Misri on Yemeni Contacts, British Police Investigation." *Al-Sharq al-Awsat* (London), July 4.

Al-Zawahiri, Ayman. 2001. *Knights Under the Prophet's Banner.* Serialized in eleven parts in *Al-Sharq al-Awsat* (London), December 2.

Al-Zubi, Fadiyah. 2001. "Report Cites Sources on al-Qaidah Spokesman Abu-Ghayth." *Al-Sharq al-Awsat* (London), October 9.

Anderson, Benedict. 1991. *Imagined Communities: Reflections on the Origin and Spread of Nationalism.* Revised edition. London: Verso.

Andrews, Edmund. 2002a. "In Rich Detail, Algerian Describes Plot to Blow up French Synagogue." *New York Times*, April 24.

———. 2002b. "German Officials Find More Terrorist Groups, and Some Disturbing Parallels." *New York Times*, April 26.

Ansari, Hamied. 1984. "The Islamic Militants in Egyptian Politics." *International Journal of Middle East Studies*, 16: 123-144.

Anticev, John. 2001. *United States of America v. Usama bin Laden, et al.* February 27-28: 1616-1690.

Arendt, Hannah. 1958. *The Origins of Totalitarianism.* Second enlarged edition. Cleveland: Meridian Books.

Bainbridge, William Sims. 1997. *The Sociology of Religious Movements.* New York: Routledge.

Baker, Mark. 2002. "Revealed: School That Bred the Bali Bombers." *The Age* (Melbourne), November 22.

Barabasi, Albert-Laszlo. 2003. *Linked: How Everything Is Connected to Everything Else and What It Means for Business, Science, and Everyday Life.* Cambridge, Mass.: Plume.

Barker, Eileen. 1984. *The Making of a Moonie—Choice or Brainwashing?* Oxford: Basil Blackwell.

Bearden, Milton. 2001. Interview, *PBS Frontline: Hunting bin Laden* at www.pbs.org/wgbh/pages/frontline/shows/binladen/interviews/bearden.html.

Bearden, Milt; and Risen, James. 2003. *The Main Enemy: The Inside Story of CIA's Final Showdown with the KGB.* New York: Random House.

Behar, Richard. 1993. "Mahmud the Red." *Time*, October 4.

Belluck, Pam. 2003. "Unrepentant Shoe Bomber Sentenced to Life." *New York Times*, January 31.

Belluck, Pam, and Chang, Kenneth. 2001. "Shoes Were a 'Homemade Bomb,' FBI Agent Says." *New York Times*, December 29.

Bergen, Peter. 2001. *Holy War, Inc.: Inside the Secret World of Osama bin Laden*, New York: The Free Press.

Bernard, Philippe. 1995a. "Stéphane et Redouane, soldats de l'islamisme, entre La Courneuve et Marrakech." *Le Monde*, January 27.

———. 1995b. "Deux associations, l'une laïque, l'autre musulmane." *Le Monde*, January 27, 1995.

———. 1995c. "L'itinéraire bien ordinaire de Khaled Kelkal, terroriste présumé." *Le Monde*, September 19.

———. 1995d. "A Vaulx-en-Velin, les nouveaux banlieusards de l'islam." *Le Monde*, October 9.

Bernstein, Richard. 1995. "Trail of the Sheik—A Special Report." *New York Times*, January 8.

Bernstein, Richard; Frantz, Douglas; Van Natta, Jr., Don; and Johnston, David. 2002. "On Path to the U.S. Skies, Plot Leader Met bin Laden." *New York Times*, September 10.

Bernton, Hal; Carter, Mike; Heath, David; and Neff, James. 2002. "The Terrorist Within: The Story Behind One Man's Holy War Against America." *Seattle Times*, June 23–July 7.

Biderman, Albert. 1963. *March to Calumny: The Story of American POWs in the Korean War.* New York: Macmillan.

bin Laden, Osama. 1996. *Declaration of War Against the Americans Occupying the Land of the Two Holy Places.* Published in *Al-Quds al-Arabi* (London) on August 23, and found at www.pbs.org/newshour/terrorism/international/fatwa_1996.html.

bin Laden, Osama, et al. 1998. "Jihad Against Jews and Crusaders." Dated February 23, and found at www.fas.org/irp/world/para/docs/980223-fatwa.htm.

"Bin Laden Associate Interrogated." 1999. *Al-Sharq al-Awsat (London)*, June 24.

Boenisch, Georg; Cziesche, Dominik; Mascolo, Georg; Stark, Holger. 2002. "Ziele in Deutschland." *Der Spiegel* (Hamburg), April 29.

Bone, James; and Road, Alan. 1997. "Terror by Degree." *Times* (London), October 18.

Bonner, Raymond. 2002. "How Qaeda Linked Up with Malaysian Groups." *New York Times*, February 7.

Bonner, Raymond; and Mydans, Seth. 2002. "'Sleeper Cells' in Singapore Show Al Qaeda's Long Reach." *New York Times*, January 26.

Bouilhet, Alexandrine. 2002. "Guerre contre al Qaida." *Le Figaro*, March 21.

Boulden, Jim. 2001. "France Opened Moussaoui File in '94." CNN, December 11.

Bright, Martin. 1999. "Man of God or Islamic Killer?" *Observer* (London), December 19.

Bright, Martin; Bartlett, Antony; Wazir, Burhan; Thompson, Tony; Beaumont, Peter; Jeffries, Stuart; Vulliamy, Ed; Connolly, Kate; Tremlett, Gilles. 2001. "The European Connection." *Observer* (London), September 30.

Brinkbaeumer, Klaus; Boenisch, Georg; Cziesche, Dominik; Ludwig, Udo; Mascolo, Georg; Meyer, Cordula; Neumann, Conny; Schelznig, Erik; Schmid, Barbara; and Ulrich, Andreas. 2001. "Anschaege ohne Auftrag." *Der Spiegel* (Hamburg), October 15.

Brinkbaeumer, Klaus; Cziesche, Dominik; Mascolo, Georg; Meyer, Cordula; and Ulrich, Andreas. 2001. "Der Krieger aus Pearl Harburg." *Der Spiegel* (Hamburg), November 26.

Brown, Marion. 2001. Interview: The Mother-in-Law of Wadih El Hage. *PBS Frontline: Hunting bin Laden* at www.pbs.org/wgbh/pages/frontline/shows/binladen/interviews/mother.html.

Brzezinski, Matthew. 2001. "Bust and Boom." *Washington Post*, December 30.

Burke, Jason. 2002. "Focus: Jihad Mastermind: How the Perfect Terrorist Plotted the Ultimate Crime." *Observer* (London), April 7.

———. 2003. *Al Qaeda: Casting a Shadow of Terror.* London: I. B. Tauris.

Burke, Jason; Bright, Martin; and Vulliamy, Ed. 2002. "The Return of al-Qaeda." *Observer* (London), June 16.

Butler, Desmond. 2002a. "Germany Arrests Moroccan Suspected in September 11 Attacks." *New York Times*, October 11.

———. 2002b. "In German Trial, Hijacker's Friend Admits to Qaeda Training." *New York Times*, October 23.

———. 2002c. "Terror Suspect's Departure from Germany Raises Concern in Other Nations." *New York Times*, December 24.

———. 2003a. "Yemeni's Role in Attacks on September 11 Is Stressed." *New York Times*, February 10.

———. 2003b. "German Court Convicts Student of Aiding September 11 Terrorists." *New York Times*, February 19.

Butler, Desmond; and Van Natta, Jr., Don. 2003. "Qaeda Informant Helps Trace Group's Trail." *New York Times*, February 17.

Ceaux, Pascal. 2001. "Paris, Londres, Jalalabad: enquête sur les combatants étrangers d'Al-Qaida." *Le Monde*, December 27.

Ceaux, Pascal; and Lhomme, Fabrice. 2002. "Les déclarations d'un islamiste arrêté en France précisent l'étendue des réseaux d'Al Qaida en Europe." *Le Monde*, February 12.

Chadi, Taieb. 2002. "Les aveux d'un islamiste marocain d'Al Qaida." *Maroc Le Jour*, at www.maroclejour.press.ma/Mhinternet/Archives_512/html_512/secret.html.

Chambon, Frédéric. 2001a. "Terrorisme ou grand banditisme." *Le Monde*, October 4.

———. 2001b. "La cour d'assises du Nord examine les personnalités sous influence des membres du gang de Roubaix." *Le Monde*, October 51.

———. 2001c. "Le troisième membre du gang de Roubaix se revendique proche du FIS." *Le Monde*, October 6.

———. 2001d. "L'attentat manqué avant un sommet du G7 à Lille." *Le Monde*, October 13.

———. 2001e. "Des peines de 18 à 28 ans de reclusion pour les trois membres du gang de Roubaix." *Le Monde*, October 20.

———. 2002. "La part d'ombre de Zacarias Moussaoui." *Le Monde*, March 29.

———. 2003a. "Au programme du stage afghan, formation militaire et cours de chimie." *Le Monde*, January 4.

———. 2003b. "Comment naissent et vivent les réseaux d'Al Qaida en Europe." *Le Monde*, January 4.

Chambon, Frederic; Langellier, Jean-Pierre; and Leser, Eric. 2001. "Itinéraire d'un apprenti terroriste." *Le Monde*, November 28.

Chatelot, Christophe. 2001. "La Bosnie, base arrière d'Oussama Ben Laden." *Le Monde*, October 23.

Cleckley, Hervey. 1941. *The Mask of Sanity*. New York: C. V. Mosby.

Cloud, John. 2001. "Atta's Oddyssey." *Time*, October 8.

Cobain, Ian; and Smith, Lewis. 2003. "Mostafa's Bride Was Guilty of a Little Window Dressing." *The Times* (London), January 30.

Collins, Randall. 1998. *The Sociology of Philosophies: A Global Theory of Intellectual Change*. Cambridge, Mass.: Harvard University Press.

Corbin, Jane. 2002. *Al-Qaeda: The Terror Network that Threatens the World*. New York: Thunder's Mouth Press/Nation Books.

Cornevin, Christophe. 2002. "La confession à Paris d'un islamiste offre une aide precieuse aux enquêteurs pour reconstituer le puzzle de l'organization." *Le Figaro*, February 11.

Cowell, Alan. 2001a. "This Mild Schoolboy, Lost in the Islamic Inferno." *New York Times*, October 11.

———. 2001b. "The Shadowy Trail and Shift to Islam of a Bomb Suspect." *New York Times*, December 29.

———. 2002. "Fugitive Muslim Cleric, an Outspoken Supporter of Al Qaeda, Is Arrested in London." *New York Times*, October 26.

Cziesche, Dominik; and Smoltczyk, Alexander. 2002. "Der Verlorene Said." *Der Spiegel* (Hamburg), January 14.

Cziesche, Dominik; Krach, Wolfgang; Leick, Romain; Udo, Ludwig; Mascolo, Georg; Meyer, Cordula; Schmid, Fidelius; Stark, Holger; Ulrich, Andreas. 2002. "So Gott will." *Der Spiegel* (Hamburg), April 22.

Cziesche, Dominik; Malzahn, Claus Christian; Mascolo, Georg; and Ulrich, Andreas. 2002. "Feuer und Blut." *Der Spiegel* (Hamburg), September 23.

Cziesche, Dominik; Mascolo, Georg; and Stark, Holger. 2003. "Das Puzzle lag auf dem Tisch." *Der Spiegel* (Hamburg), February 3.

Daly, Emma. 2001a. "Spanish Police Arrest 11 Accused of Working for bin Laden." *New York Times*, November 14.

———. 2001b. "Spain Is Seeking 3 Militants Linked to bin Laden Network." *New York Times*, November 15.

Dawoud, Khaled. 2001. "Arab-Afghans Battered." *Al-Ahram Weekly Online* (Cairo), issue no. 561, November 22-28, at www.weekly.ahram.org.eg/2001/561/6war2.htm.

Dehl, Douglas; Dugger, Celia; and Barringer, Felicity. 2002. "Death of Reporter Puts Focus on Pakistan Intelligence Unit." *New York Times*, February 25.

Dekmejian, R. Hrair. 1995. *Islam in Revolution: Fundamentalism in the Arab World*, Syracuse, N.Y.: Syracuse University Press.

Della Porta, Donatella. 1988. "Recruitment Processes in Clandestine Political Organizations: Italian Left-Wing Terrorism." *International Social Movement Research*, 1: 155-169.

———. 1992a. "Introduction: On Individual Motivations in Underground Political Organizations." *International Social Movement Research*, 4: 3-28.

———. 1992b. "Political Socialization in Left-Wing Underground Organizations: Biographies of Italian and German Militants." *International Social Movement Research*, 4: 259-290.

Diani, Mario; and McAdam, Doug. 2003. *Social Movements and Networks: Relational Approaches to Collective Action*. Oxford: Oxford University Press.

Dillon, Sam. 2001. "Indictment by Spanish Judge Portrays a Secret Terror Cell." *New York Times*, November 20.

DiManno, Rosie. 2003. "Family Denies Suspect Is Terror Alchemist." *Toronto Star*, March 7.

Dobbs, Michael. 2001. "Probe Targets Cleric in London." *Washington Post*, October 28.

Dominus, Susan. 2003. "Everybody Has a Mother." *New York Times Magazine*, February 9.

Duckitt, John. 1989. "Authoritarianism and Group Identification: A New View of an Old Construct." *Political Psychology*, 10: 63-84.

Duffy, Brian. 1995. "The Long Arm of the Law." *U.S. News and World Report*, February 20.

Dugger, Celia; and Barringer, Felicity. 2002. "Confession in 1994 Case Evokes Pearl Abduction." *New York Times*, February 8.

Duke, Lynne. 1993. "Trail of Tumult on U.S. Soil." *Washington Post*, July 11.

Duke, Lynne; and Gladwell, Malcolm. 1993. "U.S. Charges Sheik in Terror Bomb Plot." *Washington Post*, August 26.

Durand-Souffland, Stéphane. 2002. "Boualem Bensaid: un karateka happé par le jihad." *Le Figaro*, October 1.

Elegant, Simon. 2002a. "The Family Behind the Bombings." *Time International*, November 25.

———. 2002b. "Inside the Bali Plot." *Time*, December 9, 2002.

Elegant, Simon; and Tedjasukmana, Jason. 2003. "The Jihadis' Tale." *Time International*, January 27.

Elliott, Michael. 2002. "The Shoe Bomber's World." *Time*, February 25.

———. 2003. "The Biggest Fish of Them All." *Time*, March 17.

Erhel, Catherine; and de La Baume, Renaud, eds. 1997. *Le procès d'un réseau islamiste.* Paris: Albin Michel.

Erlanger, Steven. 2002a. "German Officials Deny Knowing Whereabouts of Important Figure in Hamburg Plot." *New York Times*, June 13.

———. 2002b. "Traces of Terror: Berlin: German Press Investigation of Qaeda-Tied Businessman." *New York Times*, June 20.

Erlanger, Steven; and Hedges, Chris. 2001. "Missed Signals: Terror Cells Slip Through Europe's Grasp." *New York Times*, December 28.

Esposito, John. 2002. *Unholy War: Terror in the Name of Islam.* New York: Oxford University Press.

Etchegoin, Marie-France. 2001. "Les réseaux du djihad en France." *Nouvel Observateur*, no. 1928, October 18.

Fainaru, Steve. 2002. "September 11 Detainee Is Ordered Deported." *Washington Post*, September 4.

Fainaru, Steve; and Ibrahim, Alia. 2002. "Mysterious Trip to Flight 77 Cockpit." *Washington Post*, September 10.

Faraj, Muhammad Abd al-Salam. 1986. *Al-Faridah al Ghaibah*, in Johannes Jansen, *The Neglected Duty: The Creed of Sadat's Assassins and Islamic Resurgence in the Middle East.* New York: Macmillan, 159-234.

Farley, Christopher John. 1995. "The Man Who Wasn't There." *Time*, February 20.

Fazul, Abdallah. 1997. Letter, *PBS Frontline: Hunting bin Laden*, at www.pbs.org/wgbh/pages/frontline/shows/binladen/upclose/computer.html.

Feldner, Yotam. 2001. "Radical Islamist Profiles (1): London–Abu Hamza Al-Masri." *MEMRI Inquiry and Analysis Series*, 72, October 16, found at www.memri.org/bin/articles.cgi?Page=archives&area=ia&ID=IA7201.

Fielding, Nick; and Lamb, Christina. 2003. "Natural Born Killer." *Sunday Times* (London), March 9.

Finn, Peter. 2002a. "German at Center of September 11 Inquiry." *Washington Post*, June 12.

———. 2002b. "Arrest Reveal Al Qaeda Plans: Three Saudis Seized by Morocco Outline Post-Afghanistan Strategy." *Washington Post*, June 16.

———. 2002c. "Hamburg's Cauldron of Terror; Within Cell of 7, Hatred Toward U.S. Grew and September 11 Plot Evolved." *Washington Post*, September 11.

———. 2003a. "Al Qaeda Recruiter Reportedly Tortured." *Washington Post*, January 31.

———. 2003b. "Germans Charge Another Moroccan." *Washington Post*, May 10.

Finn, Peter; and Delaney, Sarah. 2001. "Al Qaeda's Tracks Deepen in Europe." *Washington Post*, October 22.

Finn, Peter; and Khan, Kamran. 2003. "Bold Tracks of Terrorism's Mastermind." *Washington Post*, March 9.

Finn, Peter; and Rolfe, Pamela. 2001. "Spain Holds 8 Linked to Sept. 11 Plot." *Washington Post*, November 19.

Follain, John; and Rufford, Nicholas. 2001. "Tapes Reveal Poison Plan." *Sunday Times* (London), October 14.

Fouda, Yosri. 2002. "Masterminds of a Massacre–9/11–One Year On." *Sunday Times* (London), September 8.

Fouda, Yosri; and Fielding, Nick. 2003. *Masterminds of Terror: The Truth Behind the Most Devastating Terrorist Attack the World Has Ever Seen.* New York: Arcade.

Franck, Johannes. 2001. "De Peshawar à Marrakech, la route vers le jihad de deux jeunes de La Courneuve." *Le Monde*, September 26.

Frank, Steven. 2003. "The Challenge of Terror." *Time International (Canada)*, January 27.

Frantz, Douglas. 2002a. "U.S. Enlists Morocco's Help to Counter Terrorist Plots." *New York Times*, June 24.

———. 2002b. "German Police Quiz Roommate of Top Hijacker." *New York Times*, July 4.

Frantz, Douglas; and Butler, Desmond. 2002. "September 11 Attack Planned in '99, Germans Learn." *New York Times*, August 30.

Frantz, Douglas; and Hedges, Chris. 2002. "Faintly Connected Dots Portray a Qaeda Man." *New York Times*, January 11.

Fried, Joseph. 1995. "The Terror Conspiracy: The Overview." *New York Times*, October 2.

———. 1996. "Sheik Sentenced to Life in Prison in Bombing Plot." *New York Times*, January 18.

Galanter, Marc. 1989. *Cults: Faith, Healing, and Coercion.* New York: Oxford University Press.

Gattegno, Hervé. 1996. "Une seule et même équipe a organizé la campagne d'attentats de 1995." *Le Monde*, July 26.

Gattegno, Hervé; and Inciyan, Erich. 1995. "Les filières françaises de la guerre sainte." *Le Monde*, October 11.

———. 1996. "L'enquête sur les attentats révèle l'architecture des réseaux du GIA." *Le Monde*, January 17 .

Gaudia, Stephen. 2001. *United States of America v. Usama bin Laden, et al.* March 7: 1971-2030.

Gauthier, Ursula; and Jauvert, Vincent. 2001. "A l'intérieur d'Al-qaida." *Nouvel Observateur Hebdo*, no. 1934, November 29.

Gebauer, Matthias. 2002. "Das kleine Raedchen, ohne das nichts life." *Der Spiegel* (Hamburg), October 22.

Gharib, Sayyid. 1999. "Abu-Hamza on Life, Islam, Islamic Groups." *Al-Majallah*, March 21-27.

Gilmartin, Kevin. 1996. "The Lethal Triad: Understanding the Nature of Isolated Extremist Groups." *FBI Law Enforcement Bulletin*, September: 1-5.

Gladwell, Malcolm. 1995. "Sheik, 9 Others Convicted in N.Y. Bomb." *Washington Post*, October 2.

Goldstein, Amy; Sun, Lena; and Lardner, George, Jr. 2001. "Hanjour: A Study in Paradox." *Washington Post*, October 15.

Gould, Roger. 2003. "Why Do Networks Matter? Rationalist and Structuralist Interpretations," in Mario Diani and Doug McAdam, eds., *Social Movements and Networks: Relational Approaches to Collective Action*. Oxford: Oxford University Press, 233-257.

Granovetter, Mark. 1973. "The Strength of Weak Ties." *American Journal of Sociology*, 78: 1360-1380.

———. 1983. "The Strength of Weak Ties: A Network Theory Revisited." *Sociological Theory*, 1: 201-233.

———. 1985. "Economic Action and Social Structure: The Problem of Embeddedness." *American Journal of Sociology*, 91: 481-510.

Guenena, Nemat. 1986. *The "Jihad": An "Islamic Alternative" in Egypt*. Cairo Papers in Social Science, Volume 9, Monograph 2.

Gunaratna, Rohan. 2002. *Inside al Qaeda: Global Network of Terror*. New York: Columbia University Press.

Gurr, Ted. 1970. *Why Men Rebel*. Princeton, N.J.: Princeton University Press.

Harding, Luke. 2000. "Chasing Monsters: The American Helped Create the Terrorist bin Laden. Now They Try to Destroy Him." *Guardian* (London), November 24.

Harris, Paul; Wazir, Burhan; and Connolly, Kate. 2002. "Al-Qaeda's Bombers Used Britain to Plot Slaughter." *Observer* (London), April 21.

Hassan, Steven. 2000. *Releasing the Bonds: Empowering People to Think for Themselves*. Somerville, Mass.: Freedom of Mind Press.

Hedges, Chris. 2002. "Tunisian Killed in Synagogue Blast Was Unlikely Convert to Militancy." *New York Times*, June 9.

Hendawi, Hamza. 2002. "Hamburg Plotters Provide Useful Insight into al-Qaida's Sleepers." Associated Press, October 20.

Hersh, Seymour. 2002. "The Twentieth Man." *New Yorker*, September 30.

Higgins, Andrew; and Cooper, Christopher. 2001. "Cloak and Dagger." *Wall Street Journal*, November 21.

"The Highway of Death." 2002. *Sunday Times (London)*, January 27.

"Hijackers Were from Wealthy Saudi Families." 2001. *Sunday Times (London)*, October 28.

Hodgson, Marshall. 1974. *The Venture of Islam: Conscience and History in a World Civilization.* 3 vols. Chicago: University of Chicago Press.

Horgan, John. 2003. "The Search for the Terrorist Personality," in Andrew Silke, ed., *Terrorists, Victims and Society: Psychological Perspective on Terrorism and Its Consequences.* Chichester, England: John Wiley and Sons.

Ibrahim, Saad Eddin. 1980. "Anatomy of Egypt's Militant Islamic Groups: Methodological Note and Preliminary Findings." *International Journal of Middle East Studies*, 12: 423-453.

———. 1982. "Egypt's Islamic Militants." *MERIP Reports*, 103 (February): 5/14.

———. 1988. "Egypt's Islamic Activism in the 1980s." *Third World Quarterly*, 10 (2): 632-657.

Ilhami, Iqbal. 2002. "Al Qaida Member Talks from Moroccan Cell on Monitoring NATO Fleet Movements." *Al-Hayat* (London), June 30.

Inciyan, Erich. 1995a. "Au procès de Fes, une justice expéditive est en quête de coupables." *Le Monde*, January 27.

———. 1995b. "Le procureur général du roi requiert la peine de mort contre six beurs jugés à Fes." *Le Monde*, January 28.

———. 1996a. "Les auteurs de la fusillade de Roubaix ne seraient pas liés à un réseau islamiste." *Le Monde*, April 12.

———. 1996b. "L'enquête sur les attentats de l'été 1995 a beaucoup progressé." *Le Monde*, July 11.

International Crisis Group. 2001. "Indonesia: Violence and Radical Muslims." *IGC Indonesia Briefing*, October 10 at www.crisisweb.org.

———. 2002a. "Al-Qaeda in Southeast Asia: The Case of the 'Ngruki Network' in Indonesia." *ICG Indonesia Briefing*, August 8 at www.crisisweb.org.

———. 2002b. "Indonesia Backgrounder: How the *Jemaah Islamiyah* Terrorist Network Operates." *ICG Asia Report No. 43*, December 11 at www.crisisweb.org.

———. 2003. "Jemaah Islamiyah in South East Asia: Damaged but Still Dangerous." *ICG Asia Report No. 63*, August 26 at www.crisisweb.org.

Israely, Jeff. 2002. "The Second Time Around." *Time* (Europe), March 4.

Jacobson, Philip. 1993. "Muhammad's Ally." *Times* (London), December 4.

Jankowski, Martin Sanchez. 1991. *Islands in the Street: Gangs and American Urban Society.* Berkeley: University of California Press.

Jansen, Johannes. 1986. *The Neglected Duty: The Creed of Sadat's Assassins and Islamic Resurgence in the Middle East.* New York: Macmillan.

Juergensmeyer, Mark. 2000. *Terror in the Mind of God: The Global Rise of Religious Violence.* Berkeley: University of California Press.

Kepel, Gilles. 1993. *Muslim Extremism in Egypt: The Prophet and the Pharaoh.* Berkeley: University of California Press.

———. 2002. *Jihad: The Trail of Political Islam.* Cambridge, Mass.: Harvard University Press.

Khalil, Mahmud. 2002. "Report Profiles Abu-Zubaydah." *Al-Majallah* (London), August 25-31.

Khashoggi, Jamal. 2001a. "Hijacker List Raises More Questions." *Jeddah Arab News*, September 20.

———. 2001b. "Saudi Suspect's Family Denies Son's Involvement in U.S. Incidents." *Jeddah Arab News*, September 22.

Kher, Unmesh. 2002. "The Reluctant Terrorist?" *Time*, February 18.

Kherchtou, L'Houssaine. 2001. *United States of America v. Usama bin Laden, et al.* February 21-27: 1104-1538.

Khosrokhavar, Farhad. 1997. *L'islam des jeunes*. Paris: Flammarion.

———. 2002. *Les nouveaux martyres d'Allah*. Paris: Flammarion.

Krebs, Valdis. 2002a. "Uncloaking Terrorist Networks." *First Monday*, 7 (4) at http://firstmonday.org/issues/issue7_4/krebs/index.html.

———. 2002b. "Mapping Networks of Terrorist Cells." *Connections*, 24 (3): 43-52.

Kwang, Han Fook. 2002. "The Plot Thickens, but Mostly Outside Singapore." *Straits Times*, January 26.

Laabs, Dirk. 2002. "Testimony Offers Intimate Look at a September 11 Hijacker's Life." *Los Angeles Times*, November 21.

———. 2003. "Witness in Terror Trial Threatened, Germany Says." *Los Angeles Times*, January 30.

Laabs, Dirk; and McDermott, Terry. 2003. "Prelude to 9/11: A Hijacker's Love, Lies." *Los Angeles Times*, January 27.

Laidi, Ali. 2002. *Le jihad en Europe: les filières du terrorisme islamiste*. Paris: Editions du Seuil.

Lamb, Christina. 2002. "The Six Sons of Asir." *Sunday Telegraph* (London), September 15.

Lappin, Elena. 2002. "Portrait: Atta in Hamburg." *Prospect*, August 29.

Leclerc, Jean-Marc. 2001. "Terrorisme: Deux ans d'enquête de la DST et des polices européennes ont permis d'identifier un réseau qui ciblait la France." *Le Figaro*, February 23.

———. 2002. "Kamel Daoudi, soupçonné d'avoir participé à un projet d'attentat contre l'ambassade des Etats Unis à Paris, raconte son parcours." *Le Figaro*, September 10.

Le Guilledoux, Dominique. 1996. "Les mystères du 59, rue Henri-Carette." *Le Monde*, April 26.

Levitt, Matthew. 2003. "The Zarqawi Node in the Terror Matrix: Who Is Zarqawi?" *National Review*, February 6.

Leyendecker, Hans. 2002. "Progress in Tracking Islamic Terrorists Noted." *Sueddeutsche Zeitung* (Munich), April 24.

———. 2003. "Abu Mussab al-Zarqawi: Liebling der Terroristen im Heiligen Kreig." *Sueddeutsche Zeitung* (Munich), February 6.

Loch, Dietmar. 1995. "Moi, Khaled Kelkal." *Le Monde*, October 7.

Loch, Dietmar; and Rosenzweig, Luc. 1995. "L'énergie qui émane de l'exclusion." *Le Monde*, October 7.

Locy, Tony; and Johnson, Kevin. 2002. "Moussaoui's Link to 9/11 in Doubt." *USA Today*, November 21.

Lofland, John. 1981. *Doomsday Cult: A Study of Conversion, Proselytization, and Maintenance of Faith*. Enlarged edition. New York: Irvington Publishers.

Lofland, John; and Stark, Rodney. 1965. "Becoming a World-Saver: A Theory of Conversion to a Deviant Perspective." *American Sociological Review*, 30 (6): 862-875.

Lombard, Marie-Amélie. 2000. "Terrorisme. Ouverture du procès de Karim Koussa et Boualem Bensaid aux assises spéciales de Paris." *Le Figaro*, November 9.

———. 2001a. "Islamisme: L'un affirme avoir été entraîné, l'autre se dit totalement étranger au groupe des gangs terroristes." *Le Figaro*, October 5.

———. 2001b. "Assises: Retour sur la fusillade du 29 mars 1996." *Le Figaro*, October 13.

———. 2001c. "Islamisme: Devant la cour d'assises du Nord." *Le Figaro*, October 19.

Lombard, Marie-Amélie; and du Tanney, Philippe. 2001. "Islamisme à Douai." *Le Figaro*, October 4.

Lopez, Leslie. 2003. "An Experiment Gone Radically Wrong." *Wall Street Journal*, January 19.

Luthra, Dumeetha. 2003. "The Al-Qaeda Poison Master Roaming Saddam's Back Yard." *Sunday Times* (London), February 9.

Macintyre, Ben; and Tendler, Stewart. 1996. "Middle Eastern Activists Funded by Exile Tycoon." *The Times* (London), January 5.

MacLeod, Scott. 2002. "Inside an al-Qaeda Bust." *Time*, June 15.

Marchand, Stéphane, 1997, "Lionel Dumond et un complice comparaîssent pour des braquages à Zenica." *Le Figaro*, July 9.

Marshall, Andrew. 2003. "A Jihadi's Tale." *Time International*, March 10.

Mascolo, Georg. 2002. "Tod den Amerikanern." *Der Spiegel* (Hamburg), October 28.

Mascolo, Georg, and Stark, Holger. 2003. "Operation Holy Tuesday." *Der Spiegel* (Hamburg), October 27.

McDermott, Terry. 2002a. "Early Scheme to Turn Jets into Weapons." *Los Angeles Times*, June 24.

———. 2002b. "The Plot: How Terrorists Hatched a Simple Plan to Use Planes as Bombs." *Los Angeles Times*, September 1.

McDermott, Terry; and Laabs, Dirk. 2002. "September 11 Suspect Is Said to Be Central to Terrorist Cell." *Los Angeles Times*, October 24.

McDermott, Terry; Meyer, Josh; McDonnell, Patrick. 2002. "The Plots and Designs of Al Qaeda's Engineer." *Los Angeles Times*, December 22.

McGrory, Daniel. 2001. "Spanish Suspects 'Plotted Attacks Across Europe.'" *Times* (London), November 19.

McHugh, Paul. 2001. "A Psychiatrist Looks at Terrorism: There's Only One Way to Stop Fanatical Behavior." *Weekly Standard*, December 12.

McKinley, James, Jr. 1998. "In-Laws Say Bomb Suspect Led a Quiet, Religious Life." *New York Times*, August 26.

McNiel, Jr., Donald. 1998. "Assets of a Bombing Suspect: Keen Wit, Religious Soul, Angry Temper." *New York Times*, October 6.

———. 2001. "Body Confirms Suspicions About Frenchmen in Al Qaeda." *New York Times*, December 28.

Meissner, W. W. 1979. "Narcissism and Paranoia: A Comment on Paranoid Psychodynamics." *Contemporary Psychoanalysis*, 15 (3): 527-538.

Merari, Ariel. 1990. "The Readiness to Kill and Die: Suicidal Terrorism in the Middle East," in Walter Reich, ed., *Origins of Terrorism: Psychologies, Ideologies, Theologies, States of Mind*. Washington, D.C.: Woodrow Wilson Center Press, 192-207.

———. 1991. "Academic Research and Government Policy on Terrorism," in Clark McCauley, ed., *Terrorism and Public Policy*. London: Frank Cass, 88-102.

Merkl, Peter. 1995. "West German Left-Wing Terrorism," in Martha Creshaw, ed., *Terrorism in Context*. University Park: Pennsylvania State University Press.

Meyer, Josh; and Rotella, Sebastian. 2003. "Iraq, Al Qaeda a 'Lethal' Combo, U.S. Says." *Los Angeles Times*, February 6.

Meyer, Thierry. 2002. "Recrutement, financement, propagande, comment l'islamisme extrémiste utilise la Grande-Bretagne." *Le Temps*, November 13.

Miga, Andrew. 2002. "Captured al-Qaeda Leader Now Aiding CIA." *Boston Herald*, November 22.

Miller, Jill. 2001. *United States of America v. Usama bin Laden, et al.* June 28: 8380-8398.

Miller, Judith. 2001a. "On Jordan's Death Row, Convicted Terrorist Says He Has No Regrets." *New York Times*, January 15.

———. 2001b. "Holy Warriors: Dissecting a Terror Plot from Boston to Amman." *New York Times*, January 15.

———. 2002. "A Witness Against Al Qaeda Says the U.S. Let Him Down." *New York Times*, June 3.

Miller, Judith; and Van Natta, Don, Jr. 2002. "In Years of Plots and Clues, Scope of Qaeda Eluded U.S." *New York Times*, June 9.

Millot, Lorraine. 2002. "Al-Qaeda: procès test à Hambourg." *Libération*, October 23.

Ministry of Home Affairs. 2003. *White Paper: The Jemaah Islamiyah Arrests and the Threat of Terrorism*. Ministry of Home Affairs, Republic of Singapore, January 7.

Mohamed, Ali. 2000. *United States of America v. Ali Mohamed*, U.S. District Court, Southern District of New York, S (7) 98 Cr. 10232 (LBS), October 20.

Morris, Ivan. 1975. *The Nobility of Failure: Tragic Heroes in the History of Japan*. New York: Holt, Rinehart and Winston.

Moussaoui, Abd Samad; and Bouquillat, Florence. 2002. *Zacarias Moussaoui, Mon Frère*. Paris: Denoël.

Mowbray, Joel. 2002. "How They Did It: An 'Evil One' Confesses, and Boasts." *National Review*, December 23.

Mubarak, Hisham. 1996. "What Does the Gamaa Islamiyya Want? An Interview with Talat Fuad Qasim." *Middle East Report*, 198 (January-March): 40-46.

Murphy, Caryle; and Coll, Steve. 1993. "The Making of an Islamic Symbol." *Washington Post*, July 9.

Murphy, Caryle; and Ottaway, David. 2001. "Some Light Shed on Saudi Suspects; Many Raised in Area of Religious Dissent." *Washington Post*, September 25.

Murphy, Dan. 2003. "How Al Qaeda Lit the Bali Fuse." 3 parts, *Christian Science Monitor*, June 17-19.

Mylroie, Laurie. 1995. "The World Trade Center Bomb: Who Is Ramzi Yousef? And Why It Matters." *National Interest*, 42 (Winter): 3-15.

Nakashima, Ellen. 2003a. "Bali Blast Linked to Another in 2000; Police Trace Rebels' Activity." *Washington Post*, March 12.

———. 2003b. "Inquiry Shows Indonesian's Ties to Al Qaeda." *Washington Post*, March 29.

Noël, André. 2001. "Terrorisme: Le réseau Montréal." 14-part series. *La Presse* (Montreal), December 1-14.

"Notes on the Interrogation of one Suspect." *PBS Frontline: Hunting bin Laden*, at www.pbs.org/wgbh/pages/frontline/shows/binladen/bombings/interrogation.html.

Notz, Anton; Steinborn, Deborah; and Williamson, Hugh. 2003. "Guilty of Terrorism." *Financial Times* (London), February 20.

Ohnuki-Tierney, Emiko. 2002. *Kamikaze, Cherry Blossoms, and Nationalisms*. Chicago: University of Chicago Press.

Olson, Mancur, Jr. 1971. *The Logic of Collective Action: Public Goods and the Theory of Groups*. New York: Schocken Books.

O'Neill, Sean. 2003. "Architect of Terror Held in British Jail Cell." *Daily Telegraph* (London), January 9.

Ottaway, David; and Coll, Steve. 1995. "Retracing the Steps of a Terror Suspect; Accused Bomb Builder Tied to Many Plots." *Washington Post*, June 5.

Paddock, Richard. 2003. "Terror Network's Academic Outposts." *Los Angeles Times*, April 1.

Pape, Robert. 2003. "The Strategic Logic of Suicide Terrorism." *American Political Science Review*, 97 (3): 343-361.

Parry, Richard Lloyd. 2001. "Treasure Island." *Independent* (London), March 4.

Pascale, Robert Diard. 2002. "Les portraits des accusés des attentats de 1995 restent flous." *Le Monde*, October 28.

Passerini, Luisa. 1992. "Lacerations in the Memory: Women in the Italian Underground Organizations." *International Social Movement Research*, 4: 161-212.

Pearlstein, Richard. 1991. *The Mind of the Political Terrorist*. Wilmington, Del.: Scholarly Resources.

Peraino, Kevin; and Thomas, Evan. 2002. "Married to Jihad: Odyssey into Jihad." *Newsweek*, January 14.

Pereira, Brendon. 2002. "Unmasking Radical Preachers." *Straits Times* (Singapore), February 10.

Perkins, Abigail. 2001. *United States of America v. Usama bin Laden, et al.* March 19: 2795-2860.

Peyrot, Maurice. 1997. "Le plaidoyer de Safé Bourada." *Le Monde*, November 28.

Pivois, Marc. 2001. "Chafik B. de l'humanitaire au réseau islamiste." *Libération*, February 10.

Pontaud, Jean Marie; and Epstein, Marc. 2002. *Ils ont assassiné Massoud.* Paris: Robert Laffont.

Post, Jerrold. 1984. "Notes on a Psychodynamic Theory of Terrorist Behavior." *Terrorism: An International Journal*, 7 (3): 241-256.

————. 1986a. "Hostilite, Conformite, Fraternite: The Group Dynamics of Terrorist Behavior." *International Journal of Group Psychotherapy*, 36 (2): 211-224.

————. 1986b. "Narcissism and the Charismatic Leader-Follower Relationship," *Political Psychology*, 7 (4): 675-688.

————. 1990/1998. "Terrorist psycho-logic: Terrorist behavior as a product of psychological forces," in Walter Reich, ed., *Origins of Terrorism: Psychologies, Ideologies, Theologies, States of Mind.* Washington, D.C.: Woodrow Wilson Center Press.

————. 2001. *United States of America v. Usama bin Laden, et al.*, June 27: 8311-8361.

Post, Jerrold; Ruby, Keven; Shaw, Eric. 2002a. "The Radical Group in Context: 1. An Integrated Framework for the Analysis of Group Risk for Terrorism." *Studies in Conflict and Terrorism*, 25: 73-100.

————. 2002b. "The Radical Group in Context: 2. Identification of Critical Elements in the Analysis of Risk for Terrorism by Radical Group Type." *Studies in Conflict and Terrorism*, 25: 101-126.

Purdy, Matthew. 2003. "Custody Fight Disguised as Terror Case." *New York Times*, January 29.

Purdy, Matthew, and Bergman, Lowell. 2003. "Where the Trail Led Between Evidence and Suspicion; Unclear Danger: Inside the Lackawanna Terror Case." *New York Times*, October 12.

Qutb, Sayyid. n.d. *Milestones.* Cedar Rapids, Iowa: Mother Mosque Foundation.

Ratnesar, Romesh. 2002. "Confessions of an Al-Qaeda Terrorist." *Time*, September 23.

Reeve, Simon. 1999. *The New Jackals: Ramzi Yousef, Osama bin Laden and the Future of Terrorism.* Boston: Northeastern University Press.

Ressam, Ahmed. 2001. *U.S.A. v. Mokhtar Haouari.* U.S.D.C., Southern District of New York, S 4 00 Cr. 15 (JFK), July 3: 531-651.

Richburg, Keith. 1995. "Spoilers of the Peace, Militant Young Muslim Force Emerges in Philippines as Older Rebels Negotiate." *Washington Post*, May 25.

Richey, Warren. 2001. "Jordan Bomb Trial Offers U.S. a Case Study." *Christian Science Monitor*, October 24.

Robins, Robert; and Post, Jerrold. 1997. *Political Paranoia: The Psychopolitics of Hatred.* New Haven, Conn.: Yale University Press.

Roig-Franzia, Manuel; and Goldstein, Amy. 2002. "A Bomb Suspect's Search for Identity." *Washington Post*, June 15.

Rotella, Sebastian. 2002a. "Europe Battles Al Qaeda Forces in Courtrooms." *Los Angeles Times*, March 17.

————. 2002b. "Main News." *Los Angeles Times*, September 23.

Rotella, Sebastian; and Meyer, Josh. 2002. "Wiretaps May Have Foretold Terror Attacks." *Los Angeles Times*, May 30.

Rotella, Sebastian; and Stobart, Janet. 2002. "Cleric Linked to Al Qaeda Jailed." *Los Angeles Times*, October 26.

Rotella, Sebastian; and Zucchino, David. 2001. "In Paris, a Frightening Look at Terror's Inconspicuous Face." *Los Angeles Times*, October 21.

Roy, Olivier. 1995. *Afghanistan: From Holy War to Civil War*. Princeton, N.J.: Darwin Press.

———. 2002. *L'Islam Mondialisé*. Paris: Editions du Seuil.

Rubin, Alissa. 2003. "Jordanian's Mother Denies He Has Ties to Terrorism." *Los Angeles Times*, February 8.

Rushdi, Osama. 2001. "Islamist Usamah Rushdi Responds to al-Zawahiri's Memoirs." *Al-Sharq al-Awsat*, December 13.

Salem, Mona. 2001. "Yasser al-Serri, 'L'attaché de presse' des islamistes arabes armés." *Agence France Presse*, October 30.

Salomon, John. 2003. "U.S.: Moussaoui Linked to Second Attack Plan." Associated Press, March 28.

Samman, Muhamad. 2002. "Bin Ladin's In-Law Responds to New York Times Report on Terrorist Links." *Al-Sharq al-Awsat* (London), May 4.

Saporito, Bill; and McGirk, Tim. 2003. "Architect of Terror." *Time*, March 10.

Sargant, William. 1971. *Battle for the Mind: A Physiology of Conversion and Brainwashing*. New York: Perennial Library.

Schacter, Daniel, ed. 1995. *Memory Distortion: How Minds, Brains, and Societies Reconstruct the Past*. Cambridge, Mass.: Harvard University Press.

———. 1996. *Searching for Memory: The Brain, the Mind, and the Past*, New York: Basic Books.

———. 2001. *The Seven Sins of Memory: How the Mind Forgets and Remembers*, Boston: Houghton Mifflin.

Schelzig, Erik; and Finn, Peter. 2002. "Repentant Algerian Tells of Bomb Plot." *Washington Post*, April 24.

Schmidt, Sam. 2001. *United States of America v. Usama bin Laden, et al.*, February 5: 49-64.

Schmidt, Susan. 2002. "Moussaoui Linked to Plot." *Washington Post*, November 20.

———. 2003. "Prosecution of Moussaoui Nears a Crossroad." *Washington Post*, January 21.

Schmidt, Susan; and Nakashima, Ellen. 2003. "Moussaoui Said Not to Be Part of 9/11 Plot." *Washington Post*, March 28.

Schou, Nick. 2000. "The Terrorist Next Door: The U.S. Says a Former Anaheim Resident Is Trying to Kill Us All." *Orange County Weekly*, July 14-20.

———. 2001. "One Degree of Separation: Whether He Knew It or Not, Khalil Deek Had Close Ties to bin Laden." *Orange County Weekly*, October 5-11.

Sciolino, Elaine. 2002. "Portrait of the Arab as a Young Radical." *New York Times*, September 22.

Sedar, Alice. 2002. "Kamel Daoudi déchu de sa nationalité." *Le Figaro*, August 2.

Sennott, Charles. 2002a. "Driving a Wedge: Why bin Laden Plot Relied on Saudi Hijackers." *Boston Globe*, March 3.

———. 2002b. "Before Oath to Jihad, Drifting and Boredom." *Boston Globe*, March 3.

———. 2002c. "Driving a Wedge: Saudi Schools Fuel Anti-U.S. Anger." *Boston Globe*, March 4.

———. 2002d. "Driving a Wedge: Doubts Are Cast on the Viability of Saudi Monarchy for Long Term." *Boston Globe*, March 5.

Sharaf-al-Din, Khalid. 1999. "Islamic Jihad Trial 'Confessions.'" 4-part series. *Al-Sharq al-Awsat*, March 6-9.

Shenon, Philip; and Risen, James. 2002. "Terrorist Yields Clues to Plots, Questioners Say." *New York Times*, June 12.

Silke, Andrew. 1998. "Cheshire-Cat Logic: The Recurring Theme of Terrorist Abnormality in Psychological Research." *Psychology, Crime and Law*, 4: 51-69.

Simon, Bob. 2002. "The Plot: Masterminds Behind the 9/11 Attacks on the U.S. and How They Came Up with Their Plan." *CBS 60 Minutes II*, October 9.

Singer, Margaret Thaler. 1996. *Cults in Our Midst: The Hidden Menace in Our Everyday Lives*. New York: Jossey-Bass.

Singh, Jasbant. 2002. "In Plush Malaysian Condo, Hijackers Talked Terror with Asian Militants." Associated Press, January 23.

Sivan, Emmanuel. 1985. *Radical Islam: Medieval Theology and Modern Politics*. New Haven, Conn.: Yale University Press.

Smolar, Piotr. 2003. "Le kamikaze tunisien de Djerba avait bénéficié de l'aide de sa famille en France." *Le Monde*, February 11.

Stalinsky, Steven. 2003. "Arab and Muslim Jihad Fighters in Iraq." *MEMRI Special Report–No. 19*, June 27, at www.memri.org/bin/opener.cgi?Page=archivesandID =SR1903.

Stark, Rodney; and Bainbridge, William Sims, 1980, "Networks of Faith: Interpersonal Bonds and Recruitment to Cults and Sects." *American Journal of Sociology*, 80(6): 1376-1395.

———. 1985. *The Future of Religion: Secularization, Revival, and Cult Formation*. Berkeley: University of California Press.

———. 1996. *Religion, Deviance and Social Control*. New York: Routledge.

Stark, Rodney; and Finke, Roger. 2000. *Acts of Faith: Explaining the Human Side of Religion*. Berkeley: University of California Press.

Stroobants, Jean Pierre. 2001. "Tarek Maaroufi, considéré comme un membre important d'Al-Qaida, est arrêté en Belgique." *Le Monde*, December 22.

———. 2002a. "Al-Qaida: Jérome Courtailler, le premier Français jugé en Europe." *Le Monde*, December 4.

———. 2002b. "Face aux accusations d'appartenance à Al-Qaida, Jérome Courtailler invoque hazards et coincidences." *Le Monde*, December 6.

———. 2002c. "L'acquittement de Jérome Courtailler, accusé de terrorisme provoque un malaise aux Pays-Bas." *Le Monde*, December 20.

Struck, Doug; Schneider, Howard; Vick, Karl; and Baker, Peter. 2001. "Borderless Network of Terror." *Washington Post*, September 23.

Swartz, Mimi. 2002. "The Traitor Next Door." *Texas Monthly*, April.

Tabor, Mary. 1993. "Transcript of Tapes Reveals Sheik Talked of Merits of Bomb Targets." *New York Times*, August 4.

Tagliabue, John. 2001a. "Italian Tapes Portray Young Arabs Operating on the Edges of Islamic Terror." *New York Times*, October 29.

———. 2001b. "Arrests in Belgium Highlight Its Role as a Militants' Base." *New York Times*, December 20.

———. 2002. "French Link 6 to 'Shoe Bomb' Attempt." *New York Times*, November 27.

Taylor, Maxwell. 1988. *The Terrorist*. London: Brassey's.

———. 1991. *The Fanatics: A Behavioural Approach to Political Violence*. London: Brassey's.

Tazghart, Uthman. 2001. "Report Cites French Sources on Extradition of Bin-Laden's Algerian Deputy." *Al-Majallah* (London), July 22.

Thibaudat, Jean-Pierre. 2001a. "Gang de Roubaix, un procès à deux faces." *Libération*, October 2.

———. 2001b. "Il revenait de Bosnie, j'étais très excité." *Libération*, October 5.

Torriero, E. A.; and Roe, Sam. 2001. "Blips of Information Form Sketches of 2 Detainees." *Chicago Tribune*, October 12.

Tourancheau, Patricia. 2001. "Kamel Daoudi, du rap à la Kalachnikov." *Libération*, October 18.

Tyler, Patrick. 2002. "Qaeda Suspect Was Taking Flight Training Last Month." *New York Times*, December 23.

———. 2003. "Intelligence Break Led U.S. to Tie Envoy Killing to Iraqi Qaeda Cell." *New York Times*, February 6.

United States of America v. Abu Doha. U.S. District Court, Southern District of New York, 01 MAG 1242, July 2, 2001.

United States of America v. Usama bin Laden, et al. U.S. District Court, Southern District of New York, S (7) 98 Cr. 1023, February 5-July 10, 2001.

United States of America v. Richard Colvin Reid. U.S. District Court, District of Massachusetts, Criminal No. 02-10013-WGY, Government's Sentencing Memorandum, January 17, 2003.

Valbay, Jean. 1999. "L'un des survivants du gang de Roubaix en cavale." *Le Figaro*, May 29.

Van Natta, Jr., Don; and Johnston, David. 2003. "A Terrorist with a Deadly Past." *New York Times*, February 10.

Van Natta, Jr., Don; and Zernike, Kate. 2001. "Hijackers' Meticulous Strategy of Brains, Muscle and Practice." *New York Times*, November 4.

Vermaat, Emerson. 2002. "Bin Laden's Terror Networks in Europe." Mackenzie Institute at www.mackenzieinstitute.com/commentary.html.

Vick, Karl. 1998. "FBI Trails Embassy Bombing Suspect; Investigators Find Clues to Double Life." *Washington Post*, September 17.

Vincent, Isabel. 2002. "The Good Son." *National Post* (Canada), December 28.

Vise, David. 2000. "Ex-Soldier Admits Role in Embassy Blasts; Bin Laden Implicated as Man Behind Bombings that Killed 223 People." *Washington Post*, October 21.

Viviano, Frank. 2001a. "Bin Laden Operative Faces Trial in Jordan." *San Francisco Chronicle*, October 3.

———. 2001b. "Mysterious Path from San Jose to Jordanian Gallows." *San Francisco Chronicle*, October 13.

Volkan, Vamik. 1994. *The Need to Have Enemies and Allies: From Clinical Practice to International Relationships*. Northvale, N.J.: Jason Aronson.

———. 1997. *Blood Lines: From Ethnic Pride to Ethnic Terrorism*. Boulder, Colo.: Westview Press.

Walker, Tom; and Pelham, Nick. 2002. "Al-Qaeda Stirs in Dust in Casablanca." *Sunday Times* (London), June 16.

Wallace, Charles. 1995. "Weaving a Wide Web of Terror." *Los Angeles Times*, May 28.

Wasmund, Klaus. 1986. "The Political Socialization of West German Terrorists," in Peter Merkl, ed., *Political Violence and Terror: Motifs and Motivations*. Berkeley: University of California Press, 191-228.

Weaver, Mary Anne. 2000. *A Portrait of Egypt*. New York: Farrar, Straus and Giroux.

Weiser, Benjamin; and Risen, James. 1998. "The Masking of a Militant: A Special Report; A Soldier's Shadowy Trail in U.S. and in the Mideast." *New York Times*, December 1.

Wesselingh, Isabelle. 2002. "Jérome Courtailler reconnaît être un escroc mais pas un terroriste." *Agence France Presse*, December 2.

Wieviorka, Michel. 1993. *The Making of Terrorism*. Chicago: University of Chicago Press.

———. 1995. "Les logiques virtuelles du terrorisme réel." *Le Monde*, October 14.

Williams, Carol. 2002. "German Terror Cell's Link to 9/11 Detailed." *Los Angeles Times*, August 30.

Williams, Lance. 2001. "Bin Laden's Bay Area Recruiter: Khalid Abu al-Dahab Signed up American Muslims to be Terrorists." *San Francisco Chronicle*, November 21.

Williams, Lance; and McCormick, Erin. 2001. "Al Qaeda Terrorist Worked with FBI." *San Francisco Chronicle*, November 4.

Willing, Richard. 2002. "Westernized Kid Grows into 9/11 Suspect." *USA Today*, June 25.

Winfield, Nicole. 2002. "Italian Court Convicts Tunisian Suspected of Heading bin Laden's European Arm." Associated Press, February 22.

Wright, Lawrence. 2002. "The Man Behind bin Laden." *New Yorker*, September 16.

Wright, Robin; and Serrano, Richard. 2002. "Al Qaeda Figure in Custody." *Los Angeles Times*, November 22.

Yardley, Jim; MacFarquhar, Neil; and Zielbauer, Paul. 2001. "A Portrait of the Terrorist: From Shy Child to Single-Minded Killer." *New York Times*, October 10.

Yousaf, Brigadier Mohammad; and Adkin, Mark. 2001. *Afghanistan—The Bear Trap: The Defeat of a Superpower*, Havertown, Pa.: Casemate.

Zaynah, Abduh. 2001. "Report Profiles Bin Ladin's Aide Muhammad Atif, Alias Abu-Hafs al-Masri." *Al-Sharq al-Awsat*, October 8.

Zill, Oriana. 2001. "A Portrait of Wadih El Hage, Accused Terrorist." *PBS Frontline: Hunting bin Laden* at www.pbs.org/wgbh/pages/frontline/shows/binladen/up-close/elhage.html.

Index

Acknowledgments

This book could not have been written without the encouragement and collaboration of a great number of people. When I began my investigations of the 9/11 terrorists, multilateral online discussions with a number of distinguished colleagues stimulated ideas and eventually led to an invitation from Philip Zimbardo to participate in a panel discussion on terrorism at the American Psychological Association Convention in Chicago in August 2002.

Colleagues at the University of Pennsylvania also encouraged me to pursue this topic and invited me to present my findings in their various stages. Their comments shaped the evolution of my thoughts on this subject. Most prominent among these supporters were Mark Liberman, Cynthia MacLemore, and William Labov at the Institute for Research in Cognitive Science, and Clark McCauley, Paul Rozin, and especially Jonathan Drummond at the Solomon Asch Center for the Study of Ethno-political Conflict.

For their insightful comments and questions, encouragement and collaboration, I am also indebted to Andrew Silke from the Home Office, London; John Horgan at University College, Cork, Ireland; Philip Zelikow, Susan Ginsburg, Douglas MacEachin and Tom Dowling at the National Commission on Terrorist Attacks Upon the United States; Rohan Gunaratna at the Institute of Defense and Strategic Studies, Nanyang Technological University, Singapore; Gilles Kepel at the Institut des Sciences Politiques and Olivier Roy at the Centre National de Recherches Scientifiques, Paris, France; Gerold Yonas, Benjamin Wu, Wendell Jones and Nancy Kay Hayden at the Sandia National Laboratory; Hsinchun Chen and Jennifer Xu, Artificial Intelligence Lab, University of Arizona; Henry Schuster from CNN; David Hammon, Clete DiGiacomo, and Jeffrey Milstein from the Defense Threat Reduction Agency; and Steven Brooke and Robert Leiken from the Nixon Center, Washington, D.C.

After one of my presentations, Peter Agree of the University of Pennsylvania Press encouraged me to write a book on this topic. Without his support, this project would never have reached its present form. Also at the Press, Noreen O'Connor provided many wise editorial suggestions, for which I am most grateful. I must also thank Deborah Fromstein, my research assistant, for her help. Very special thanks must be extended to Randall Collins and Elisa Bienenstock for reading the whole draft and making excellent suggestions for improving the logic and flow of the argument.

However, my greatest collaborator has been my wife, whom I thank for reading and revising many of my drafts, and whose suggestions and support throughout this project have been invaluable. Finally, I am indebted to my son for his most helpful cooperation, without which this book could not have been written. It is my hope that this work will contribute to an understanding that will lead to a more peaceful world for all of his generation.